*Towards an Asian American
Biblical Hermeneutics*

Towards an Asian American Biblical Hermeneutics

AN INTERSECTIONAL ANTHOLOGY

Gale A. Yee

CASCADE *Books* · Eugene, Oregon

TOWARDS AN ASIAN AMERICAN BIBLICAL HERMENEUTICS
An Intersectional Anthology

Copyright © 2021 Gale A. Yee. All rights reserved. Except for brief quotations in critical publications or reviews, no part of this book may be reproduced in any manner without prior written permission from the publisher. Write: Permissions, Wipf and Stock Publishers, 199 W. 8th Ave., Suite 3, Eugene, OR 97401.

Cascade Books
An Imprint of Wipf and Stock Publishers
199 W. 8th Ave., Suite 3
Eugene, OR 97401

www.wipfandstock.com

PAPERBACK ISBN: 978-1-7252-6340-6
HARDCOVER ISBN: 978-1-7252-6341-3
EBOOK ISBN: 978-1-7252-6342-0

Cataloguing-in-Publication data:

Names: Yee, Gale A., 1 949-, author.

Title: Towards an Asian American biblical hermeneutics : an intersectional anthology / Gale A. Yee.

Description: Eugene, OR: Cascade Books, 2021. | Includes bibliographical references and indexes.

Identifiers: ISBN: 978-1-7252-6340-6 (paperback). | ISBN: 978-1-7252-6341-3 (hardcover). | ISBN: 978-1-7252-6342-0 (ebook).

Subjects: LCSH: Bible—Hermeneutics. | Bible—Old Testament—Criticism, interpretation, etc. | Asian Americans—Religion.

Classification: BS511.3 Y44 2021 (print). | BS511.3 (epub).

Scripture quotations marked (NRSV) are taken from the New Revised Standard Version Bible © 1989 National Council of the Churches of Christ in the United States of America. Used by permission. All rights reserved worldwide.

Scripture quotations marked (NJB) are taken from the New Jerusalem Bible, published and copyright 1985 by Darton, Longman & Todd Ltd and Les Editions du Cerf, and used by permission of the publishers.

Dedicated to the Faculty, Staff, and Students of
Episcopal Divinity School
Cambridge, Massachusetts
USA

Contents

Acknowledgments | *ix*
Abbreviations | *xi*

1. Introduction: My Autobiographical Journey | 1
2. Methodological Interventions:
    Definitions, Explorations, and Intersections | 14
3. Inculturation and Diversity in the Politics of National Identity | 54
4. Refiguring the Missionary Position or We Asian North American
    Women Won't Take This Lying Down! | 60
5. Yin/Yang Is not Me: An Exploration into an
    Asian American Biblical Hermeneutics | 65
6. "She Stood in Tears amid the Alien Corn":
    Ruth the Perpetual Foreigner and Model Minority | 85
7. Racial Melancholia and the Book of Ruth | 111
8. The Woman Warrior Revisited:
    Jael, Fa Mulan, and American Orientalism | 123
9. Coveting the Vineyard:
    An Asian American Readings of 1 Kings 21 | 142
10. Of Foreigners and Eunuchs:
    An Asian American Reading of Isaiah 56:1–8 | 165
11. Jerusalem, Samaria, and Sodom:
    A Sisterly Urban Triad in Ezekiel 16:44–63 | 180

Subject Index | 203
Author Index | 208

Acknowledgments

THIS VOLUME WAS MADE possible by the many individuals and professional organizations that have shaped my development as an Asian American biblical scholar. I would like to thank my colleagues of the Ethnic Chinese Biblical Colloquium for their annual meetings at the Society of Biblical Literature (SBL) and for their biannual gatherings—at all of which we gorged ourselves at Chinese hot pots, at banquets, and over dim sum. I am so thankful for the exquisite Ruth and Naomi art piece by He Qi that they gave me after my SBL presidential address in 2019. I am grateful for all my sisters at Pacific Asian and North American Asian Women in Theology and Ministry (PANAAWTM), who have helped me develop as an Asian American feminist all these years. I especially thank them for organizing the wild Friday night celebration of my presidential address before the annual meeting with several Asian American groups of the American Academy of Religion. Imagine a whole roomful of Asian Americans doing the Cupid Shuffle together! I would like to thank my coeditor of the Texts@Contexts series, Athalya Brenner-Idan, an absolute joy to work with. This series is dedicated to vibrant global readings of the biblical text from diverse social locations. Three of the essays in this book were originally printed in this series. I would like to thank my editor K. C. Hanson, who contacted me about doing this volume with him. He was very influential getting my book *Poor Banished Children of Eve* taken on at Fortress Press and is now faithfully shepherding me through this project at Cascade Books/Wipf and Stock Publishers.

This book is dedicated to the faculty, staff, and students at Episcopal Divinity School, Cambridge, Massachusetts. The bulk of these essays were written while I taught and lived on its beloved location near Harvard Square. Their commitments to anti-racism and anti-oppression formed me and generations of progressive and justice-seeking students in the world. I was especially proud to be colleagues with the likes of Angela Bauer-Levesque, Stephen Burns, Patrick Cheng, Joanna Dewey, Christopher Duraisingh, Thomas Eoyang, Carter Heyward, Bill Kondrath, Sheryl Kujawa-Holbrook, Kwok Pui Lan, Joan Martin, Fredrica Harris Thompsett, and Larry Wills.

Chapters 1, 4, and 11 have not been published elsewhere. I am grateful for the publishers' permissions to republish the following essays with slight revisions and corrections:

"Yin/Yang Is Not Me: An Exploration into an Asian American Biblical Hermeneutics." In *Ways of Being, Ways of Reading: Asian-American Biblical Interpretation*, edited by Mary F. Foskett and Jeffrey K. Kuan, 152–63. St. Louis: Chalice, 2006.

"'She Stood in Tears amid the Alien Corn': Ruth, the Perpetual Foreigner and Model Minority." In *They Were All Together in One Place? Toward Minority Biblical Criticism*, edited by Randall C. Bailey, Tat-Siong Benny Liew, and Fernando F. Segovia, 119–40. Atlanta: Society of Biblical Literature, 2009.

"The Woman Warrior Revisited: Jael, Fa Mulan, and American Orientalism." In *Joshua and Judges*, edited by Athalya Brenner and Gale A. Yee, 175–90. Texts@Contexts. Minneapolis: Fortress, 2013.

"Coveting the Vineyard: As Asian American Reading of 1 Kings 21." In *Samuel, Kings, and Chronicles, I*, edited by Athalya Brenner-Idan and Archie C. C. Lee, 46–64. Texts@Contexts. London: Bloomsbury T. & T. Clark, 2016.

"Racial Melancholia in the Book of Ruth." In *The Five Scrolls*, edited by Athalya Brenner-Idan, Gale A. Yee, and Archie C. C. Lee, 61–70. Texts@Contexts. London: Bloomsbury T. & T. Clark, 2018.

"Introduction: Definitions, Explorations, and Intersections," in *The Hebrew Bible: Feminist and Intersectional Perspectives*, edited by Gale A. Yee, 1–38. Minneapolis: Fortress, 2018.

"Of Foreigners and Eunuchs: An Asian American Reading of Isa. 56.1–8." In *T & T Clark Handbook of Asian American Biblical Hermeneutics*, edited by Uriah Y. Kim and Seung Ai Yang, 261–72. London: T. & T. Clark, 2019.

Abbreviations

AB	Anchor Bible
ABD	*Anchor Bible Dictionary*. Edited by David Noel Freedman. 6 vols. New York: Doubleday, 1992
ANET	*Ancient Near Eastern Texts Relating to the Old Testament*. Edited by James B. Pritchard. 3rd ed. Princeton: Princeton University Press, 1969
API	Asian American and Pacific Islanders
BAR	*Biblical Archaeology Review*
Bib	*Biblica*
BibInt	*Biblical Interpretation*
BTB	*Biblical Theology Bulletin*
CBQ	*Catholic Biblical Quarterly*
CBR	*Currents in Biblical Research*
FCB	Feminist Companion to the Bible
JAAAT	*Journal of Asian and Asian American Theology*
JBL	*Journal of Biblical Literature*
JFSR	*Journal of Feminist Studies in Religion*
JSOT	*Journal for the Study of the Old Testament*
JSOTSup	Journal for the Study of the Old Testament Supplements
LHBOTS	Library of Hebrew Bible / Old Testament Studies
MM	Memar Marqah

OTL	Old Testament Library
PANAAWTM	Pacific Asian North American Asian Women in Theology and Ministry
SBLDS	Society of Biblical Literature Dissertation Series
SymS	Symposium Series (Society of Biblical Literature)
VT	*Vetus Testamentum*
ZAW	*Zeitschrift für die alttestamentliche Wissenschaft*

1

Introduction

My Autobiographical Journey

FOR YEARS MY GOOD friend Kwok Pui Lan urged me to edit my articles on Asian American biblical hermeneutics into a book. Each time I resisted. Given the plurality of Asian American ethnicities, their diverse immigration histories to the United States, and their different generational experiences in this dominant white world, I felt that the project would be rather arrogant and presumptuous. How can I even think to offer a monograph on Asian American biblical hermeneutics and cover it adequately? The diversity of this vibrant field of study has already been documented by several excellent collections.[1] It was only when I reflected on my own journey as an intersectional Chinese American biblical scholar who ended up as the first Asian American and first woman of color to be named president of the Society of Biblical Literature (SBL) that such a retrospective might be worthwhile for later generations of racial/ethnic women. Hence, the *Towards* in the title of this book reflects the modesty of this enterprise. An Asian American biblical hermeneutics is still in process, not only for myself, but also for the field. I still continue to learn how to interpret the biblical text through an Asian American lens. This book documents only a part of that journey.

When I taught at Episcopal Divinity School (1998–2017), I would have all of my students complete Norman Gottwald's self-inventory on

---

1. See especially, Foskett and Kuan, eds., *Ways of Being*; Kim and Yang, *T. & T. Clark Handbook of Asian American*; Sun, "Recent Research."

biblical hermeneutics and discuss their results together.² This instrument has students identify the factors at play when they interpret the biblical text. The inventory contains eighteen of them, including church tradition, gender, ethnicity, social class, education, explicit and implicit political stances, and so forth. Discussing this survey was not only a way to get the students to introduce themselves and one another, but also to make them aware of the forces operative in their study of the Bible whether they were conscious of them or not. Revelatory are those factors that students choose to complete and the ones they pass over. To explain how I came to be an Asian American intersectional biblical scholar, I therefore had to reflect autobiographically on my social location over the years by considering how I would complete a similar survey if I was in their shoes.

The following is a distillation of a number of autobiographies that I have written regarding my social location as a female Asian American biblical scholar,³ along with other aspects of my bio that will appear in the following chapters of this book. Unlike most Asian Americans and Pacific Islanders (API) whom I know, I am a third-generation Chinese American, raised in the slums of Chicago with playmates who were Black and Puerto Rican. Unlike first-generation Asian American immigrants, I was not "assimilated" into the dominant white society. I did not have to adapt a previous Asian context to the new and often hostile one in America. As a third-generation descendant of Chinese immigrants, I was born into this society and had to come to terms with it straightaway. I had to become an "American" long before I actually became an "Asian American." But I had to become an American by growing up and living as a racial-ethnic minority in a white-dominated society that had a violent history of racial conflict.

I am the oldest of twelve children, the first of my family to go to college. The Catholicism of my Roman Catholic parents is an important aspect of my identity because the Christian API's I usually encounter are Protestant, many of whom were or are evangelical. Unlike Protestants, I was never bound by their doctrines of biblical authority, particularly in

---

2. Gottwald, "Framing Biblical Interpretation."

3. Yee, "An Autobiographical Approach"; Yee, "Where Are You Really From?"; Yee, "Negotiating Shifts in Life's Paradigms"; Yee, "The Process of Becoming"; Yee, "The Woman Warrior Within." Lest one disparage an autobiographical approach, allow me to mention a firmly entrenched "male" autobiographical genre that turns up quite frequently at the Society of Biblical Literature: "How my mind has changed and how it has remained the same."

debates in the public square on the use of the Bible in social and cultural issues. For this reason, the hermeneutics of suspicion regarding the text came more easily and with less struggle for me than for some of my Protestant colleagues. I was able to name the sexism, racism, homophobia, and other isms in the text as *not* the Word of God, while still deeply appreciating the Bible's beauty and spirituality. Released from such doctrinal challenges, my eventual approach to the text was in asking the ethical questions, "Whom does my interpretation help, whom does it hurt, and whose interests does it serve?"

I became an English major in college when it became clear that I would never pass the math courses needed for my pre-med major. During my senior year I attended a Taizé gathering with a college friend and had a religious conversion. I actually ended up in Taizé, France, with the first contingent from the US for one of their Councils of Youth (1971). I then hitchhiked afterwards to several Christian communities in Switzerland, Germany, and the Netherlands, returning to the US in the "fire of the Spirit." While leading Catholic charismatic prayer meetings, I completed a master's degree in New Testament (Loyola University of Chicago, 1975) and a doctoral degree in Hebrew Bible (University of St. Michael's College, Toronto School of Theology, 1985).

While a doctoral student in the '70s, I became engrossed in the paradigm shift from historical criticism to literary criticism of the biblical text, because of my methodological familiarity with English literature during my undergraduate days. I was not a feminist during that period. However, the shift to a literary paradigm facilitated viewing the biblical text as a site of struggle among competing interpretations, and the misogyny of the text became very apparent. I became a feminist after team teaching a Women in Religion course with a member of the English department at my first job at the College (now University) of St. Thomas in St. Paul, Minnesota, and in the late '80s I became cochair and then chair of the Women in the Biblical World Section of the SBL.

As I reflected on my Asian American-ness, I recognized that my "becoming" an Asian American scholar was a process that had been percolating since my youth. Even though I was always a woman, I had to name myself as a feminist when I finally realized that I was. Similarly, even though I was always an Asian American, I had to claim it eventually as an advocacy stance. The growing consciousness of my different positionalities were the result of both personal and institutional factors. I noticed that my academic and personal formation followed theoretical shifts in my guild, the SBL. It took a while for the SBL to acknowledge and support the female[4] and racial/ethnic scholars in its midst, since its establishment in 1880. Only in 1992 were both the Status of Women in the Profession Committee and the Committee on Underrepresented Racial and Ethnic Minority in the Profession (CUREMP) finally launched. I was one of the founding members of CUREMP with Vincent Wimbush, Fernando Segovia, Randall Bailey, and Henry Sun (who is no longer in the field). The men comprised the requisite African American, Latinx American, and Asian American ethnicities. I was probably added as the token feminist of the group. I became the next chair of CUREMP from 1995 to 1997 and still look forward to their lunches for racial/ethnic biblicists on Mondays of the annual SBL meetings to this day.

In 1994, Kwok Pui Lan invited me to be on a panel on the topic of the impact of national histories on the politics of identity at the American Academy of Religion annual meeting. I mark this panel as my official "coming out" as an Asian American. The paper I presented at this panel forms Chapter 3 of this book. From this point on in my career, I became energetically involved with several Asian American groups. In 1995, I joined the Ethnic Chinese Biblical Colloquium as a founding member, the lone female at its first meeting at Andover Newton Theological School. I was one of the founding members of the SBL's Asian and Asian American Biblical Studies Consultation and on its steering committee from 1994 to 1999. I became one of the faculty advisors in 1998 for PAN-AAWTM (Pacific Asian and North American Asian Women in Theology and Ministry), organizing several of its meetings in Boston; Stony Point, New York; Berkeley, California; and Orange, California. I have presented for The Gathering for API Episcopalians in the Los Angeles area. I was also fortunate to bring my expertise to a global Asian context. I was the plenary speaker for the 2014 International Congress of Ethnic Chinese Biblical Scholars at the Chinese University of Hong Kong and coedited the volume of its conference proceedings.[5] In 2019, I was invited to present on feminist and intersectional biblical interpretation at different conferences at Shanghai University and Shandong University (Shanghai and Jinan, People's Republic of China).

The chapters of this book comprise several of my attempts to read the biblical texts through an Asian American lens. Because I really had

---

4. Documented in Taylor, "Celebrating 125 Years."
5. Yee and Yieh, eds., *Honouring the Past*.

no models for such analyses, this book is titled *Towards an Asian American Biblical Hermeneutics*. These essays are my initial stabs. It may seem incongruous that Chapter 2, "Methodological Interventions," is from the introduction of my book *The Hebrew Bible: Feminist and Intersectional Perspectives*.[6] However, that chapter summarizes my academic interests in the methods of biblical interpretation, which lays the foundation for my feminist intersectional Asian American essays. Unlike many biblical scholars of my acquaintance, I did not specialize in a particular corpus of biblical books, such as the Pentateuch, historical books, prophets, or wisdom literature, even though I have published in all these areas. I was continually fascinated by the many different exegetical and interdisciplinary methods of studying the Bible. I was intrigued by the specific questions each of these methods asked of a text, and discovered, as well, their limitations and the questions they were unable to answer. This fascination can be seen not only in my edited books on methods,[7] but also in several articles on methods, where I employed them in texts that have absorbed me.[8] All of my Asian American essays are grounded in and flow from my scholarly training and expertise in different modes of biblical exegesis.

As stated above, Chapter 3, "Inculturation and Diversity in the Politics of National Identity," was my first foray in reflecting on my social location as an Asian American in 1994.[9] I had never really thought seriously about my Asian American-ness before this invitation to speak at the American Academy of Religion, which was another first. I remember that I had to contact my Auntie Toy to brief me on the immigration history of my maternal grandparents and their children, including my mother.[10] I saw how this personal history was interwoven with what was politically happening in the US. It was also the first time I declared my troika'd gendered, raced and classed identities as a female Chinese American from the lower classes. I remember that I was astounded that the big

6. Yee, ed., *The Hebrew Bible*.

7. Yee, ed., *Judges & Method*, an expansion of the 1995 first edition.

8. Yee, "'Fraught with Background'"; Yee, "An Analysis of Prov 8:22–31"; Yee, "Gender, Class, and the Social-Scientific Study"; Yee, "Ideological Criticism"; Yee, "Ideological Criticism and Woman as Evil"; Yee, "Materialist Analysis"; Yee, "Postcolonial Biblical Criticism"; Yee, "Recovering Marginalized Groups"; Yee, "Anatomy of Biblical Parody"; Yee, "The Author/Text/Reader and Power"; Yee, "The Bible and Art"; Yee, "The Social Sciences"; Yee, "What Is Cultural Criticism."

9. Yee, "Inculturation and Diversity."

10. My aunt has since published a memoir of her experiences as a picture bride. Kay and Gates, *An American Picture Bride*.

conference room was filled with all these Asian female faces. It was my first time meeting Kwok Pui Lan, chair of the panel, and Jung Ha Kim, copresenter, both later becoming my PANAAWTM sisters. A treasured memory was future New Testament scholar Mary Foskett coming up to introduce herself to me, appreciating that I brought up the topic of the adoption of Asian children by white parents, which resonated with her own experience as an adoptee.[11] Mary would later invite me to contribute an essay for the first anthology of Asian American biblical interpretation, *Ways of Being, Ways of Reading*, which became Chapter 5 of the present book.[12]

Chapter 4, "Refiguring the Missionary Position or We Asian North American Women Won't Take This Lying Down," was a talk given at my very first PANAAWTM meeting in 1998. It was held at Emmanuel College, one of the schools of the Toronto School of Theology where I did my doctoral studies. The talk was geared to Asian immigrant students studying theology in a Canadian context. This was my first encounter with the wonderful Asian and Asian American women theologians of PANAAWTM, who have organized these yearly gatherings of female Asian and Asian North American students in seminaries and graduate departments of theology and religious studies since 1984 (https://www.panaawtm.org/). This conference was an important milestone for me, when the faculty advisors and speakers all went out for dim sum when it was over. Over the meal Kwok Pui Lan passed around this advertisement for an interim two-year position in studies in feminist liberation theologies at Episcopal Divinity School where she taught. She was hoping that one of the faculty had students who might be interested. I applied for it, even though I was already a tenured full professor at my institution. I got the job and spent eighteen great years at one of the most antiracist and anti-oppression seminaries in the US, and as faculty advisor for PANAAWTM, which celebrated its thirty-fifth anniversary in 2020.

Chapter 5, "Yin/Yang Is Not Me," was the first paper I presented at the SBL from an Asian American perspective. As its subtitle conveys, it was "An Exploration into an Asian American Biblical Hermeneutics."[13] It was my first crack at developing an Asian American hermeneutics of the biblical text. It related two personal experiences from my social location,

---

11. Foskett, "Obscured Beginnings"
12. Foskett and Kuan, eds., *Ways of Being*.
13. Yee, "Yin/Yang Is Not Me."

which became starting points for my theorizing through an Asian American lens. Using W. E. B. Du Bois's criteria for an authentic Black theater as a springboard, it suggested what an Asian American biblical hermeneutics *about us, by us, for us, and near us* might look like. It then described my own process of becoming an Asian American by reflecting upon the two prongs of my hyphenated Asian American situation. The essay challenged Asian American biblical scholars to make "whiteness" visible in the production of their readings. I write this introduction during a terrible COVID-19 pandemic, in which white bullies harass, attack, and blame Asian Americans for "Kung flu."[14] Just a few weeks before writing this Introduction, white supremacists and white nationalists abused the teachings of the Bible to legitimate a violent raid on the US Capitol as the Senate and Congress were counting the electoral votes for the new president.[15] Asian American biblical scholars must condemn such racism and nationalism lodged against us with a hermeneutics that is *about us, by us, for us, and near us* in the public square.

Chapter 6, "'She Stood in Tears amid the Alien Corn,'" was my first attempt to do an Asian American reading on a biblical text, the book of Ruth.[16] It was written for a two-week-long Wabash Center workshop over 2004–2005 titled "Reading and Teaching the Bible as Black, Asian American and Latino/a Scholars in the US." The workshop gathered racial-ethnic minority scholars to explore how they might cross the Black vs. white color line to form a coalition to transform the discipline of biblical studies.[17] With genuine camaraderie but also recognizing tensions, we shared and discussed one another's work, which eventually appeared in a Semeia Studies volume.[18] For my own paper, I delved not only into the history of the Chinese in the US, but also the huge field of Asian American studies. I was very much aware of the stereotype "model minority," but was not familiar with the label "perpetual foreigner." Nevertheless, I was completely familiar with its microaggression "Where are you *really* from?" when asked even after I informed questioners that I am from Cambridge, Massachusetts. Their transparent intent to discover my ethnicity presumed that I was a foreigner and not a real citizen of the US.

14. Oppenheim, "Professor Tracks Rise."
15. The raid took place on January 6, 2021. See Kuruvilla, "White Christian Radicalization."
16. Yee, "'She Stood in Tears.'"
17. Bailey et al., "Toward Minority Biblical Criticism," 3–4.
18. Bailey et al., eds., *They Were All Together in One Place?*

Reading these two stereotypes in the person of Ruth came quite naturally to me, because of the narrative's rich social matrixes and the different power relations formed among them.

Chapter 7, "Racial Melancholia in the Book of Ruth," was a distinctly different Asian American interpretation of the book.[19] I place these two analyses next to each other in this volume to demonstrate how different methodologies produced diverse readings of the same text. Among my experimentation with different exegetical methods, psychoanalytic criticism did not appeal to me until I read Anne Anlin Cheng's *The Melancholy of Race: Psychoanalysis, Assimilation, and Hidden Grief*.[20] Melancholia was the inability to "get over" a loss, and Cheng applied Freud's notion to the phenomenon of racial melancholia that affects both whites and the racial other. I argued that the many losses Ruth experienced comprised a list of unarticulated grief, losses that were not named and therefore not properly mourned. Cheng's declaration that the US was "a nation at ease with grievance but not with grief"[21] found resonances in an op-ed Judith Butler recently wrote, "Why Donald Trump Will Never Admit Defeat."[22] Utilizing Freud's notion of melancholia, Butler argues that Trump was not able to mourn the loss, not only of the hundreds of thousands to the pandemic, but also of his own election. Mourning, for Freud, was the acknowledgment of loss, a "letting go" and "getting over." But, "whether it is deaths from Covid-19 or his own election defeat, admitting loss is something Trump finds impossible to do." He and his white followers were racial melancholics more at ease with political fantasies of grievance and victimhood. Rather than mourn for those who died from COVID-19, or mourn the loss of an election that did not turn out their way and the loss of their white privilege and entitlement, and enraged that they were being replaced by Black and Brown bodies, the former president and his white followers unleashed their grievances in a violent assault on the Capitol.

Chapter 8, "The Woman Warrior Revisited," was an Asian American reading of Judges 4–5 on Sisera's assassin, Jael, expanding upon previous work analyzing Deborah and Jael as women warriors.[23] This new article provided an opportunity not only to delve into the fascinating person of

---

19. Yee, "Racial Melancholia."
20. Cheng, *The Melancholy of Race*.
21. Cheng, *The Melancholy of Race*, x.
22. Butler, "Why Donald Trump."
23. Yee, "By the Hand of a Woman."

Jael again, but also learn about the intriguing Chinese warrior Fa Mulan, who secretly took her disabled father's place to fight for the emperor. Both women shared a warriorhood that defied the conventions of male militarism at their time. Their ethnicities were also ambiguous, even though they were claimed as ethnic heroes in their respective Israelite and Chinese texts. Both shared the liminal gendered zone between male and female. Amplifying the reception histories of Jael and Mulan, I was able to discuss positively a feature of American Orientalism for myself, the Disney version of *Mulan*, and how I would have loved to have seen this movie in my early years.[24]

Chapter 9, "Coveting the Vineyard," was an experiment by the Minoritized Criticism Section of the SBL annual meeting in 2013.[25] Different racial/ethnic scholars were asked to interpret 1 Kgs 21, on Naboth and his vineyard, from their African American, Pacific Islander, Latinx American and Asian American perspectives. As the Asian American presenter, I ran into roadblocks working on this paper, resolving them by beginning with a metacommentary on actually doing a minoritized reading. I just could not compartmentalize the various aspects of the gendered and methodologically trained parts of me to siphon out an Asian American reading. I also objected to being forced to do an Asian American reading on a text that was just handed to me. I came to the conclusion that I was a hybrid, bringing together different identities and methodological expertise. Any analysis I accept to do will have an Asian American component to it, whether it is obvious or not, because Asian American is who I am. In the end, however, I was able to connect in the essay the story of the illegitimate seizure of Naboth's vineyard to the Japanese internment and relate the characters of Jezebel and Ahab to Orientalist stereotypes of Dragon Lady and Fu Manchu.

Chapter 10, "Of Foreigners and Eunuchs," was my contribution to the *T & T Clark Handbook of Asian American Biblical Hermeneutics*, edited by Uriah Kim and Seung Ai Yang.[26] I was asked to do something on the prophets, and I selected Isa 56:1–8 because it advocated for the inclusion of two populations (namely, foreigners and eunuchs) into the worshiping community amid the nationalistic and ethnocentric struggles in Persian-period Yehud. I had already dealt with the Asian American

---

24. Yee, "The Woman Warrior Revisited."
25. Yee, "Coveting the Vineyard."
26. Yee, "Of Foreigners and Eunuchs."

perpetual-foreigner stereotype in my analysis of the book of Ruth.[27] This passage from Third Isaiah provided a biblical affirmation for the inclusion of Asian immigrants and refugees, especially from South Asia and Southwest Asia (the Middle East) into the religious assembly. Moreover, I interpreted the eunuchs of Isa 56 as sexual minorities, which they were during the time of Third Isaiah. LGBTQ communities have been condemned on the basis of a few verses in the Bible. Moreover, Asian immigrant churches here in the US have been resistant to including LGBTQ worshipers in their assemblies. My hope in writing this essay was to provide a biblical text that affirmed and welcomed them, just as God brought the outcasts in Isa 56:7–8 to God's holy mountain to worship.

Chapter 11, "Jerusalem, Samaria, and Sodom: A Sisterly Urban Triad in Ezekiel 16:44–63" concludes this volume. It is dedicated to Kwok Pui Lan in appreciation for her persistence in urging me to get this book done and for her deep friendship. My previous work on the sordid histories of Ezekiel's notorious women characters, Jerusalem (Ezek 16:1–43) and Oholah and Oholibah (Ezek 23), made me curious about the extended characterization of Jerusalem's sisters in Ezek 16:44–63. I could understand the addition of Samaria as the Northern capital city and rival of Jerusalem, since their pairing as sisters occurred in Jer 3:6–11 and Ezek 23. However, the addition of Sodom as Jerusalem's sister was puzzling, especially in its characterization as being proud, gluttonous, and enjoying "the life of Riley," but neglecting the poor and needy. This characterization of Sodom is usually understood as an alternate tradition that diverges from the threatening male/male gang rape of Gen 19. This essay argues that the context of these verses are the mixed ethnic communities in the post-582 BCE social landscape, not only in Samaria and Yehud, but particularly in Egypt, which was embodied in the personification of Sodom as Jerusalem's sister. Instead of the typical binary of peoples of the land versus the returnees from Babylonia, the social context also included internally remixed groups in Samaria and the various diasporic Jews in Egypt.

As one can see from this introduction, I have only taken individual whacks at an Asian American biblical hermeneutics. Hopefully, they will provide a basis for intrepid Asian American biblical scholars to develop a more systematic approach to Asian American biblical hermeneutics. Onward!

27. See Chapter 6 of this volume.

Works Cited

Bailey, Randall C., et al., eds. *They Were All Together in One Place? Toward Minority Biblical Criticism.* Semeia Studies 57. Atlanta: Society of Biblical Literature, 2009.

———. "Toward Minority Biblical Criticism: Framework, Contours, Dynamics." In *They Were All Together in One Place?: Toward Minority Biblical Criticism*, edited by Randall C. Bailey et al., 3–43. Semeia Studies 57. Atlanta: Society of Biblical Literature, 2009.

Butler, Judith. "Why Donald Trump Will Never Admit Defeat." *Guardian*, January 20, 2021. https://www.theguardian.com/commentisfree/2021/jan/20/donald-trump-election-defeat-covid-19-deaths/.

Cheng, Anne Anlin. *The Melancholy of Race: Psychoanalysis, Assimilation, and Hidden Grief.* Race and American Culture. New York: Oxford University Press, 2001.

Foskett, Mary F. "Obscured Beginnings: Lessons from the Study of Christian Origins." In *Ways of Being, Ways of Reading: Asian American Biblical Interpretation*, edited by Mary F. Foskett and Jeffrey Kah-jin Kuan, 178–91. St. Louis: Chalice, 2006.

Foskett, Mary F., and Jeffrey Kah-jin Kuan, eds. *Ways of Being, Ways of Reading: Asian American Biblical Interpretation.* St. Louis: Chalice, 2006.

Gottwald, Norman K. "Framing Biblical Interpretation at New York Theological Seminary: A Student Self-Inventory on Biblical Hermeneutics." In *Reading from This Place.* Vol. 1, *Social Location and Biblical Interpretation in the United States*, edited by Fernando F. Segovia and Mary Ann Tolbert, 251–61. 2 vols. Minneapolis: Fortress, 1995. Republished in Gottwald, *Social Justice and the Hebrew Bible*, 3:77–88. 3 vols. Center and Library for the Bible and Social Justice. Eugene, OR: Cascade Books, 2018.

Kay, Toy, and Janine Gates. *An American Picture Bride.* Centralia WA: Gorham, 2017.

Kim, Uriah Y, and Seung Ai Yang, eds. *T & T Clark Handbook of Asian American Biblical Hermeneutics.* London: T. & T. Clark, 2019.

Kuruvilla, Carol. "White Christian Radicalization Is a Violent Threat." *HuffPost*, January 15, 2021. *Yahoo! News* (website). https://www.yahoo.com/huffpost/white-christian-nationalism-capitol-riot-155511787.html/.

Oppenheim, Jamie. "Professor Tracks Rise in Racism Linked to Pandemic." *SF State News*, March 27, 2020. https://news.sfsu.edu/news-story/professor-tracks-rise-racism-linked-pandemic/.

Sun, Chloe. "Recent Research on Asian and Asian American Hermeneutics Related to the Hebrew Bible." *CBR* 17 (2019) 238–65.

Taylor, Marion Ann. "Celebrating 125 Years of Women in the Society of Biblical Literature (1894–2019)." In *Women and The Society of Biblical Literature*, edited by Nicole L. Tilford, 1–44. Biblical Scholarship in North America 29. Atlanta: SBL Press, 2019.

Yee, Gale A. "An Analysis of Prov 8:22–31 according to Style and Structure." *ZAW* 94 (1982) 58–66.

———. "The Anatomy of Biblical Parody: The Dirge Form in 2 Samuel 1 and Isaiah 14." *CBQ* 50 (1988) 565–86.

———. "The Author/Text/Reader and Power: Suggestions for a Critical Framework in Biblical Studies." In *Reading from This Place: Social Location and Biblical Interpretation.* Vol. 1, *Social Location and Biblical Interpretation in the United*

States, edited by Fernando F. Segovia and Mary Ann Tolbert, 109–18. 2 vols. Minneapolis: Fortress, 1995.

———. "An Autobiographical Approach to Feminist Biblical Scholarship." *Encounter* 67 (2006) 375–90.

———. "The Bible and Art." In *Anselm Companion to the Old Testament*, edited by Corrine L. Carvalho, 80–97. Winona, MN: Anselm Academic, 2014.

———. "'By the Hand of a Woman': The Biblical Metaphor of the Woman Warrior." *Semeia* 61 (1993) 99–132.

———. "Coveting the Vineyard: As Asian American Reading of 1 Kings 21." In *Samuel, Kings, and Chronicles, I*, edited by Athalya Brenner-Idan and Archie C. C. Lee, 46–64. Texts@Contexts. London: Bloomsbury T. & T. Clark, 2016.

———. "'Fraught with Background': Literary Ambiguity in II Sam 11." *Interpretation* 42 (1988) 240–53.

———. "Gender, Class, and the Social-Scientific Study of Genesis 2–3." *Semeia* 87 (1999) 177–92.

———, ed. *The Hebrew Bible: Feminist and Intersectional Perspectives*. Minneapolis: Fortress, 2018.

———. "Ideological Criticism." In *Dictionary of Biblical Interpretation. A–J*, edited by John H. Hayes, 534–37. Nashville: Abingdon, 1999.

———. "Ideological Criticism and Woman as Evil." In *Poor Banished Children of Eve: Woman as Evil in the Hebrew Bible*, 9–28. Minneapolis: Fortress, 2003.

———. "Inculturation and Diversity in the Politics of National Identity." *JAAAT* 2 (1997) 108–12.

———, ed. *Judges & Method: New Approaches in Biblical Studies*. 2nd ed. Minneapolis: Fortress, 2007 (1st ed., 1995).

———. "Materialist Analysis of the Prophets." In *The Oxford Handbook of the Prophets*, edited by Carolyn J. Sharp, 491–506. Oxford Handbooks. New York: Oxford University Press, 2016.

———. "Negotiating Shifts in Life's Paradigms." In *Women and The Society of Biblical Literature*, edited by Nicole L. Tilford, 103–12. Biblical Scholarship in North America 29. Atlanta: SBL Press, 2019.

———. "Of Foreigners and Eunuchs: An Asian American Reading of Isa. 56.1–8." In *T & T Clark Handbook of Asian American Biblical Hermeneutics*, edited by Uriah Y. Kim and Seung Ai Yang, 261–72. London: T. & T. Clark, 2019.

———. *Poor Banished Children of Eve: Women as Evil in the Hebrew Bible*. Minneapolis: Fortress, 2003.

———. "Postcolonial Biblical Criticism." In *Methods for Exodus*, edited by Thomas B. Dozeman, 193–233. Methods in Biblical Interpretation. Cambridge: Cambridge University Press, 2010.

———. "The Process of Becoming for a Woman Warrior from the Slums." In *Asian and Asian American Women in Theology and Religion: Embodying Knowledge*, edited by Kwok Pui-Lan, 15–30. Asian Christianity in the Diaspora. Cham, Switzerland: Palgrave Macmillan, 2020.

———. "Racial Melancholia in the Book of Ruth." In *The Five Scrolls*, edited by Athalya Brenner-Idan, Gale A. Yee, and Archie C. C. Lee, 61–70. Texts@Contexts. London: Bloomsbury T. & T. Clark, 2018.

———. "Recovering Marginalized Groups in Ancient Israel: Methodological Considerations." In *To Break Every Yoke: Essays in Honor of Marvin L. Chaney*, edited by Robert B. Coote and Norman K. Gottwald, 10–27. The Social World of Biblical Antiquity, 2nd ser., 3. Sheffield: Sheffield Phoenix, 2007.

———. "'She Stood in Tears amid the Alien Corn': Ruth, the Perpetual Foreigner and Model Minority." In *They Were All Together in One Place? Toward Minority Biblical Criticism*, edited by Randall C. Bailey et al., 119–40. Semeia Studies 57. Atlanta: Society of Biblical Literature, 2009.

———. "The Social Sciences and the Biblical Woman as Evil." In *Poor Banished Children of Eve: Woman as Evil in the Hebrew Bible*, 29–58, 171–83. Minneapolis: Fortress, 2003.

———. "What Is Cultural Criticism of the Old Testament?" In *Why Read the Old Testament? Questions Asked and Unasked: The Legacy of Fr. Lawrence Boadt*, edited by Corrine L. Carvalho, 43–55. Mahwah, NJ: Paulist, 2013.

———. "Where Are You Really From? An Asian American Feminist Biblical Scholar Reflects on Her Guild." In *New Feminist Christianity: Many Voices, Many Views*, edited by Mary E. Hunt and Diann L. Neu, 79–85. Woodstock, VT: Skylight Paths, 2010.

———. "The Woman Warrior Revisited: Jael, Fa Mulan, and American Orientalism." In *Joshua and Judges*, edited by Athalya Brenner-Idan and Gale A. Yee, 175–90. Texts@Contexts. Minneapolis: Fortress, 2013.

———. "The Woman Warrior within and about Me." *Inheritance: Heritage, Culture, Faith* 64/2 (2019) 82–87.

———. "Yin/Yang Is Not Me: An Exploration into an Asian American Biblical Hermeneutics." In *Ways of Being, Ways of Reading: Asian-American Biblical Interpretation*, edited by Mary F. Foskett and Jeffrey K. Kuan, 152–63. St. Louis: Chalice, 2006.

Yee, Gale A., and John Y. H. Yieh, eds. *Honouring the Past, Looking to the Future: Essays from the 2014 International Congress of Ethnic Chinese Biblical Scholars*. Chung King Lecture Series 12. Shatin N. T., Hong Kong: Divinity School of Chung Chi College, Chinese University of Hong Kong, 2016.

2

Methodological Interventions
Definitions, Explorations, and Intersections[1]

Definitions

THE BIBLE HAS BEEN a foundational text, not only for the religious communities of Jews and Christians, but particularly for its influence in the formation and perpetuation of certain gender relations that privileged men and disenfranchised women. Serious critique against this inequality between the genders arose particularly in the latter half of the twentieth century by the proponents of feminism and intersectionality and continues in the present day. Let's begin this introductory essay by defining "feminism" and "intersectionality," the major themes of this book. After this, I will present a short history of the women's movement and the various modes of feminist theorizing, and then turn to feminist and intersectional perspectives on the Bible

In its most general sense, the word "feminism" refers to the political activism by women on behalf of women.[2] When used in biblical studies, feminist criticism is one of a series of recent methods of biblical exegesis (interpretation) that fall under the term "ideological criticism." The ideological criticisms investigate the power differentials in certain social relationships in the production of the text (who wrote it, when, and why),

---

1. This essay was originally published as Yee, "Introduction: Definitions, Explorations, and Intersections."

2 McCann and Kim, "Introduction: Feminist Theory," 1.

how these power relations are reproduced in the text itself, and how they are consumed by readers of various social groups. For example, materialist criticism (aka Marxist or socioeconomic criticism) investigates ideologies of economic class relations that keep certain classes wealthier and others poorer. Postcolonial criticism looks at relations between colonizer and colonized and the ideologies that keep the conquerors and the natives in their respective places. Cultural criticism examines the ideologies of how the Bible was received and used in high and popular culture throughout the ages and globally. And so, for our purposes, feminist criticism studies the ideologies of gender that legitimize unequal relations between men and women. Many schools of thought exist in feminist studies, such as liberal feminism, radical feminism, Marxist/socialist feminism, postmodern feminism, psychoanalytic feminism, postcolonial feminism, feminisms of color, ecofeminism, to name a few.[3] This rich diversity of feminist thinking will be reflected in the various theoretical approaches of feminist biblical scholars.

"Intersectionality" was a term coined in 1989 by the African American lawyer, Kimberlé Crenshaw, to theorize the complex interconnections between gender, race, and class that have marginalized Black and non-white women in the subjugation they routinely experienced. Rich white men experience "oppression" differently from poor women of color, because both occupy different but intersected and often conflicted locations on gender, race, and class continuums. These interconnections, however, had been explored by African American theorists long before the term became fashionable.[4] Moreover, intersectional interfaces have sometimes been broadened theoretically to include other categories of analysis along with gender, race, and class, such as sexuality, colonial status, ethnicity, physical ability, and so forth.[5]

---

3. Tong, *Feminist Thought*.

4. Cf. The Combahee River Collective, "A Black Feminist Statement"; Davis, *Women, Race and Class*; hooks, *Feminist Theory*.

5. Cho et al., "Toward a Field of Intersectionality Studies"; Dill and Zambrana, "Critical Thinking about Inequality."

Can Women Become Like Men? Do Women Want To? Should They Want To?

The feminist movement has often been described through the metaphor of "waves."[6] The first wave possibly began in the eighteenth century with the treatise by Mary Wollstonecraft, *A Vindication of the Rights of Women*, who argued that the dependence of (privileged) women on men kept them in their homes and deprived them of becoming educated and being independent rational agents like men. The movement towards women's rights continued in the nineteenth century with the women's suffrage movement through other liberal feminists, such as Sarah and Angelina Grimké, Lucretia Mott, and Elizabeth Cady Stanton. The so-called second wave of US feminism began during the politically turbulent 1960s, sparked by the publication of Betty Friedan's *The Feminist Mystique* and the formation of the National Organization for Women (NOW) and other liberal feminist women's rights groups. Liberal feminism advocated equal rights for women in employment, education, reproduction and other legal matters. Some of its gains were the right to vote, to education, to work outside the home, access to birth control and legalized abortion, the enactment of affirmative action laws, and laws against sexual and domestic violence. However, liberal feminism primarily advanced the concerns of white, heterosexual, middle class, educated women and neglected the concerns of poor women of color. Furthermore, it made being "male" the ideal by presuming that women could become like men if they wanted to, that women wanted to become like men, and that they should want to become like men.[7]

However, for many women, becoming male was not the ideal to be strived for. Rather, the sexism and misogyny of men was the very source of their oppression. The radical feminists criticized the "rights" focus in the liberal feminist agenda, because they did not think that women's oppression would be eliminated simply by changing the laws, educating women, and letting them have careers outside the home. Women's oppression went much deeper because it was embedded in a male system characterized by power, dominance, hierarchy, and competition. According to Andrea Dworkin, "Sexism is the foundation on which all tyranny

---

6. However, the "waves" metaphor has been criticized particularly because it tended to exclude white antiracist women and women of color in the typical histories of the women's movement. See Nicholson, "Feminism in 'Waves': Useful Metaphor or Not?"

7. See chapter 1, on "Liberal Feminism," in Tong, *Feminist Thought*, 11–49.

is built. Every social form of hierarchy and abuse is modeled on male-over-female domination." Investigating the biblical text as embedded in a patriarchal system that subordinated women would be influential in the work of feminist biblical scholars, as we will see.

A good starting point to understand the different forms of radical feminism is the essay by Gayle Rubin, "The Traffic in Women." Rubin traced the roots of women's oppression by analyzing the male thinkers Karl Marx, Claude Levi-Strauss, Sigmund Freud, and Jacques Lacan on how they theorized what she called "the sex/gender system." The sex/gender system "is the set of arrangements by which a society transforms biological sexuality into products of human activity."[8] Sex referred to one's biological anatomy; gender referred to the social constructions based on one's biological anatomy. Patriarchy[9] took certain aspects related to male and female physical biology (such as, men are stronger than women, women have no penis) to construct gendered identities of maleness and femaleness, and social arrangements that served to empower men and disempower women. Patriarchy convinced men and women to believe that these social constructions of gender were somehow "natural," "essential," or "normal," and any deviance from them was "evil" and "abnormal." Using these constructions to give themselves power and authority, men kept women under their control. Women became objects of exchange by men "given in marriage, taken in battle, exchanged for favors, sent as tribute, traded, bought and sold."[10]

This conceptual separation of sex from gender helps us understand the different forms of radical feminism and their contrasting views on how to combat sexism. Radical-libertarian feminists believed that just focusing on female gender identity would limit their development as a full human person. They encouraged women to become androgynous, encouraging both masculine and feminine characteristics. This view worked on the presumption that male characteristics were aggressive, independent, and competitive, while female characteristics were compassionate, nurturing, and obedient. The radical-cultural feminist theologian, Mary Daly, scoffed at the notion of androgyny for women,

---

8. Rubin, "The Traffic in Women," 159.

9. Patriarchy refers a social system where males dominate and have authority over women as a group. It has a literal sense of "rule of the father," in kinship societies, such as ancient Israel's, where power in the family resides in the oldest living male, usually the father.

10. Rubin, "The Traffic in Women," 175.

as "John Travolta and Farrah Fawcett-Majors scotched-taped together" (or George Clooney and Beyoncé taped together). Radical-cultural feminists saw men and women as *essentially different* and wanted to reassert values of female culture that have been suppressed by male culture. Some radical-cultural feminists would go so far as advocating the overthrow of the existing male order, and creating a new society governed by the supposedly superior ethics of the female. Unlike liberal feminists who advocated sexual equality, these feminists believed that women were superior to men.[11]

From this point on, I will be discussing the ensuing forms of feminism rather quickly, touching mainly on feminist thought that has influenced feminist biblical scholars. Marxist feminists identified two systems oppressing women, class exploitation and patriarchy, examining the ways in which they colluded in subjugating women and where their interests collided.[12] They sharpened Marx's understanding of ideology[13] in the cultural production of gender in sophisticated ways.[14] They were particularly important in developing standpoint theory, which presumed that all knowledge was constructed from situated positions within different social locations that influenced how people viewed the world, such as different race, gender and class positions. Like the standpoint of the proletariat in Marxist theory, Hartsock argued that women's lives offered a particular vantage point that could provide a powerful critique of patriarchal institutions.[15] Standpoint theory and epistemology (how we know what we know) contested the prevailing views of scientific knowledge as objective, value-free, or neutral. They would become especially important when feminists of color developed their own theories of situational knowledge and of women's oppression.

Another reaction to the views of knowledge as objective and value-free were the postmodern feminisms.[16] In postmodern theory, social

---

11. For fuller discussions of the streams of radical-feminist thought, see Tong, *Feminist Thought*, 50–92; Mann, *Doing Feminist Theory*, 78–111.

12. Hartmann, "The Unhappy Marriage."

13. Ideology is a complex system of meaning that constructs "reality" for people and helps them understand their place in the world as natural, inevitable, and necessary. It is not "reality" itself.

14. Barrett, *Women's Oppression Today*.

15. Hartsock, "The Feminist Standpoint."

16. Postmodernism has been used interchangeably with poststructuralism, although poststructuralism applies narrowly to five French theorists: Jacques Derrida,

reality and human subjectivity (one's sense of self) were formed in and through language. What we know about the world and ourselves was defined and contested in the language of historically specific discourses. Discourse broadly referred to the various symbolic and linguistic systems and narratives used in human communication, such as legal discourse, political discourse, medical discourse, and right-wing discourse. There was no "reality" or "real world" because what we thought was "real" was known only through different and often conflicting discourses. What became socially or culturally legitimated as knowledge resulted from specific maneuvers by those in power who controlled the discourse, such as the institutional church regarding matters of belief. A shift thus occurs in theory from "*What* truth is being claimed and what truth is being suppressed?" to "*Whose* truth is being claimed and whose truth is being suppressed?" "Truth" was not objective; rather "truth" was what the dominant discourse maintained it to be. However, other suppressed voices, such as women's, had this tendency to make "truth" unstable and slippery. Postmodern feminists claimed that there was not a single discourse of gender or sexuality, but multiple and competing discourses. The gender identity of one's maleness and femaleness became the site of continual conflicts among discourses, such as religious discourse, medical discourse, literary discourse, right-wing discourse, liberal or radical feminist discourse, etc., for the allegiance of its subjects. Gender or maleness and femaleness did not exist outside of discourses. Determining what gender *was* depended on which discourse was attempting to define it and then analyzing the dominant powers that controlled it.[17]

Emerging in the 1990s, queer theory was an amalgam of postmodernism, feminist theory, and gay/lesbian studies. Postmodernism argued that all language was composed of binary pairs of opposition, like white/black, heaven/hell, soul/body, male/female, saved/sinner. The problem with binaries was that one part of the binary was privileged over the other. Queer theorists wanted to subvert the binaries of male/female and heterosexual/homosexual by highlighting gender and sexual fluidity. Taking her cues from Simone de Beauvoir's assertion that "one is not born, but rather *becomes* a woman," Judith Butler argued that because of its instability gender was "an identity instituted through a *stylized repetition*

Michel Foucault, Jacques Lacan, Julia Kristeva, and Roland Barthes.

17. For fuller discussions of postmodern feminisms see McCann and Kim, "Introduction: Theorizing Feminist Knowledge and Agency"; Tong, *Feminist Thought*, 192–210.

of acts."[18] Gender came into being through the repeated performances of acts, norms, and conventions associated with heterosexual maleness and femaleness, such as wearing pants for men and dresses for women. Typifying postmodern thinking and applying it to a transvestite on stage, Butler asserted:

> If the "reality" of gender is constituted by the performance itself, then there is no recourse to an essential and unrealized "sex" or "gender" which gender performances ostensibly express. Indeed, the transvestite's gender is as fully real as anyone whose performance complies with social expectations. Gender reality is performative which means, quite simply, that it is real only to the extent that it is performed.[19]

Sexualities themselves were socially constructed in queer feminist thinking.[20] According to Gayle Rubin, whom we encountered before, many sexualities and sexual expressions did not fit into the strict male/female and heterosexual/homosexual binaries and were regulated by societies and cultures in hierarchies of sexual value.[21] This observation became the basis for queer analyses of heteronormativity: the assumption that heterosexuality is "natural," "normal," and "right," privileging and institutionalizing heterosexuality as the "correct" form of sexual relations, and defining other sexual forms as "bad" and "unnatural." "Like gender, sexuality is political. It is organized into systems of power, which reward and encourage some individuals and activities, while punishing and suppressing others."[22]

Theorizing Intersecting Identities

> We believe that sexual politics under patriarchy is as pervasive in black women's lives as are the politics of class and race. We also often find it difficult to separate race from class from sex oppression because in our lives they are most often experienced

---

18. Butler, "Performative Acts."
19. Butler, "Performative Acts," 488–89.
20. Mann, *Doing Feminist Theory*, 235–38.
21. Rubin, "Thinking Sex." The following is a list of Rubin's non-normative sexualities: homosexual, unmarried, promiscuous, non-procreative, commercial, alone or in groups, casual, cross-generational, in public, pornography, with manufactured objects, sadomasochistic (p. 281).
22. Rubin, "Thinking Sex," 309.

simultaneously. We know that there is such a thing as racial-sexual oppression, which is neither solely racial nor solely sexual ... We need to articulate the real class situation of persons who are not merely raceless, sexless workers, but for whom racial and sexual oppression are significant determinants in their working/economic lives.[23]

African American feminists, such as the Combahee River Collective just cited, have long noted the interconnections among gender, race, class, and sexuality in the early days of the women's movement. They observed that they were oppressed as Blacks in a society dominated by whites, as women in a patriarchal society and by the civil rights and Black power movements, which were run mostly by men, and as lesbians in a society where heteronormativity was standard.

It took a while, however, for white feminists to catch on to such intersections. In an important study, Elizabeth Spelman critiqued the essentialist arguments of some important white feminists, who claimed that sexism was the more fundamental form of oppression than racism.[24] Citing Lorraine Bethel's colorful exclamation, "What Chou Mean WE, White Girl?"[25] Spelman remarked that it was not surprising that women of color have been distrustful of white women, who pointed out their commonalities when it seemed politically expedient to do, but overlooked their dissimilarities. In trying to argue that all women shared the same oppression under patriarchy, white feminists neglected to consider the differences among women in their presumption of "sameness." They seemed to assume that *all* women shared their white, middle-class, educated social locations.[26] White feminists often invoked the notion of "sisterhood" to mobilize women politically and stress women's common concerns. However, according to Audre Lorde, "[T]here is a pretense to homogeneity of experience covered by the word *sisterhood* that does not in fact exist...Certainly there are very real differences between us of race, age, and sex. But it is not those differences between us that are separating us. It is rather our refusal to recognize those differences."[27] She described her social location as a Black, female, lesbian mother of a

23. The Combahee River Collective, "A Black Feminist Statement," 117.
24. Spelman, *Inessential Woman*, 114–32.
25. Bethel, "What Chou Mean WE, White Girl?"
26. Spelman, *Inessential Woman*, 138–39, fn 6.
27. Lorde, *Sister Outsider*, 115–16.

daughter and a son, poet, and partner in a racially mixed relationship as a "sister outsider."

Before recognizing intersectionality as a critical aspect of feminist theory, white feminists had different ways of dealing with multiple oppressions. As Spelman pointed out, one model was to rank oppressions in a hierarchy, treating one form of oppression as earlier or more fundamental than others. Recall Andrea Dworkin's claim above that "Sexism is the foundation on which all tyranny is built. Every social form of hierarchy and abuse is modeled on male-over-female domination." Some Marxist feminists privileged class oppression, with gender and race oppressions as less important derivatives. Another way of dealing with multiple oppressions was known variously as the "tootsie roll," "pop-bead," and "ampersand" approach.[28] This was an additive model in which multiple oppressions, such as racism, sexism, and classism, were treated as separate and distinct. Oppressions were simply added together, and people just described as doubly or triply subjugated.

Neither model adequately dealt with the reality that oppressions formed an integrated whole with each continually interwoven with the other. The Combahee River Collective, cited above, described the interconnectedness of oppressions as occurring "simultaneously." Kimberlé Crenshaw described it as "intersectionality," which highlighted the fact that women of color were situated within at least two subordinated groups that frequently pursued conflicting political agendas. She noted that the experiences of Black women were assumed to be synonymous with either Black males by antiracist strategies or with white women by feminist ones. The single-issue focus of these strategies ignored the full dimension of racist and sexist oppression experienced by women of color.[29]

African American feminist Patricia Hill Collins developed Crenshaw's intersectionality with her own theory of the "matrix of domination."

> Intersectional paradigms remind us that oppression cannot be reduced to one fundamental type, and that oppressions work together in producing injustice. In contrast, the matrix of domination refers to how these intersecting oppressions are actually organized.[30]

---

28. Spelman, *Inessential Woman*, 114–15, 136–37; King, "Multiple Jeopardy."
29. Crenshaw, "Mapping the Margins."
30. Collins, *Black Feminist Thought*, 21.

According to Collins, any particular matrix of domination was organized through four interrelated domains of power: the *structural* (institutional structures of society), the *disciplinary* (ideas and practices that characterized and sustained bureaucratic hierarchies), the *hegemonic* (the ideas, symbols, and ideologies that shaped consciousness), and the *interpersonal* (the interactions of people at the macro- and microlevels of social organization).[31] "Each domain serves a particular purpose. The structural domain organizes oppression, whereas the disciplinary domain manages it. The hegemonic domain justifies oppression, and the interpersonal domain influences everyday lived experience and the individual consciousness that ensues."[32] In the politics of power and empowerment, people could simultaneously be both oppressors and oppressed, powerful and powerless, because of their different and shifting locations in a matrix of domination. For example, June Jordan meditated on being an African American female in the Sheraton British Colonial Hotel in the Bahamas, being serviced by lower-class Afro-Caribbean maids, waiters, and market vendors. Even though in the US, she would endure systemic racism for her blackness, she was privileged in race and class compared to the service workers in the Bahamas.[33] Collins argued that Black feminism needed to develop more complex notions of empowerment and resistance, by being cognizant of the ways in which a matrix of domination was structured through those interrelated domains of power. The simplistic model of oppressors and oppressed did not adequately deal with the complexity of the matrix of domination, which worked, not only along certain axes—race, gender, class, sexuality—but also through the four interconnected domains of power.[34]

African American feminists were not alone in theorizing the intersections of gender, race, class, and sexualities. Asian American[35] and Latina American feminists have also been actively involved since the 1960s and '70s on behalf of their constituencies.[36] This short history can only name a few of their number. Lisa Lowe's highly anthologized "Heterogeneity, Hybridity, Multiplicity: Asian American Differences" was a

31. Collins, *Black Feminist Thought*, 295–307.
32. Collins, *Black Feminist Thought*, 294.
33. Jordan, "Report from the Bahamas."
34 Collins, *Black Feminist Thought*, 308.
35. See Bow, ed., *Asian American Feminisms*, for the most up-to-date anthology of Asian American feminisms.
36. Thompson, "Multiracial Feminism," 51–62.

landmark essay highlighting the fact that, although Asian Americans differed from white Anglo society, they were extremely different and diverse from the perspectives of Asian Americans themselves. Heterogeneity, hybridity, and multiplicity signified the material contradictions that characterized Asian American groups that disrupted the dominant discursive construction of Asian Americans as a homogeneous group.[37] Gloria Anzaldúa and Cherríe Moraga were two Chicana (Mexican American) feminists, who brought to the forefront of feminist theory the writings of Third World women in their trailblazing anthology, *This Bridge Called My Back: Writings by Radical Women on Color*.[38] In *Borderlands/La Frontera*, Anzaldúa used English and Spanish to highlight the linguistic dislocations that characterized the Latina American feminist experience. She also developed the notion of "borderlands," such as the US/Mexican border, as an important epistemological location to critique US colonialism, heteronormativity, and male dominance.[39]

In this section on theorizing intersectionality, I have singled out noteworthy US women of color and their ideas. Let us now turn to women of color feminists on the global stage. Variously known as third world feminists, postcolonial feminists, and transnational feminists, these feminists highlighted the impact of global capitalism, racism, war, genocide, colonization, and poverty in the experiences of indigenous third world women.[40] As I mentioned at the start of this essay, postcolonial criticism looks at relations between colonizer and colonized and the ideologies that keep the conquerors and the natives in their respective places. As an entrée into this significant field of feminist theorizing, let's consider one of the most noteworthy essays of postcolonial feminism, Chandra Talpade Mohanty's "Under Western Eyes: Feminist Scholarship and Colonial Discourses."[41] Mohanty's aim was to make visible and dismantle the privilege and ethnocentrism in the discourses of many Western feminists when they write about women living in the third world. She argued that these feminists discursively colonized the historical and material diversities of the lives of real women in the third world, producing a singular monolithic subject, "the third world woman":

37. Lowe, "Heterogeneity, Hybridity, Multiplicity."
38. Moraga and Anzaldúa, eds., *This Bridge Called My Back*.
39. Anzaldúa, *Borderlands*. See also Lugones, *Pilgrimages = Peregrinajes*.
40. Tong, *Feminist Thought*, 231–54; Mann, *Doing Feminist Theory*, 355–99.
41. Mohanty, "Under Western Eyes." Mohanty revisited this landmark essay sixteen years later in Mohanty, "'Under Western Eyes' Revisited."

> This average third world woman leads an essentially truncated life based on her feminine gender (read: sexually constrained) and her being 'third world' (read: ignorant, poor, uneducated, tradition-bound, domestic, family-oriented, victimized, etc.). This, I suggest, is in contrast to the (implicit) self-representation of Western women as educated, as modern, as having control over their own bodies and sexualities, and the freedom to make their own decisions.[42]

This ideological social construction of the third-world woman in certain feminist discourses was mistaken for real, historical groups of third-world women, reducing them to powerless, victimized, exploited, and sexually oppressed beings. In this discursive reduction, Mohanty located the "colonialist move." The "subject" of these studies was supposed to be about third-world women, but it was really about Western white women and their own ideological self-presentation. The discursive colonization of third-world women, lumping their many differences and specificities in class and ethnicities into the category of average third-world female Other, robbed them of their historical and political agency. They were never able to rise above their status of "object."[43] The purpose of her essay was to make this discursive colonization in the feminist scholarship of her time visible and "decolonize" it.

Becoming Visible, Recognizing Differences, Raising Voices

Although we have only seen the tip of the iceberg regarding feminist/intersectional theorizing, we are in a better position to understand its development and observe its connections with feminist biblical scholarship. In the usual histories of second wave feminism, the focus was primarily on the visibility of (white) women and the notion of gender. Liberal feminism highlighted the rights of women in the political sphere. The emphasis was on the equality of women with men. In contrast, radical feminists argued that women's oppression was enmeshed in a deeper system of male dominance and would not be eliminated simply by laws or the education of women. For them, gender was a social construction apart from biological sex, and based on how they understood that

---

42. Mohanty, "Under Western Eyes," 56.
43. Mohanty, "Under Western Eyes," 71–72.

construction of gender, they offered different theories to combat women's oppression by men.

Marxist feminists added class exploitation to women's oppression. They were particularly important in developing standpoint theory and epistemologies to feminist theorizing: the acknowledgment that one could never be neutrally located, that one must continually be aware of how social, historical, and cultural processes are constructing us, our thoughts, and our production of knowledge. Knowledge was always produced from someone's or a group's "standpoint." Postmodern feminism took a radically different approach by combining the production of knowledge with power. What we "know" of the world was primarily through different discourses, such as medical, legal, scientific, religious, etc., which were controlled by different regimes of power. Maleness or femaleness did not exist outside of these discourses. Later, queer theorizing elaborated this discursive understanding of gender further to argue that gender was primarily a performance, a stylized repetition of acts.

Unfortunately, the feminism in the typical histories of the second wave was primarily white-led, marginalizing the activism and standpoints of women of color. The common notion in these histories was that women of color emerged in reaction to and therefore later than white feminism. However, as we have seen in this overview, this would be a mistake. Women of color—African American, Latina American, Asian American—have been involved in feminist, antiracist work since the 1970s and raising their distinctive voices in their many-faceted theorizing.[44] As Audre Lourde pointed out, it was not the differences that separated women, but the refusal to recognize those differences.[45] Women of color in varying ways diagnosed and theorized the interconnections of gender, race, class, and sexuality. They developed more complex theories of women's oppression that went beyond the simplistic oppressor/oppressed models by considering not only gender, race, and class as categories of analysis, but also their locations in different domains of power. Finally, we became acquainted with an important postcolonial, transnational feminist, Chandra Mohanty, who took white feminism to task for its ideological construction of the typical "third-world woman." This construction reduced the historical material lives of real third-world

---

44. Thompson, "Multiracial Feminism," 51–56.
45. Lorde, *Sister Outsider*, 115–16.

women to the status of victims, stripping them of their historical and political agency.

In various ways, through feminist theorizing and activism, white feminists and feminists of color were able to make their voices heard and challenge deeply sexist, racist, hierarchical and heteronormative systems of male dominance. And they continue to do so. Feminist biblical scholars were and continue to be indebted to them.

Feminist Perspectives on the Hebrew Bible

Early Milestones

Created as the first woman who supposedly tempted man to sin, which led to his and humanity's "fall," the character of Eve in Gen 1–3 became the flash point not only for scores of misogynous interpretations, but also for early feminist ones. Twelfth-century German abbess, Hildegard of Bingen, saw Eve as prefiguring Mary, the mother of Jesus. Before the Fall, sex between her and Adam was free of lust, their relationship complementary and interdependent. She would give birth painlessly through her side in the manner that she was created from Adam.[46] Christine de Pizan later argued that Eve, created from Adam's rib, would therefore "stand by his side as companion and never lie at his feet like a slave, and also that he would love her as his own flesh" (*The Book of the City of Ladies*, 1405). Pizan asserted that Eve was created in God's image, even surpassing Adam who was created from the ground, because she was created from Adam's very substance, "the noblest substance which had ever been created."[47] Through the voice of Pilate's wife, who warned her husband to have "nothing to do with that just man," Jesus (Matt 27:19), Amelia Lanyer gave a spirited defense of Eve in *Salve Deus Rex Judaeorum* (1611). Though her fault was great, Adam was the one to be most blamed, because he should have refused the serpent, being of greater strength, and the one who actually received God's command about the fruit. If Eve stumbled, it was for the knowledge the fruit could give her and her spouse:

---

46. Cited in "One Thousand Years of Feminist Bible Criticism," in Lerner, *The Creation of Feminist Consciousness*, 142–43.

47. Cited in Lerner, "One Thousand Years of Feminist Bible Criticism," in Lerner, *The Creation of Feminist Consciousness*, 144–45.

> If Eve did err, it was for knowledge' sake,
> The fruit being fair persuaded him to fall:
> No subtle Serpent's falsehood did betray him,
> If he would eat it, who had power to stay him?
> Not Eve, whose fault was only too much love,
> Which made her give this present to her Dear,
> That what she tasted, he likewise might prove,
> Whereby his knowledge might become more clear.[48]

During the nineteenth-century in the US, two feminist interpreters of note, one white and one African American, presented their insights on the first woman. Both were involved in the abolitionist and the women's suffrage movements of the time. Elizabeth Cady Stanton assembled a committee of learned (white) women to publish *The Woman's Bible*, to provide commentaries on those portions of the Bible that dealt with women. "Whatever the Bible may be made to do in Hebrew or Greek, in plain English it does not exalt and dignify women."[49] Her characterization of Eve before the serpent in Genesis 3 would resonate with one of the first feminist biblical scholars, Phyllis Trible, more than eighty years later:

> In this prolonged interview, the unprejudiced reader must be impressed with the courage, the dignity, and the lofty ambition of the woman. The tempter evidently had a profound knowledge of human nature and saw at a glance the high character of the person he met by chance in his walks in the garden. He did not try to tempt her from the path of duty by brilliant jewels, rich dresses, worldly luxuries or pleasures, but with the promise of knowledge, with the wisdom of the Gods.[50]

One of thirteen children, Sojourner Truth (née Isabella Baumfree) was born a slave in a Dutch colony, speaking Dutch until she was eleven when her abusive new master forced her to use English. She was sold to two more masters until she was freed on July 4, 1827, by the New York legislature along with all the other slaves in the state. A travelling evangelist, she eventually added abolition and women's suffrage to her sermons. At the Women's Rights Convention in Akron, Ohio, she delivered her famous "Ain't I a Woman" speech in 1851:

---

48. Lanyer, "Eve's Apology in Defense of Women."
49. Stanton, *The Woman's Bible*, 12.
50. Stanton, *The Woman's Bible*, 24.

> That man over there says that women need to be helped into carriages, and lifted over ditches, and to have the best place everywhere. Nobody ever helps me into carriages, or over mud puddles or gives me any best place and ain't I a woman? Look at me! Look at my arm! I have plowed, and planted, and gathered into barns, and no man could head me—and ain't I a woman? I could work as much and eat as much as a man (when I could get it), and bear the lash as well—and ain't I a woman? I have borne thirteen children and seen them almost all sold off into slavery, and when I cried out with a mother's grief, none but Jesus heard—and ain't I a woman?

She concluded this famous speech with a reference to Eve.

> If the first woman God ever made was strong enough to turn the world upside down, all alone, these together ought to be able to turn it back and get it right side up again; and now they are asking to do it, the men better let them.[51]

If one woman could upset the world order, the women assembled in Akron could make it right again. She enjoined the men to let the convention get on with the business of women's suffrage and support them in this endeavor.[52]

Feminist Literary and Historical Interpretations of the Bible

Because of the profusion of feminist biblical scholarship since the 1970s, the following survey is necessarily selective, highlighting some of the major moments in feminist and intersectional analyses of the Hebrew Bible. This first section considers those feminist biblical studies that mainly apply the literary and historical methods of the biblical guild.

The biblical studies guild is very diverse in the traditional methods used to analyze a difficult text that was composed over a long period of time, in different languages, in several geographical areas, and often under and in response to many domestic and international conflicts. Methods, such as source, form, redaction and sociological criticism, regard the Bible as an historical text, examining the different historical, social, and

---

51. "Sojourner Truth: Ar'n't I a Woman?, 1851 (1797–1883)" in Gottheimer et al., eds., *Ripples of Hope*; Baker-Fletcher, "Anna Julia Cooper and Sojourner Truth."

52. For other nineteenth-century women writers on Eve, see Taylor and Weir, eds., *Let Her Speak for Herself*, 21–105.

cultural Israelite and ancient Near Eastern contexts in which the texts were written and edited. In contrast, methods, such as narrative criticism, rhetorical criticism, poetics, and reader response criticism, primarily study the Bible as a literary text and the significant rhetorical features of its prose and poetic genres. Literary criticism of the Bible particularly emerged during the 1970s in reaction to the dominance of the historical-critical methods up to that point.[53]

The historical and literary criticisms reveal that the Hebrew Bible is mainly the work of elite men. Although they were only a tiny minority of the population of ancient Israel, their upper-class male sociohistorical and religious imprints are dominant and normative throughout the text. Furthermore, biblical scholars and religious interpreters of the bible, such as clergy, have primarily been male. Thus, the composition of the biblical text as well as its interpretation throughout the ages tend to focus on male interests and ideologies. This changed during the 1970s and 80s, when professionally trained female biblicists began to apply feminist perspectives in their historical and literary exegesis (interpretation) of the Hebrew Bible.[54] Just as there are a plurality of exegetical methods employed in the study of the biblical text, so too will these feminist biblical scholars adopt diverse literary and historical toolboxes to analyze the male-centeredness of the Hebrew Bible and its interpretation.[55]

We saw in the discussion above that the radical feminists criticized the "rights" focus of the liberal feminists by insisting that women's oppression would not simply be eliminated by equal educational or legal opportunities. It went much deeper because it was embedded in a male system characterized by power, dominance, hierarchy, and competition that was often called patriarchy. Recognizing patriarchy in the Hebrew Bible, Phyllis Trible argues for "Depatriarchalizing in Biblical Interpretation," in one of the first essays of feminist biblical interpretation, although she does not label herself a radical feminist.[56] Trible does not perceive an either/or opposition between biblical faith and the movement of women's liberation. As a Christian believer, she maintains that the objective of

---

53. For an introduction to different methods of biblical interpretation, see Carvalho, *Primer on Biblical Methods*; LeMon and Richards, eds., *Method Matters*.

54. For a nuanced overview of feminist and intersectional biblical interpretation, see Junior, *Introduction to Womanist Biblical Interpretation*, 76–121.

55. For an anthology devoted to the various methods employed by feminist biblical scholars, see Scholz, ed., *Feminist Interpretation*, vol. 3, *Methods*.

56. Trible, "Depatriarchalizing in Biblical Interpretation."

biblical faith was not to create or perpetuate patriarchy but rather assist in the salvation of both women and men. The biblical text itself contains the means of depatriarchalizing its sexism in, for example, the maternal imagery for the deity, the Song of Songs, and the Exodus tradition. However, because male biases of the translator and interpreter amplify the sexism of the text, a feminist hermeneutic must be applied to counteract them.

Applying a careful literary reading of the Hebrew, Trible reinterprets the person of Eve in her classic work, *God and the Rhetoric of Sexuality*.[57] Rather than being the cunning temptress whose sole purpose was simply as man's helpmate, Eve's creation becomes the highpoint in Gen 2, resulting in the creation of sexuality itself. Instead of a subservient helper, she becomes the man's companion. Trible's rehabilitation of Eve, as an intelligent, theological interpreter of God's command when confronting the snake (Genesis 3), is similar to Elizabeth Cady's Stanton's assessment of Eve in *The Woman's Bible Commentary*, cited previously.

In the companion volume to this classic book, Trible deals with the male violence against women in the Hebrew Bible directly in *Texts of Terror: Literary-Feminist Readings of Biblical Narratives*. She singles out four stories of the cruelty men inflict upon women: Hagar, the cast-off Egyptian slave woman (Gen 16 and 21); Tamar, the Judean princess raped by her half-brother (2 Sam 13); the concubine from Bethlehem, gang-raped and dismembered by her husband (Judg 19); Jephthah's daughter, sacrificed as a burnt offering by her father (Judg 11).[58] Usually not read or preached in churches and synagogues, these stories are "texts of terror" for women. Trible enjoins the reader to hold these neglected women "*in memoriam*," by interpreting these "stories of outrage on behalf of their female victims in order to recover a neglected history, to remember a past that the present embodies, and to pray that these terrors shall not come to pass again. In telling sad stories, a feminist hermeneutic seeks to redeem the time."[59]

Other significant feminist scholars of the 1970–1980s adopt historical approaches to the biblical text. In her pioneering essay, "Images of Women in the Old Testament," Phyllis Bird attempts to deal with the diversity of these images by situating them in the historical times in

---

57. Trible, *God and the Rhetoric of Sexuality*, 72–143.
58. Trible, *Texts of Terror*.
59. Trible, *Texts of Terror*, 3.

which they were composed and in the literary genres, such as law codes, in which they are found. For example, these laws disclose the place of women in Israelite notions of family and kinship, sexuality and its transgressions, where she was "a legal non-person; where she did become visible it was as a dependent, and usually an inferior, in a male-centered and male-dominated society."[60] Bird's historical work on women's place in Israelite cult reveals that the centralization of Israelite cult restricted women's participation in pilgrim feasts and local shrines. However, cross-cultural studies draw attention to rituals and devotions revered by women, especially in the different cycles of their lives, which may have been hidden beneath the biblical text or regarded as frivolous or heterodox by the dominant male cult.[61]

Carol Meyers enlists archaeology and the social sciences to reconstruct the lives of ancient Israelite women, particularly during Israel's premonarchic or tribal period. Anthropological studies of preindustrial societies demonstrate that even though women have been denied access to formal avenues of power, they can exert informal power to achieve their ends. Meyers argues that the focus on subsistence living in the premonarchic period rendered women and their roles to be pivotal for the survival of the agrarian family household. Women controlled food preparation and resources; they were involved in subsistence crafts, such as making pottery, tools, and clothing; they had a crucial role in the religious, moral, and social education of young children. "In short, female power will be as significant as male power, and perhaps even greater."[62]

Athalya Brenner's *The Israelite Woman* is the first book-length treatment of women's professions and social institutions, such as queens, wise women, poets, prophets, magicians, sorcerers, witches, and prostitutes, and the different literary types of women and their behaviors, as mothers, temptresses, foreigners, and ancestresses.[63] In the second edition of this book thirty years later, Brenner relates how she was turned down for tenure at Haifa University because of this book, since her committee felt that "feminist research was not truly academic, not meaningful, a passing fad and waste of time and energy and money, and that its practitioners in

---

60. Bird, "Images of Women," 56.

61. Bird, "Place of Women."

62. Meyers, *Discovering Eve*, 176. Meyers will considerably update this book in Meyers, *Rediscovering Eve*.

63. Brenner, *The Israelite Woman*.

any field should be excised from the guild."[64] Devastated, especially after losing her appeal, Brenner began working on one of the most influential series of feminist biblical criticism, *The Feminist Companion to the Bible* (series 1 and 2, 1993–2001). For the different books of the Hebrew Bible, she brought together previously published articles, but primarily new ones on the expanding and diverse literature on feminist biblical interpretation.

The 1980s also witnessed the publication of several essay collections that highlight the diversity of feminist literary and historical approaches to the biblical text. These include the papers from the 1980 session on "The Effects of Women's Studies on Biblical Studies" during the centennial celebrations for the Society of Biblical Literature;[65] a *Semeia* volume on *The Bible and Feminist Hermeneutics*, edited by New Testament scholar Mary Ann Tolbert;[66] *Feminist Perspectives on Biblical Scholarship*, edited by New Testament scholar Adela Yarbro Collins;[67] and *Feminist Interpretation of the Bible*, edited by theologian Letty Russell.[68]

Perhaps the highpoint of feminist scholarship during the 1990s is the publication of *The Women's Bible Commentary* in 1992.[69] In contrast to Cady Stanton's *The Woman's Bible*, professionally trained female scholars pen the commentaries for each book of the Old and New Testaments, selecting those passages that they judge to be of particular relevance to women. The change in nomenclature from Stanton's *Woman's Bible* to *Women's Bible* reflects the editors' recognition of the diversity of among women who read and study it. A second edition of the commentary appeared in 1998, adding commentaries for each book of the Apocrypha or deuterocanonical books and the addition of a bibliography at the end of the volume to supplement the ones in the original articles. A twentieth-anniversary third edition appeared in 2012, which replaced some articles with those of newer scholars and updated those that remained. Furthermore, thirteen female biblical characters were singled out for their reinterpretation in art and in other ancient and modern texts.

---

64. Brenner-Idan, *The Israelite Woman* (2nd ed.), xii.
65. See the story behind this centennial in Trible, "The Effects of Women's Studies," 3–5.
66. Tolbert, "The Bible and Feminist Hermeneutics."
67. Collins, *Feminist Perspectives*.
68. Russell, *Feminist Interpretation*.
69. Newsom and Ringe, eds., *The Women's Bible Commentary*.

Feminist Interdisciplinary Explorations of the Bible

Particularly during the 1990s–2000s, feminist biblical scholars begin to adopt some of the critical theories and approaches of disciplines beyond the traditional historical and literary methods. These postmodern feminist approaches include deconstructive criticism, Marxist/materialist criticism, gender and queer criticism, and cultural criticism.

We begin first with Esther Fuchs, an Israeli secular Jew, who contributed two essays in one of the earliest collections of feminist biblical scholarship, writing on the sexual politics of mothers and the alleged "deceptiveness" of biblical women.[70] Lamenting that Fuchs was a lone voice crying in the wilderness about the insidious ways in which the biblical text communicates patriarchy, Pamela Milne argued in 1997 that feminist biblical scholarship needed to have greater connections and interactions with the larger feminist movement and feminist scholarship in other disciplines.[71] Fuchs is significant because she is one of the few feminist biblical scholars who directly engages the daunting field of postmodern feminist theory in her writings.[72] Fuchs is critical of what she calls a "resurgence of neoliberal feminist recuperations of the Hebrew Bible" in the 1990s–2000s. Recall in the discussion in the first section of this chapter that liberal feminism tries to convince women that they could be and should be like men in order to win access to the public sphere and civil rights, highlighting equality with men, encouraging the liberal ideals for women, such as independence, rationalism, individualism, and influence. Fuchs' analysis reveals how several feminist biblical scholars impose neoliberal idealizations of strength, assertiveness, self-determination, and independence upon biblical women, such as Miriam, Deborah, Jael, Abigail, and Delilah, without recognizing the male ideological and political framing on their stories.

> By ignoring or denying the analytical prisms of ideology, gender as power, and discourse—the important interventions of Marxist, radical, and poststructuralist feminisms—neoliberal feminist approaches return us to the traditional myth of the

---

70. Fuchs, "Literary Characterization of Mothers"; Fuchs, "Who Is Hiding the Truth?"

71. Milne, "Toward Feminist Companionship."

72. Along with her critical survey of feminist theory, several of her important essays are reprinted in Fuchs, *Feminist Theory and the Bible*.

"feminine mystique"—to typologies and representations of sexual difference that continue to inform Western culture.[73]

Fuchs acknowledges that seeking feminist models in biblical women is understandable, "but in the process of this quest we must make sure not to project narrow and largely discarded definitions of feminism on what are ultimately patriarchal constructs."[74]

Firmly ensconced in postmodern theories of language, deconstructive criticism is an act of reading that exposes the ways in which biblical texts contradict themselves and highlights elements of the text that traditional readings have overlooked or have intentionally ignored. Such a reading explores the complex and sometimes conflictual nature in the text's production of meaning, as opposed to a reading that reduces a text's meaning to a single or dominant interpretation.[75] Important feminist biblical scholars employing deconstructive criticism include Danna Nolan Fewell,[76] Mieke Bal,[77] and Yvonne Sherwood.[78] In an accessible example of deconstructive analysis, Danna Fewell contrasts two feminist readings of the book of Ruth. Phyllis Trible produces a positive or text-affirming reading of the book, while on the opposite end of the spectrum, Esther Fuchs represents a negative or text-resistant one. Fewell argues that both scholars omitted those elements that did not accord with their thesis, and therefore one must constantly reread. Any reading that results in a text that is thematically unified is a misreading, because the text itself contains the seeds of its own contradiction. She then applies deconstruction in an analysis of Esther 1, the story of Queen Vashti's banishment for her disobedience to her husband, to expose the fragility of male sovereignty in a story utterly soaked in patriarchy.[79]

Marxist/materialist criticism investigates the socioeconomic class relations in the biblical texts, such as rich and poor, elite and peasant, royal court and landowners, empire and vassal state, and so forth. Feminist biblical scholars adopting such criticism incorporate the issues

---

73. Fuchs, "Reclaiming the Hebrew Bible."
74. Fuchs, "Reclaiming the Hebrew Bible," 65.
75. Yee, *Judges and Method*, 238.
76. Fewell and Gunn, *Gender, Power, and Promise*. For a discussion of the presuppositions and application of the method, see Fewell, "Deconstructive Criticism."
77. Bal, *Lethal Love*; Bal, *Murder and Difference*; Bal, *Death and Dissymmetry*.
78. Sherwood, *The Prostitute and the Prophet*.
79. Fewell, "Feminist Reading."

surrounding gender into their class analysis.[80] For example, applying the standpoint theory of Marxist feminism, Avaren Ipsen analyzes the stories of biblical prostitutes, such as the Canaanite Rahab (Joshua 2 and 6), the prostitutes before Solomon (1 Kings 3), and the whore of Babylon (Revelation 17–19) with a racially-mixed reading group of activist sex workers in Berkeley, California (SWOP, the Sex Worker Outreach Project). Standpoint theory presumes that the women who do sex work have important subjugated knowledge that deserve theoretical articulation, producing thought-provoking results when undertaken within the discipline of biblical interpretation. Ipsen's sex workers highlight the systemic economic circumstances of their trade: No young girls grow up wanting to be prostitutes, but they become prostitutes because they are poor, starving, and need to feed their families. They are quick to deduce Rahab's anxiety with the king's officers of Jericho, because they are often squeezed for information or blackmailed for sexual favors by the police. In the story of the prostitutes before Solomon, they highlight from their own daily experiences the violence of Solomon's courtroom, the corruption of the court system itself, and that a prostitute's testimony is always questionable. Avoiding the usual characterizations of the two prostitutes as the "good" and "bad" mother, the SWOP activists sympathize with both from their own personal experiences of motherhood in their sex work. Ipsen hopes that these readings will inform the field of biblical studies, while empowering the liberation struggles of sex workers, whose population "has dramatically increased in the current neoliberal global economy where poverty and the feminization of poverty is ubiquitous."[81]

Gender criticism is an approach to reading that explores the role of gender in society and cultural products, while simultaneously revealing the instability of categories and norms associated with gender, such as "man" and Woman," "masculine" and feminine."[82] Along with feminist theory, gender criticism includes insights from queer theory, masculinity studies, and intersectional analyses. In a provocatively titled article, "From Gender Reversal to Genderfuck," Deryn Guest applies gender criticism to the story of the assassin Jael in Judges 4–5, revealing one of the hallmarks of gender criticism, the volatility of the gender binary.[83]

80. Yee, *Poor Banished Children of Eve*; Boer and Økland, eds., *Marxist Feminist Criticism*.
81. Ipsen, *Sex Working and the Bible*, 11.
82. Stone, "Gender Criticism"; Ruane, "When Women Aren't Enough."
83. Guest, "From Gender Reversal to Genderfuck."

Guest rejects interpretations of Jael that persist in confining gender to the binaries male/female, masculine/feminine. As long as scholars remain within this closed dichotomous system, Jael's transgressive acts will only be seen as gender "reversal" that for Guest simply shifts the ground from one gender to the other. According to Guest, all commentators have not been able to break through the male/female binary in consistently referring to Jael as female, because they fail to see, à la Judith Butler, that gender is a performance. Guest prefers instead to resist, subvert, undo, and deconstruct these binaries to reveal them as social constructions. While several scholars have described Jael's violent assassination of Sisera with a phallic tent peg as a reversal of male rape, Guest maintains that

> Jael is not a *woman* warrior and equally Jael is not a *male* rapist. The narrator has conjured a figure who carries a resonance he could probably never have anticipated for readers in the early twenty-first century. Jael is a figure who unsettles and destabilizes, whose performativity provides one of those unintelligible genders that give the lie to ideas of sex as abiding substance.[84]

It is this gender blur and confusion of Jael as "not-woman/not-man" that aggravates and provokes the dominant structures of patriarchy in the Jael narrative.[85]

Cultural criticism explores the different ways in which the Bible has been received and interpreted in the different high and popular cultures that encounter it. It investigates Scripture's history of reception in its various duplications from very early times all the way up to the present.[86] Perhaps the most memorable introduction of feminist cultural studies to the biblical guild is J. Cheryl Exum's presentation "Bathsheba Plotted, Shot, and Painted," at the 1994 session of the Society of Biblical Literature. Comparing 1 Samuel 11 with different paintings and movie versions of David and Bathsheba's adulterous encounter, Exum demonstrates how the different media used by painters and film directors focus on Bathsheba's body as an object of sexual desire and male aggression. "Since the essay self-consciously looks at looking, I invite its readers to join me in looking at our own gaze—at our collusion, or complicity, or resistance when faced with the exposure of female flesh for our literary or visual

---

84. Guest, "From Gender Reversal to Genderfuck," 26 (italics original).

85. Guest pushes the disciplinary boundaries of feminist biblical criticism to argue for "genderqueer" readings of the Bible in Guest, *Beyond Feminist Biblical Studies*.

86. Yee, "What Is Cultural Criticism"; Gunn, "Cultural Criticism."

consumption."[87] Feminist cultural studies on the Bible has been applied to the persons of Adam of Eve,[88] to Hollywood films,[89] religion, politics, the media,[90] and advertising.[91]

Intersectional Perspectives on the Hebrew Bible

Just as feminists of color have been active in the beginnings of the US women's movement in the 1960s, so too have feminists of color been involved in feminist biblical studies since its initial stages. Feminists biblical scholars of color bring their different racial/ethnic and class locations in a dominant white society to bear on the interpretation of the biblical text, using an array of exegetical methods and approaches. This short survey will primarily discuss African American, Asian American and postcolonial feminist biblical scholars of the Hebrew Bible.

Among female African American biblical scholars, how they identify themselves as "feminist" in their racial locations is an important consideration. African American women have historically been reticent to adopt the identification of "feminist" for themselves, because of the racism they see in white feminism. One of the early Black feminist theorists, bell hooks, avoids saying "I am a feminist," by using the descriptive "I advocate feminism." For her, this response implies a choice to be committed to the feminist struggle, which she sees as a movement to end sexist oppression, while being open to supporting other political movements as well.[92] Other African American women embrace the term *womanist*, coined by Alice Walker in 1983, which designates "a black feminist or feminist of color" at its first level.[93] Still others prefer the nomenclature of *Black feminist*, acknowledging the contributions of a generation of Black feminist foremothers, which the term womanist may preclude.[94] Nyasha

---

87. Exum, "Bathsheba Plotted, Shot, and Painted," 47; See also Exum, *Plotted, Shot, and Painted*, where she examines Michal, Ruth and Naomi, and Delilah.

88. Schearing and Ziegler, *Enticed by Eden*.

89. Bach, *Biblical Glamour*.

90. Bach, *Religion, Politics, Media*.

91. Edwards, *Admen and Eve*.

92. hooks, *Feminist Theory: From Margin to Center*, 29.

93. Walker, *In Search of Our Mother's Gardens*, xi–xii. Walker's inclusion of "a woman who loves other women, sexually and/or nonsexually" in her second part of the definition, will be offensive to some Black church women.

94. West, "Is a Womanist a Black Feminist?"

Junior, author of a recent introduction to womanist biblical interpretation, does not label herself as either a feminist or a womanist, because neither term conveys who she is professionally.[95] The latest collection of African American female biblical scholars is explicitly titled *Womanist Interpretations of the Bible*, even though some of its contributors self-identify differently.[96] Acknowledging this complexity, I will refer to the identification of African American scholars with the terms they use for themselves. For example, Wil Gafney offers a fluid self-definition, depending upon her racial/ethnic context:

> My own practice of self-definition varies according to context. Like hooks and Dube my primary self-designation is as a black feminist. I am a black feminist who works and worships in solidarity with my womanist sisters. My location in feminist, rather than womanist, space reflects my intent to participate in the redemption of a radically egalitarian ethic from the pale hands of those who infected it with racism and classism. But in environments in which the radically egalitarian ideals of feminism have been hijacked by racism and classism, I self-identify as a womanist to avoid being coopted by white feminists. Occasionally my experience of my hybridized identity results in a hybridized identifier, fem/womanist, which stands at the intersection of feminist and womanist practices.[97]

Renita J. Weems is the first African American woman to earn a PhD in Hebrew Bible in 1989 at Princeton Theological Seminary. While not an academic monograph, her crossover book for African American Christian women, *Just a Sister Away*, is considered the first womanist biblical interpretation, since she employs "some of the best fruits of feminist biblical criticism, along with the best of the Afro-American oral tradition, with its gifts for story-telling and its love of dramas."[98] Her chapters deal with female pairs, such as Hagar and Sarah, Naomi and Ruth, Jephthah's daughter and the mourning women, Vashti and Esther, Lot's wife and her daughters. Analyzing these characters through the lenses of gender, race,

---

95. Junior, *Introduction to Womanist Biblical Interpretation*, xxi.

96. Byron and Lovelace, eds., *Womanist Interpretations*.

97. Gafney, "A Black Feminist Approach," 397. Adopting and modernizing a rabbinic exegetical commentary, Gafney develops a "womanist midrash," not only in several articles, but most recently in a book on well-known and lesser-known women in the Hebrew Bible: Gafney, *Womanist Midrash*.

98. Weems, *Just a Sister Away*, ix.

and class, she connects their stories to present-day experiences of African American women.

Weems's article "Gomer: Victim of Violence or Victim of Metaphor" foregrounds the problematic nature of the marriage metaphor in Hosea 2 to describe the covenantal relationship between God and Israel.[99] She continues to explore its hermeneutical issues, that "it's not just a metaphor," in her monograph, *Battered Love: Marriage, Sex, and Violence in the Hebrew Prophets*, concluding:

> Not only does the image of the promiscuous wife have the potential to reinforce violence against women. It also has the potential to exclude whole segments of the population from hearing and responding to the biblical message. It does this by asking women who have been raped and violated or who live with the threat of rape and violation to join with writers in inhabiting a world where women's rape and violation are theologically justifiable. On these grounds alone, metaphors require our constant vigilance.[100]

In her contribution to the first essay collection of African American biblical interpretation, "Reading *Her Way* through the Struggle: African American Women and the Bible," Weems tackles the question of why African American women, who are marginalized by gender and ethnicity, and often class, continue to find the Bible meaningful.[101] She argues that because African American culture has primarily been a hearing one, *particular* readings and reading strategies of the text become more important than the text itself. African American women have consistently identified with those passages where the oppressed were freed, the humbled exalted, the long-suffering rewarded, even though the sexism of the Bible creates some ambivalence in the way they read it. On the one hand, African American women read the Bible to resist what they have been taught about their ineligibility to read; and on the other, to comply in some ways with what they have been taught about how to read it, namely, to identify with the dominant voice against the oppressed, the humbled, the long-suffering. The challenge for African American women is to use

---

99. Weems, "Gomer."
100. Weems, *Battered Love*, 115–16.
101. Weems, "Reading Her Way," 58.

whatever means necessary to recover the voice of the oppressed within the biblical texts.[102]

"As a Christian (Protestant) and feminist/womanist African-American female," Cheryl B. Anderson tackles the biblical laws in the book of the covenant and Deuteronomic law, on the ways in which they construct gender ideologically and are inherently violent against women.[103] As a former attorney, she adopts the criteria of feminist legal theorists to make her argument that the law codes do indeed equate masculinity with male dominance.[104] Taking, for example, some of the laws regarding rape in the Hebrew Bible, she argues that the law is male if it systematically favors men and oppresses women, if it is neutral in form but has a disproportionately negative impact on females, and if it embodies only the male experience.[105] For Anderson, all three criteria are present in the biblical law codes. "These laws are clearly male and as such they follow a gender-role pattern that supports and sustains male dominance."[106] Anderson then engages the critical theorists of the Frankfort School, specifically the work of Theodor Adorno, Max Horkheimer, and Walter Benjamin, to make the argument that these male laws do not just allow violence against women to occur, but that they are forms of violence in and of themselves.

Intersectional connections among gender, race, class, and sexual orientation are particularly evident in Anderson's second book, in which she calls for the development of an inclusive biblical interpretation. Here, she tackles problematic biblical laws from the perspectives of those regarded as the marginalized Other: women, the poor, non-Israelites (foreigners), gays, indigenous folks, and the colonized. Her liberationist readings collectively involve feminist/womanist, queer, and postcolonial methodologies. Because liberationist struggles are often pitted against each other, Anderson declares that transformative change for inclusive communities can only occur when these liberationist groups strategically incorporate the issues of another marginalized population. Her convictions on this matter are worth quoting at length, because they exemplify

102. Weems, "Reading Her Way," 72–73.

103. Anderson, *Women, Ideology and Violence*, 19–20.

104. Anderson here relies on Peggy Sanday's contention that in some cultures, male dominance/female subordination is not an inevitable human occurrence (*Women, Ideology and Violence*, 78).

105. Anderson, *Women, Ideology and Violence*, 80–91.

106. Anderson, *Women, Ideology and Violence*, 91.

the interconnectedness of oppressions in Patricia Hill Collins' matrix of domination and the politics of power and empowerment:[107]

> Instead of supporting the dominant condemnation of homosexuality, heterosexual women need to understand that the same underlying rationale for this condemnation supports the subordination of women. Therefore, fighting heterosexism and homophobia should be an integral part of a feminist agenda. Instead of supporting the dominant condemnation of homosexuality, African American church leaders need to understand that the same underlying rationale for this condemnation supports white supremacy, that is, the dominance of white people over people of color. Therefore, their continuing struggle against racism should include the struggle against heterosexism and homophobia. Instead of supporting the dominant condemnation of homosexuality, African church leaders need to understand that the same underlying rationale for this condemnation supports the dominance of the West and its exploitation of Africa's resources. Therefore, any critique of global capitalism as neocolonialism should also address heterosexism and homophobia. Similarly, instead of condemning the homophobia of African and African American communities, leaders in the lesbian/gay/bisexual/transgender (LGBT) communities need to understand that the same underlying rationale for the condemnation of homosexuality supports racism. Therefore, white LGBT leaders have every reason to struggle against racism as part of their own activities.[108]

African American advocacy appears in other ways in Anderson's writings. Her reflections on the intermarriage ban and its exclusionary racial/ethnic policies in Ezra are correlated with the segregationist and anti-miscegenation laws that were used against African Americans, and whose harmful consequences still linger, even though they have been officially abolished.[109] Finally, Anderson is particularly noted for her work on reading the Hebrew Bible in the contexts of the HIV/AIDS pandemic and especially the responses of the African and African American churches.[110]

---

107. See pp. 22–23 above.
108. Anderson, *Ancient Laws*, 153.
109. Anderson, "Reflections in an Interethnic/Racial Era."
110. Anderson, "Transatlantic Reflections"; Anderson, "Biblical Interpretation as Violence"; Anderson, "Song of Songs."

If one skimmed the titles in the two volumes of collected essays on Asian American biblical interpretation, several overlapping themes stand out: "finding a home," "home as memory, metaphor, and promise," "the politics of identity," "neither here nor there," "liminality," "betwixt and between," "yin/yang is not me," "constructing hybridity and heterogeneity," "boundary and identity," "obscured beginnings."[111] Asian Americans do not fit neatly into the white/black racial binary. Racially, they are neither white nor Black, neither here nor there, but betwixt and between. As immigrants or descendants of immigrants, Asian Americans continue to struggle to find their place, home, and belonging in the white dominant society of the US. And attempting to do so, they have to contend with the covert, overt, and virulent racism targeted against them. It is because of this racism that Asian Americans as a minority group in the US have to explicitly address the construction of racial and ethnic identity for survival and empowerment. "The Bible is of particular importance because the exclusion of and discrimination against Asian in the United States have long been enacted in terms of a struggle to protect not only the nation but also Christendom from these racial *and* religious others."[112]

To read through the lenses of the Chinese American experience, Gale A. Yee singles out the book of Ruth, because it conjoins issues of gender, sexuality, race/ethnicity, immigration, nationality, assimilation, and class in fascinating ways that allow different social groups to read their own stories into the multi-layered narrative of Ruth and Naomi. For Yee, the person of Ruth the Moabite embodies the dialectical stereotype that has plagued Asian Americans as both a model minority and a perpetual foreigner. On the one hand, Ruth is this devoted widow who rejects her homeland to accompany her Jewish mother-in-law to a strange new land, and her faithfulness attracts the man who will become her new husband and provide for her. As the model immigrant, she teaches the Jewish people the true meaning of God's covenantal love. Similarly, set up against Blacks and Latino/as, Asian Americans become the model minority, those who work hard, venerate and respect family, and do not rock the boat. On the other hand, just like those who consistently ask even third-generation Asian Americans, "Where are you *really* from?," the book of Ruth never lets the reader forget that she is a perpetual foreigner, a Moabite, one not fully assimilated into the Israelite community,

---

111. Liew and Yee, eds., *The Bible in Asian America*; Foskett and Kuan, *Ways of Being*.

112. Liew, "Asian American Biblical Interpretation," 37.

and one who disappears from the story once she gives birth to Naomi's grandson.¹¹³

Chinese American biblical scholar Lai Ling Elizabeth Ngan develops an Asian American hermeneutics through the story of Hagar in the book of Genesis. She notes that for much of the twentieth century, those who are not white, Black, or Hispanic were classified as "others" in US demographic data. It was through the civil rights movement of the 1960s that the category of "Asian" or "Asian American" was added to US censuses, recognizing those who trace their ethnic origins to parts of East or South Asia. The labeling or marking of difference is not a neutral or value-free act, because lines and boundaries make some things visible and others invisible. "Since the marking of boundaries and ethnicity is socially constructed, Asian Americans must ask if these boundary markers are valid and whether lines should be drawn differently."¹¹⁴ Ngan points out that Hagar does not identify herself as an Egyptian, but is marked repeatedly as one from the dominant perspective of the exilic or postexilic storyteller whose own ethnicity serves as the norm of the story. Narrated from his perspective, Hagar's Egyptian identity marks her as belonging to a people who oppressed the Israelites in the land of bondage and slavery. However, for Ngan, Hagar herself redraws the boundary lines that demarcates her Egyptian identity. Empowered by God who relates to her, addresses her by name, promises offspring, she audaciously names God and forges a new identity for herself as the mother of a numerous people.¹¹⁵

Postcolonial analysis of the Bible emerges particularly with the insertion and challenge of voices from the so-called third-world and indigenous peoples into the academic guild, interpreting the Bible from out of their indigenous, postcolonial, or neocolonial contexts. With its shared concerns for the preferential option for the poor, postcolonial biblical criticism is sympathetic to liberation hermeneutics, but proceeds beyond the focus on the economic poor to embrace those marginalized by gender, sexuality, race, ethnicity, culture, colonialism and religion. Its special focus is on the power relations and disparities between empire and colony, conquered and conquered, between center and periphery.¹¹⁶

113. Yee, "'She Stood in Tears.'" See Chapter 6 in this volume.

114. Ngan, "Neither Here nor There," 73.

115. Ngan explores her Asian American hermeneutics further in Ngan, "Bitter Melon"; Ngan, "Until Everyone Has a Place."

116. Yee, "Postcolonial Biblical Criticism"; Crowell, "Postcolonial Studies"; Perdue and Carter, *Israel and Empire*.

One of the most well-known feminist postcolonial biblical scholars is Musa Dube, a Black Motswana African, a survivor of colonialism, and in a continuous struggle against neocolonialism, where global capitalism is impoverishing most Two-Thirds World countries with huge debts.[117] In analyzing ancient imperializing texts like the Bible, she asks the following questions:

1. Does this text have a clear stance against the political imperialism of its time?
2. Does this text encourage travel to distant and inhabited lands, and if so, how does it justify itself?
3. How does this text construct difference: is there dialogue and mutual interdependence, or condemnation and replacement of all that is foreign?
4. Does this text employ gender representations to construct relationships of subordination and domination?[118]

Dube then applies these questions to select passages in the books of Exodus and Joshua to disclose how "the story of Israel's trek from Egypt to the land of Canaan is in every way a God, gold, and glory narrative." It becomes an imperializing story because it is expressly focused on taking and maintaining power over foreign and inhabited lands by divine decree and assistance. The colonizers portray themselves as "chosen," while depicting those they conquer and colonize as deserving invasion, dispossession, subjugation, and annihilation if need be.[119]

In a highly anthologized piece, Cherokee American scholar Laura Donaldson applies postcolonial criticism to the book of Ruth, reading it prismatically through the encounter between Native women and European colonizers. Ruth the Moabite carries the taint of sexuality, because her tribal ancestry can be traced back to the incestuous encounter between Lot and his daughter (Gen 19:36–37) and the Moabite women who seduce Israelite men into idolatry (Num 25:1–3). Thomas Jefferson, the third president of the US and a framer of its Constitution, compared Ruth's seduction of Boaz to the alleged sexual brazenness of Native women and the sexual impotence of Native men. Facilitating the conquest of indigenous peoples by promoting assimilation, Jefferson encouraged intermarriage between Native woman and European men, addressing a

---

117. Dube, "Toward a Postcolonial Feminist Interpretation," 14.
118. Dube, *Postcolonial Feminist Interpretation*, 57.
119. Dube, *Postcolonial Feminist Interpretation*, 69–70.

delegation of Natives: "in time, you will be as we are; you will become one people with us. Your blood will mix with ours." For Donaldson, the book of Ruth similarly underscores the usefulness of intermarriage in the process of assimilating a non-Jew into the community, where Ruth ultimately disappears.

Both Ruth and her "other" mother-in-law Rahab, the Canaanite prostitute who gives birth to Boaz (Matt 1:5), have analogues with one of Euramerica's signature narratives about Native women, the Pocahontas Perplex. This narrative ideologically constructs Native women as the ones who save or aid white men in their colonization of the land. Ruth, in her intermarriage with Boaz, and Rahab, who helps the spies in the conquest of Canaan, represent the stereotype of the indigenous woman who forsakes her native land and aligns herself with the men who will eventually subjugate her and her people. Donaldson does envision a counter-narrative in Ruth in the person of Orpah, Ruth's Moabite sister-in-law. Rather than accompanying Naomi and Ruth to Judah, Orpah kisses her mother-in-law goodbye and returns to her mother's house (Ruth 1:8, 14–15). Although Orpah's return has been regarded negatively, "to Cherokee women . . . Orpah connotes hope rather than perversity, because she is the one who does not reject her traditions or her sacred ancestors," but rather chooses "the indigenous mother's house over that of the alien Israelite Father."[120]

Gale A. Yee employs both feminist materialist and postcolonial criticisms in her analysis of Ezek 23. Here, the prophet describes the terrible destruction of Jerusalem and the exile of its elites in a passage notable for its pornographic portrait of Israel and Judah as sexually insatiable sisters. Set within the historical context of colonial relations that led to their destruction and exile, she argues that the pornography of the narrative should be coded not simply as another form of patriarchal violence, but as colonial ethnic conflict framed as a sexualized encounter. Similar to constructions of gender in other colonial narratives, Judah and Israel are feminized as the invaded colonized female body, while their foreign conquerors are hypersexualized, with penises "like those of donkeys and whose emission was like that of stallions" (23:20). Ezekiel 23 is the prophet's attempt to deal with the personal and collective trauma of colonization, conquest, and exile of the Judean elite. He absolves his own institutional complicity in the sins of the nation, and that of the male elite

---

120. Donaldson, "The Sign of Orpah."

class to which he belongs, by projecting the sins of the nation metaphorically onto two sisters, promiscuous from their youth, who suffer sexually violent acts of rape, dismemberment, and destruction.[121]

Conclusion

As we have seen, feminist biblical scholarship rests on a strong foundation of feminist and intersectional scholarship, a scholarship that became conscious of and reacted to its own racism, class bias, colonial privilege, and homophobia over the course of its development. Feminist biblical scholarship began to flourish in the 1960s–1970s, in keeping with the various movements of civil, racial, and gender rights and intellectual unrest occurring during this formative time. In biblical studies, this unrest took shape in the appearance of literary critical studies, reacting to the dominance of historical-critical investigations of the biblical text. Phyllis Trible was the first biblical scholar to apply feminist literary-critical hermeneutics to the Hebrew Bible. Other scholars applied more historical-critical approaches in their own feminist works.

The field of biblical studies itself broadened by adopting interdisciplinary approaches beyond the historical and literary, and feminist biblical scholars were at the forefront of these intellectual inquiries. These scholars embraced insights from postmodern and Marxist/materialist feminists, deconstructionists, queer theorists, and cultural critics to elucidate the Hebrew Bible in invigorating ways. In parallel with these developments, feminist biblicists of color had their own critical interpretations of the text, from their particular situated locations in areas of race, class, colonial or indigenous status, and sexual orientation.

This introduction provides only the tip of the iceberg regarding the current state of feminist and intersectional perspectives on the Hebrew Bible. I hope that it has broadened your own understanding of these issues and helped you approach issues of gender, race, and class in the biblical text with greater clarity.

Works Cited

Anderson, Cheryl B. *Ancient Laws and Contemporary Controversies: The Need for Inclusive Biblical Interpretation*. New York: Oxford University Press, 2009.

---

121. Yee, "The Two Sisters in Ezekiel."

———. "Biblical Interpretation as Violence: Genesis 19 and Judges 19 in the Context of HIV and AIDS." In *La Violencia and the Hebrew Bible: The Politics and Histories of Biblical Hermeneutics on the American Continent*, edited by Susanne Scholz and Pablo R. Andiñach, 121–36. Semeia Studies 82. Atlanta: SBL Press, 2016.

———. "Reflections in an Interethnic/Racial Era on Interethnic/Racial Marriage in Ezra." In *They Were All Together in One Place? Toward Minority Biblical Criticism*, edited by Randall C. Bailey et al., 119–40. Semeia Studies 57. Atlanta: Society of Biblical Literature, 2009.

———. "The Song of Songs: Redeeming Gender Constructions in the Age of AIDS." In *Womanist Interpretations of the Bible: Expanding the Discourse*, edited by Gay L. Byron and Vanessa Lovelace, 73–92. Semeia Studies 85. Atlanta: SBL Press, 2016.

———. "Transatlantic Reflections: Contesting the Margins and Transgressing Boundaries in the Age of AIDS." *JFSR* 25 (2009) 103–7.

———. *Women, Ideology and Violence: The Construction of Gender in the Book of the Covenant and Deuteronomic Law*. JSOTSup 394. New York: Continuum, 2004.

Anzaldúa, Gloria. *Borderlands: La Frontera: The New Mestiza*. 4th ed. San Francisco: Aunt Lute Books, 2012. First published 1999.

Bach, Alice, ed. *Biblical Glamour and Hollywood Glitz*. Semeia 74 (1996).

———. *Religion, Politics, Media in the Broadband Era*. Bible in the Modern World 2. Sheffield: Sheffield Phoenix, 2004.

Baker-Fletcher, Karen. "Anna Julia Cooper and Sojourner Truth: Two Nineteenth-Century Black Feminist Interpreters of Scripture." In *Search the Scriptures: A Feminist Introduction*, edited by Elisabeth Schüssler Fiorenza, 41–51. New York: Crossroad, 1995.

Bal, Mieke. *Death and Dissymmetry: The Politics of Coherence in the Book of Judges*. Chicago Studies in the History of Judaism. Chicago: University of Chicago Press, 1988.

———. *Lethal Love: Feminist Literary Readings of Biblical Love Stories*. Indiana Studies in Biblical Literature. Bloomington: Indiana University Press, 1987.

———. *Murder and Difference: Gender, Genre, and Scholarship on Sisera's Death*. Indiana Studies in Biblical Literature. Bloomington: Indiana University Press, 1988.

Barrett, Michèle. *Women's Oppression Today: The Marxist/Feminist Encounter*. Rev. ed. London: Verso, 1988.

Bethel, Lorraine. "What Chou Mean WE, White Girl?" *Conditions* 5 (1979) 86–92.

Bird, Phyllis A. "Images of Women in the Old Testament." In *Religion and Sexism: Images of Woman in the Jewish and Christian Traditions*, edited by Rosemary Radford Ruether, 41–88. New York: Simon & Schuster, 1974.

———. "The Place of Women in the Israelite Cultus." In *Ancient Israelite Religion: Essays in Honor of Frank Moore Cross*, edited by Patrick D. Miller et al., 397–419. Philadelphia: Fortress, 1987.

Boer, Roland, and Jorunn Økland, eds. *Marxist Feminist Criticism of the Bible*. Bible in the Modern World 14. Sheffield: Sheffield Phoenix, 2008.

Bow, Leslie, ed. *Asian American Feminisms*. Asian American Feminisms 1. London: Routledge, 2013.

Brenner, Athalya. *The Israelite Woman: Social Role and Literary Type in Biblical Narrative*. Biblical Seminar 2. Sheffield: JSOT Press, 1985.

Brenner-Idan, Athalya. *The Israelite Woman: Social Role and Literary Type in Biblical Narrative*. 2nd ed. Cornerstones. London: Bloomsbury, 2015.
Butler, Judith. "Performative Acts and Gender Constitution: An Essay in Phenomenology and Feminist Theory." In *Feminist Theory Reader: Local and Global Perspectives*, edited by Carol R. McCann and Seung-Kyung Kim, 481–92. 4th ed. 1988. Reprint, London: Routledge, 2017.
Byron, Gay L., and Vanessa Lovelace, eds. *Womanist Interpretations of the Bible: Expanding the Discourse*. Semeia Studies, 85. Atlanta: SBL Press, 2016.
Carvalho, Corrine. *Primer on Biblical Methods*. Winona, MN: Anselm Academic, 2009.
Cho, Sumi, et al. "Toward a Field of Intersectionality Studies: Theory, Applications, and Praxis." *Signs: Journal of Women in Culture & Society* 38 (2013) 785–810.
Collins, Adela Yarbro, ed. *Feminist Perspectives on Biblical Scholarship*. Biblical Scholarship in North America 10. Chico, CA: Scholars, 1985.
Collins, Patricia Hill. *Black Feminist Thought: Knowledge, Consciousness, and the Politics of Empowerment*. 2nd. ed. Routledge Classics. London: Routledge, 2009.
The Combahee River Collective. "A Black Feminist Statement." In *Capitalist Patriarchy and the Case for Social Feminism*, edited by Eisenstein, Zilla, 362–72. New York: Monthly Review Press, 1978.
Crenshaw, Kimberlé Williams. "Mapping the Margins: Intersectionality, Identity Politics, and Violence against Women of Color." In *Critical Race Theory: The Key Writings That Formed the Movement*, edited by Kimberlé Crenshaw, et al., 357–83. New York: New Press, 1995.
Crowell, Bradley L. "Postcolonial Studies and the Hebrew Bible." *CBR* 7/2 (2009) 217–44.
Davis, Angela Y. *Women, Race and Class*. New York: Vintage, 1981.
Dill, Bonnie Thornton, and Ruth Enid Zambrana. "Critical Thinking about Inequality: An Emerging Lens." In *Feminist Theory Reader: Local and Global Perspectives*, edited by Carol R. McCann and Seung-Kyung Kim, 182–93. 4th ed. 2009. Reprint, London: Routledge, 2017.
Donaldson, Laura E. "The Sign of Orpah: Reading Ruth through Native Eyes." In *Ruth and Esther: A Feminist Companion to the Bible*, edited by Athalya Brenner, 130–44. FCB, 2nd ser., 3. Sheffield: Sheffield Academic, 1999.
Dube, Musa W. *Postcolonial Feminist Interpretation of the Bible*. St. Louis: Chalice, 2000.
———. "Toward a Postcolonial Feminist Interpretation of the Bible." *Semeia* 78 (1997) 11–26.
Edwards, Katie B. *Admen and Eve: The Bible in Contemporary Advertising*. Bible in the Modern World 48. Sheffield: Sheffield Phoenix, 2012.
Exum, J. Cheryl. "Bathsheba Plotted, Shot, and Painted." *Semeia* 74 (1996) 47–73.
———. *Plotted, Shot, and Painted: Cultural Representations of Biblical Women*. JSOTSup 215. Sheffield: Sheffield Academic, 1996.
Fewell, Danna Nolan. "Deconstructive Criticism: Achsah and the (E)Razed City of Writing." In *Judges and Method: New Approaches in Biblical Studies*, edited by Gale A. Yee, 113–37. 2nd ed. Minneapolis: Fortress, 2007.
———. "Feminist Reading of the Hebrew Bible: Affirmation, Resistance and Transformation." *JSOT* 39 (1987) 77–87.
Fewell, Danna Nolan, and David M. Gunn. *Gender, Power, and Promise: The Subject of the Bible's First Story*. Nashville: Abingdon, 1993.

Foskett, Mary F., and Jeffrey Kah-jin Kuan, eds. *Ways of Being, Ways of Reading: Asian American Biblical Interpretation*. St. Louis: Chalice, 2006.
Fuchs, Esther. *Feminist Theory and the Bible*. Feminist Studies and Sacred Texts. Lanham, MD: Lexington, 2016.
———. "Reclaiming the Hebrew Bible for Women: The Neoliberal Turn in Contemporary Feminist Scholarship." *JFSR* 24 (2008) 45–65.
———. "The Literary Characterization of Mothers and Sexual Politics in the Hebrew Bible." In *Feminist Perspectives on Biblical Scholarship*, edited by Adela Yarbro Collins, 117–36. Biblical Scholarship in North America 10. Chico, CA: Scholars, 1985.
———. "Who Is Hiding the Truth? Deceptive Women and Biblical Androcentrism." In *Feminist Perspectives on Biblical Scholarship*, edited by Adela Yarbro Collins, 137–44. Biblical Scholarship in North America 10. Chico, CA: Scholars, 1985.
Gafney, Wilda C. *Womanist Midrash: A Reintroduction to the Women of the Torah and the Throne*. Louisville: Westminster John Knox, 2017.
Gafney, Wilda C. M. "A Black Feminist Approach to Biblical Studies." *Encounter* 67 (2006) 391–403.
Gottheimer, Josh, et al., eds. *Ripples of Hope: Great American Civil Rights Speeches*. Online Resource. New York: Basic Civitas, 2003.
Guest, Deryn. *Beyond Feminist Biblical Studies*. The Bible in the Modern World 47. Sheffield: Sheffield Phoenix, 2012.
———. "From Gender Reversal to Genderfuck: Reading Jael through a Lesbian Lens." In *Bible Trouble: Queer Reading at the Boundaries of Biblical Scholarship*, edited by Teresa Hornsby and Ken Stone, 9–43. Semeia Studies 67. Atlanta: Society of Biblical Literature, 2011.
Gunn, David M. "Cultural Criticism: Viewing the Sacrifice of Jephthah's Daughter." In *Judges and Method: New Approaches in Biblical Studies*, edited by Gale A. Yee, 202–36. 2nd ed. Minneapolis: Fortress, 2007.
Hartmann, Heidi. "The Unhappy Marriage of Marxism and Feminism: Towards a More Progressive Union." In *The Second Wave: A Reader in Feminist Theory*, edited by Linda Nicholson, 97–122. 1981. Reprint, New York: Routledge, 1997.
Hartsock, Nancy C. M. "The Feminist Standpoint: Toward a Specifically Feminist Historical Materialism." In *Feminist Theory Reader: Local and Global Perspectives*, edited by Carol R. McCann and Seung-Kyung Kim, 368–83. 4th ed. London: Routledge, 2017.
hooks, bell. *Feminist Theory: From Margin to Center*. Boston: South End, 1984.
Ipsen, Avaren E. *Sex Working and the Bible*. London: Equinox, 2009.
Jordan, June. "Report from the Bahamas." In *Feminist Theory Reader: Local and Global Perspectives*, edited by Carol R. McCann and Seung-Kyung Kim, 304–12. 4th ed. London: Routledge, 2017. First published 1985.
Junior, Nyasha. *An Introduction to Womanist Biblical Interpretation*. Louisville: Westminster John Knox, 2015.
King, Deborah. "Multiple Jeopardy: The Context of a Black Feminist Ideology." In *Feminist Frameworks: Alternative Theoretical Accounts of Relations between Women and Men*, edited by Alison M. Jaggar and Paula S. Rothenberg, 220–36. 3rd ed. Boston: McGraw-Hill, 1993.

Lanyer, Amelia. "Eve's Apology in Defense of Women." In *Salve Deus Rex Judaeorum, 1611*. http://whs-hs.weatherfordisd.com/ourpages/auto/2013/11/20/57676221/Poem-Eve_s%20Apology.pdf/.
LeMon, Joel M., and Kent H. Richards, eds. *Method Matters: Essays on the Interpretation of the Hebrew Bible in Honor of David L. Petersen*. Resources for Biblical Study. Atlanta: Society of Biblical Literature, 2009.
Lerner, Gerda. *The Creation of Feminist Consciousness: From the Middle Ages to Eighteen-Seventy*. New York: Oxford University Press, 1993.
Liew, Tat-Siong Benny. "Asian American Biblical Interpretation." In *The Oxford Encyclopedia of Biblical Interpretation*, edited by Steven L. McKenzie, 1:36–42. Oxford: Oxford University Press, 2013.
Liew, Tat-Siong Benny, and Gale A. Yee, eds. *The Bible in Asian America*. Semeia 90/91. Atlanta: Society of Biblical Literature, 2002.
Lorde, Audre. *Sister Outsider: Essays and Speeches by Audre Lorde*. Freedom, CA: Crossing, 1984.
Lowe, Lisa. "Heterogeneity, Hybridity, Multiplicity: Marking Asian American Difference." *Diaspora* 1 (1991) 24–44.
Lugones, María. *Pilgrimages = Peregrinajes: Theorizing Coalition against Multiple Oppressions*. Lanham, MD: Rowman & Littlefield, 2003.
Mann, Susan Archer. *Doing Feminist Theory: From Modernity to Postmodernity*. Oxford: Oxford University Press, 2012.
McCann, Carol R., and Seung-Kyung Kim. "Introduction: Theorizing Feminist Knowledge and Agency." In *Feminist Theory Reader: Local and Global Perspectives*, edited by Carol R. McCann and Seung-Kyung Kim, 353–65. 4th ed. London: Routledge, 2017.
———. "Introduction: Feminist Theory, Local and Global Perspectives." In *Feminist Theory Reader: Local and Global Perspectives*, edited by Carol R. McCann and Seung-Kyung Kim, 1–30. 4th ed. London: Routledge, 2017.
Meyers, Carol. *Discovering Eve: Ancient Israelite Women in Context*. New York: Oxford University Press, 1988.
———. *Rediscovering Eve: Ancient Israelite Women in Context*. New York: Oxford University Press, 2013.
Milne, Pamela J. "Toward Feminist Companionship: The Future of Feminist Biblical Studies and Feminism." In *A Feminist Companion to Reading the Bible: Approaches, Methods and Strategies*, edited by Athalya Brenner and Carole Fontaine, 39–60. FCB 11. Sheffield: Sheffield Academic, 1997.
Mohanty, Chandra Talpade. "'Under Western Eyes' Revisited: Feminist Solidarity through Anticapitalist Struggles." In *Feminism without Borders: Decolonizing Theory, Practicing Solidarity*, 221–51. Durham: Duke University Press, 2003.
———. "Under Western Eyes: Feminist Scholarship and Colonial Discourses." In *Third World Women and the Politics of Feminism*, edited by Chandra Talpade Mohanty, Ann Russo, and Lourdes Torres, 51–80. Bloomington: Indiana University Press, 1991.
Moraga, Cherríe, and Gloria Anzaldúa, eds. *This Bridge Called My Back: Writing by Radical Women of Color*. New York: Kitchen Table: Women of Color Press, 1981.
Newsom, Carol A., and Sharon H. Ringe, eds. *The Women's Bible Commentary*. Louisville: Westminster John Knox, 1992.

Ngan, Lai Ling Elizabeth. "Bitter Melon, Bitter Delight: Reading Jeremiah Reading Me." In *Off the Menu: Asian and Asian North American Women's Religion and Theology*, edited by Rita Nakashima Brock et al., 163–81. Louisville: Westminster John Knox, 2007.

———. "Neither Here nor There: Boundary and Identity in the Hagar Story." In *Ways of Being, Ways of Reading: Asian-American Biblical Interpretation*, edited by Mary F. Foskett and Jeffrey K. Kuan, 70–83. St. Louis: Chalice, 2006.

———. "Until Everyone Has a Place under the Sun." In *The Bible and the Hermeneutics of Liberation*, edited by Alejandro F. Botta and Pablo R. Andiñach, 213–23. Semeia Studies 59. Atlanta: Society of Biblical Literature, 2009.

Nicholson, Linda. "Feminism in 'Waves': Useful Metaphor or Not?" In *Feminist Theory Reader: Local and Global Perspectives*, edited by Carol R. McCann and Seung-Kyung Kim, 182–93. 4th ed. London: Routledge, 2017. First published 2010.

Perdue, Leo G., and Warren Carter. *Israel and Empire: A Postcolonial History of Israel and Early Judaism*. London: Bloomsbury T. & T. Clark, 2015.

Ruane, Nicole J. "When Women Aren't Enough: Gender Criticism in Feminist Hebrew Bible Interpretation." In *Feminist Interpretation of the Hebrew Bible in Retrospect*. Vol. 3, *Methods*, edited by Susanne Scholz, 243–60. Recent Research in Biblical Studies 9. Sheffield: Sheffield Phoenix, 2016.

Rubin, Gayle. "The Traffic in Women: Notes on the 'Political Economy' of Sex." In *Toward and Anthropology of Women*, edited by Rayna R. Reiter, 157–210. New York: Monthly Review Press, 1975.

———. "Thinking Sex: Notes for a Radical Theory of the Politics of Sexuality." In *Pleasure and Danger: Exploring Female Sexuality*, 267–319. Boston: Routledge & Kegan Paul, 1984.

Russell, Letty M., ed. *Feminist Interpretation of the Bible*. Philadelphia: Westminster, 1985.

Schearing, Linda S., and Valarie H. Ziegler. *Enticed by Eden: How Western Culture Uses, Confuses, (and Sometimes Abuses) Adam and Eve*. Waco: Baylor University Press, 2013.

Scholz, Susanne, ed. *Feminist Interpretation of the Hebrew Bible in Retrospect*. Vol. 3, *Methods*. Recent Research in Biblical Studies 9. Sheffield: Sheffield Phoenix, 2016.

Sherwood, Yvonne. *The Prostitute and the Prophet: Hosea's Marriage in Literary-Theoretical Perspective*. JSOTSup 212. Sheffield: Sheffield Academic, 1996.

Spelman, Elizabeth V. *Inessential Woman: Problems of Exclusion in Feminist Thought*. Boston: Beacon, 1988.

Stanton, Elizabeth Cady. *The Woman's Bible*. Edited by Maurene Fitzgerald. Boston: Northeastern University Press, 1993.

Stone, Ken. "Gender Criticism: The Un-Manning of Abimelech." In *Judges and Method: New Approaches in Biblical Studies*, edited by Gale A. Yee, 183–201. 2nd ed. Minneapolis: Fortress, 2007.

Taylor, Marion Ann, and Heather E. Weir, eds. *Let Her Speak for Herself: Nineteenth-Century Women Writing on Women in Genesis*. Waco: Baylor University Press, 2006.

Thompson, Becky. "Multiracial Feminism: Recasting the Chronology of Second Wave Feminism." In *Feminist Theory Reader: Local and Global Perspectives*, edited by Carol R McCann and Seung-Kyung Kim, 51–62. 4th ed. London: Routledge, 2017.

Tolbert, Mary Ann, ed. "The Bible and Feminist Hermeneutics." *Semeia* 28 (1983) 3–126.
Tong, Rosemarie. *Feminist Thought: A More Comprehensive Introduction*. 4th ed. Boulder: Westview Press, 2014.
Trible, Phyllis. "Depatriarchalizing in Biblical Interpretation." *Journal of the American Academy of Religion* 41 (1973) 30–48.
———. "The Effects of Women's Studies on Biblical Studies: An Introduction." *JSOT* 7 (1982) 3–5.
———. *God and the Rhetoric of Sexuality*. Overtures to Biblical Theology. Philadelphia: Fortress, 1978.
———. *Texts of Terror: Literary-Feminist Readings of Biblical Narratives*. Overtures to Biblical Theology. Philadelphia: Fortress, 1984.
Walker, Alice. *In Search of Our Mother's Gardens*. Orlando: Harcourt, 1983.
Weems, Renita J. *Battered Love: Marriage, Sex, and Violence in the Hebrew Prophets*. Overtures to Biblical Theology. Minneapolis: Fortress, 1995.
———. "Gomer: Victim of Violence or Victim of Metaphor?" *Semeia* 47 (1989) 87–104.
———. *Just a Sister Away: Womanist Vision of Women's Relationships in the Bible*. San Diego: Lura Media, 1988.
———. "Reading Her Way through the Struggle: African American Women and the Bible." In *Stony the Road We Trod: African American Biblical Interpretation*, edited by Cain Hope Felder, 57–77. Minneapolis: Fortress, 1991.
West, Traci C. "Is a Womanist a Black Feminist? Marking the Distinctions and Defying Them: A Black Feminist Response." In *Deeper Shades of Purple: Womanism in Religion and Society*, edited by Stacey M. Floyd-Thomas, 291–95. New York: New York University Press, 2006.
Yee, Gale A. "Introduction: Definitions, Explorations, and Intersections." In *The Hebrew Bible: Feminist and Intersectional Perspectives*, edited by Gale A. Yee, 1–38. Minneapolis: Fortress, 2018.
———, ed. *Judges and Method: New Approaches in Biblical Studies*. 2nd ed. Minneapolis: Fortress, 2007.
———. *Poor Banished Children of Eve: Woman as Evil in the Hebrew Bible*. Minneapolis: Fortress, 2003.
———. "Postcolonial Biblical Criticism." In *Methods for Exodus*, edited by Thomas B. Dozeman, 193–233. Cambridge: Cambridge University Press, 2010.
———. "'She Stood in Tears amid the Alien Corn': Ruth, the Perpetual Foreigner and Model Minority." In *They Were All Together in One Place? Toward Minority Biblical Criticism*, edited by Randall C. Bailey et al., 119–40. Semeia Studies 57. Atlanta: Society of Biblical Literature, 2009.
———. "The Two Sisters in Ezekiel: They Played the Whore in Egypt." In *Poor Banished Children of Eve: Woman as Evil in the Hebrew Bible*, 111–34. Minneapolis: Fortress, 2003.
———. "What Is Cultural Criticism of the Old Testament?" In *Why Read the Old Testament? Questions Asked and Unasked: The Legacy of Fr. Lawrence Boadt*, edited by Corrine L. Carvalho, 43–55. Mahwah, NJ: Paulist, 2013.

3

Inculturation and Diversity in the Politics of National Identity[1]

TWO RELATED ISSUES DEEPLY affect my identity as a Chinese American. The first is my *inculturation* and that of my nuclear and extended family into US society. The second is the ethnic and regional *diversity* of Asian American inclusion. On the one hand, inculturation tried to mold my identity into a proper citizen of a society in which I was an ethnic minority. It tried to suppress and eliminate my savory Chinese heritage and replace it with a "white-bre(a)d" culture. On the other hand, the ethnic and regional diversity of Asian American women makes me resist generalizing how this inculturation takes place for Asian American women. The construction of an American identity for a Hmong woman growing up in Minnesota, or a Korean woman adopted as a child by a Southern white couple, will be completely different from that of a Taiwanese woman growing up in San Francisco's or New York's Chinatown.

As a springboard to discuss the complex intersections of inculturation and ethnic and regional diversity, I offer my own unique experience. Around 1908 my maternal grandfather was lured from the Hoy San district in the Kuantung Province of southern China to seek his fortune in Butte, Montana. Although California was home to most Chinese immigrants, Montana also had a sizeable Chinese population. Immigration policies designed to keep Chinese women out of the US and the Chinese

---

1. Originally published as "The 3rd Story" in Yee, "Inculturation and Diversity." Presented in the session on "The Impact of National Histories on the Politics of Identity" for the Women and Religion Section of the American Academy of Religion, 1994 annual meeting, Chicago, Illinois.

reluctance to bring wives to the States were both factors which influenced my grandfather to leave my maternal grandmother and their son in China. White hostility prevented a Chinese labor force from entering the industrial, agricultural, and mining sectors after the completion of the transcontinental railroad, where this labor force had been employed. Therefore, only two opportunities for self-employment were available to my grandfather here in Gold Mountain during this time. He could open the ubiquitous Chinese laundry ("No tickee, no washee!") or he could sell vegetables.[2] What he did was the latter, buying a horse and cart and peddling vegetables and fruit door-to-door. (I have since learned that my paternal grandfather was a laundry man.) After fifteen long years saving his money from vegetable peddling, my maternal grandfather was able to bring my grandmother and their son from China.

Enduring several miscarriages and abortions through Chinese herbs, my grandmother bore eight more children here in the States for my grandfather. However, she became fed up with his abusiveness and left him and went to Seattle, Washington, taking their younger children with her. She gave my mother and two of the other older siblings into the care of guardians. My grandfather in turn sicced the Bing Kung Tong (Chinese Mafia) on my grandmother, who then fled to Chicago where the Bing Kung Tong could not touch her, since it was governed by another group of Tong. My illiterate but economically shrewd grandmother opened a restaurant across the street from Holy Name Cathedral in Chicago and was able to send for my mother to join her. All of this is a roundabout way of explaining how my mother came to the Midwest region of the USA where she met my Chinese American father, who was in the Navy at the time. Originally from Cincinnati, Ohio, he was docked in Chicago during World War II.

A brief remark should be made at this point before I continue with my family history. A number of personal factors (e.g., my grandfather's abusiveness, my grandmother's resistance and resourcefulness) combine in very complex ways with political factors (e.g., discriminatory US immigration policies, racial hostility against a Chinese labor force and the marginalization of my grandfather, the Tong subculture, a naval base in Chicago, World War II) to make a difference where I grew up as a Chinese American woman in this society. I therefore cannot separate analytically my family's personal history from my country's national history. For my

---

2. Takaki, *Strangers from a Different Shore*, 93.

Asian American identity, the personal is interlocked with the political in a very real way.

I am the firstborn of twelve children, six daughters and six sons. (Being both Chinese and a recent convert to Roman Catholicism, my mother did not have a chance regarding decisions about her fertility!) After leaving the Navy, my father became a short-order cook and my mother worked inside the home with the children. For the first ten years of my life, my family lived in the territory of the Blackstone Rangers gang of Chicago's South Side, one of the poorest and meanest areas of the city. In very real ways, then, the holy Trinity of gender, race, and class—my Chinese ethnicity, my lower-class status, and my female gender—impinged upon my Asian American identity to put me outside of the mainstream of American society. This identity becomes even more complicated by the fact that my playmates were children of Black and Puerto Rican descent. My early years were therefore shaped more by African American and Hispanic identities than by an Asian American one. However, I knew I was Chinese even before I realized that I was female. I knew I was different from my Black and Hispanic friends, yet they accepted me as I was. However, when I turned eleven, my family moved to a "white" neighborhood and I painfully encountered racism for the first time. I had to renegotiate my self-identity vis-à-vis the dominant society.

I always wondered whether my inculturation into this society would have been easier if I had grown up in an Asian American community like San Francisco's or New York's Chinatown, or Seattle's international district. My family did have relatives in Chicago's large Chinatown, but we rarely visited them. This isolation from Asian American communities actually sharpened my Asian American identity, in that all through my life I knew that I was ethnically different and I had to bear this difference without the support of an Asian American critical mass. My mother tried to mitigate this difference, first of all, by refusing to teach us Chinese and by enforcing English to be spoken in the household. She thought we would be more accepted at school and receive better grades if we did not speak English with a Chinese accent. (As it was, I spoke English in grade school with a noticeable South Side Black intonation.) My mother twisted my straight hair into pincurls and subjected it to Lilt home permanents (which she always left on too long) in order to give my hair the curls that little white girls had. She imposed her Catholicism upon me so that I would not be different in my parochial school classes.

I know that my experiences as an Asian American are not typical. I know of no other Asian American feminist theologians who grew up in Blackstone Ranger territory in Chicago. I joke that I am the only Roman Catholic Asian American female in Hebrew Bible in the whole world. This, however, is precisely the point that I wish to make on this panel about our national histories and the politics of Asian American identities. One *cannot* generalize about the construction of identity for Asian American women and their personal inculturation into this society. Talking about Asian American women in the abstract levels the diverse experiences of Chinese, Japanese, Sri Lankan, Korean, Filipino, Taiwanese, Vietnamese, Cambodian, Laotian, Hmong, Thai, East Indian, Burmese, Samoan, Hawaiian, and Malaysian women who live in this nation (and I am sure I have omitted some other groups who would fall under the umbrella rubric "Asian American"). The Asian American experience in this society is far from homogeneous. Besides a plurality of different Asian American ethnic groups with their own immigration histories to this country, these groups have settled in different regions of the US—the East coast, the Midwest, the Deep South, California, the upper Northwest—each with its own particular ideas about what it means to be American.

I would like to illustrate the problem further by drawing upon two more personal experiences. Around the late 1970s I was in graduate school in Toronto and a young man had this crush on me, believe it or not. He was particularly fascinated by the fact that I was "Oriental." He had me pegged as being Mongolian until he was informed by my friend Celia that I was Chinese. The guy was absolutely captivated by Chinese culture, its history, its food, its art, etc., and here was this live Chinese woman in the flesh. I never found out what erotic fantasies he may have harbored about "Oriental" women (shades of Suzy Wong), but I did learn that he had definite ideas about what a Chinese woman should be like. He attempted to woo me through my friend Celia. He would ask the two of us to "pig out" at different Chinese restaurants in Toronto's Chinatown. Celia and I both knew what was going on but we played along, and besides, we both loved Chinese food. An incident happened at the last of these dinners that dashed any hopes on his part of sharing connubial bliss with *moi*. This person wanted to try some of the more esoteric dishes that the restaurant did not offer to its "white" patrons. These dishes were written in Chinese on the menu. This person proceeded to berate me through the whole meal for not knowing Chinese. "You're Chinese, for God's sake, why can't you read or speak the language?" He would not let up on the matter. I could not use the argument, "You wouldn't expect an Italian American to speak Italian or a German American to speak German." He was Jewish and, sure enough, he did read and speak Hebrew. He was in Rabbinic Studies. He made it seem that I was not authentic because I did not fit the mold he had of an Asian. At the time I had not reached the level of reflection that I have today on my ethnicity. I could not articulate all of those complex factors about my growing up that formed me into the authentic Asian American that I consider myself to be, e.g., growing up on Chicago's South Side, my mother deliberately not teaching us Chinese to help us inculturate, etc., etc. Not knowing the Chinese language is paradoxically very much a part of my identity as a Chinese American. He could not see it and I could not voice it. I was furious and told Celia later that I found his remarks to be racist. Celia felt that "racist" was too strong a word to describe his behavior. Racism in the late 1970s was applied to more overt discrimination, not the subtle attitudes this person exhibited. I am sure that Celia would think differently nowadays.

The second experience I would like to relate happened a few years ago at a conference of Catholic feminist theologians at the College of St. Catherine, St. Paul, Minnesota. It was a divisive gathering that set the women of colors and the Caucasian feminists against each other. There were some attempts to cool things down on the explosive final day. An African American nun began talking about the commonalities among the feminist theologians, the womanist theologians, the *mujerista* theologians, and . . . She struggled for an epithet to describe the Asian and Asian American theologians in the room and ended up saying, "Those women who haven't named themselves yet." I remember casting a meaningful look across the room at one of the Filipina women, who immediately spoke up on behalf of the "women without a name." The African American nun became very embarrassed because she certainly did not want to contribute to the bad feeling that was already in the room.

I was reminded at the time of the first chapter of Maxine Hong Kingston's *The Woman Warrior*, which was titled, "The No Name Woman." I wondered if the Asian and Asian American feminist theologians would ever have a neat name that would encapsulate their gender, their ethnicity, and their theological work. The problem, in fact, is that we Asian and Asian American women have many names: Korean, Korean American, Japanese, Japanese American, Laotian, Laotian American, and so forth. We might not have a common name that we all share here at this gathering, but we are still here together.

I do not want to be known as one of the No Name theologians. However, the different experiences of inculturation and the ethnic and regional diversity of Asian American women makes me resist applying a fancy name to my work as an Asian American feminist biblical scholar. Moreover, it is precisely the differences in national history that would prevent me from adopting a name that the Asian feminists give to themselves. I am essentially Asian American, not Asian. I need to hear more stories about the diverse experiences of Asian American women to detect any patterns, shaped by both personal and national circumstances, that give Asian American feminists a particular identity. Only then will we be able to name that identity.

How my Asian American identity affects my scholarship is a difficult question for me at this point. I cannot divide my self, my identity, into compartments focusing on that which is female, that which is Asian American, that which is Roman Catholic, that which is trained in Canada, etc. I know where my gender affects my biblical studies, but I have not yet figured out where my ethnicity affects my biblical scholarship. I suppose that just as the early biblical feminists entered strange, hostile waters to explore the Bible from a woman's perspective, so will I as an Asian American enter new territory in studying the Bible from an Asian American perspective. I helped formulate a proposal (which has since been approved) for a new Consultation on Asian and Asian American Biblical Studies in the Society of Biblical Literature and I am on its steering committee. Wish me luck in this new adventure and ask me this question in five years.

Works Cited

Takaki, Ronald. *Strangers from a Different Shore: A History of Asian Americans.* Updated and rev. ed. New York: Back Bay, 1998.

Yee, Gale A. "Inculturation and Diversity in the Politics of National Identity." *JAAAT* 2 (1997) 108–12.

4

Refiguring the Missionary Position
or We Asian North American Women Won't Take This Lying Down![1]

THE SEXUAL POSITION WHERE the man is on top and the woman reclines on her back, facing him, is often dubbed the missionary position. This description is attributed to Christian missionaries who ostensibly advocated the coital posture, even though the "natives" preferred a sexual variety. In this panel on methodological issues, the missionary position becomes a fitting metaphor to describe in part the current place/position of many Asian and Asian North American women in theology and ministry. Besides fusing issues of religion, gender, and sexuality, the expression "missionary position" personifies the fact that Asian contact with Christianity was primarily through evangelical Christian missionaries who imposed a particular form of cultural, religious, and sexual imperialism on their converts. In different ways, we here are all products of this Western religious colonialism. Any sexual position where the man was not on top these missionaries regarded as unnatural. They legitimated their belief by appealing to Genesis where, they argued, man is created first and given primacy over woman in all things. Now, of course, we cannot blame Christian missionaries for the subordination of women in

1. Originally presented at the 13th PANAAWTM conference on *Being Asian & Women: Implications for Theology and Ministry*—WOTS (Weaknesses, Opportunities, Threats, Strengths) UP? March 13–15, 1998, Emmanuel College, Victoria University, Toronto, Canada (Pacific Asian North American Asian Women in Theology and Ministry).

Asia. Missionary sexism meshed very well with an already entrenched Asian patriarchy and reinforced it socially with a peculiarly Christian religious twist. When many of these Asians came to North America, they reinscribed this multicultural brand of sexism in their immigrant church communities.

The missionary position as metaphor embodies a divinely decreed natural order. The position of women in this order is on the bottom. Christian missionary sexism reinforced cultural expectations of the Asian woman as submissive, obedient, silent, and deferent to males. With a strong sense of duty and obligation, she maintains traditional family honor. She unfailingly identifies her primary role in the social order as the mother of sons. To rebel against her place on the bottom would bring shame and loss of face, not simply to herself, but to her whole family lineage. But by acknowledging her proper place, the Asian Christian woman supported and preserved the Tao and Confucian philosophical traditions of balance and harmony in the world order.

In the missionary position, the Asian and Asian North American female on the bottom is often invisible when viewed from above because the male covers, conceals, and subsumes her. This invisibility extends to images of those in ministry and theology. When one thinks of a member of the clergy, a minister, a theologian, a biblical scholar, this person usually does not have an Asian or Asian North American *female* face. When we try to formulate and claim a theological self-identity, it is from the methodological standpoint of the underside. Here, we are often invisible, certainly more invisible than Caucasian females, and where traditional sources of theological empowerment are lacking. Moreover, Asian and missionary sexism combine with North American sexism to hit us with a triple whammy that obstructs our theological work and keeps us on the bottom.

In the missionary position, the woman is on her back facing the male. What she sees and touches within this androcentric order is solely the male, who makes exclusive claims upon her body. In our theological formation, education, and ministry, whom do we see as our teachers, leaders, and mentors, as we lie passively back? Our ways of theologizing and doing ministry are primarily through the eyes of a white Western male educational and ecclesiastical leadership. We appropriate Western discourse into our theological essays, sprinkling them with terms like *Wissenschaft*, *mutatis mutandis*, and *Heilsgeschichte*, because, we are taught, this is "doing theology," this is "being a scholar." What this really is, however, is "being a white Western male," the image of what an Asian or Asian North American primarily sees while doing theology and ministry in the missionary position.

During this era of multiculturalism and global awareness, this same Western Christian male discourse wonders quizzically why we cannot immediately come up with the Asian or Asian North American "take" on a particular religious issue, or in my case, with a particular reading of a biblical text. We in this room have the added burden of expressing the Asian or Asian North American *woman's* "opinion" when this is demanded by this discourse. In other words, we Asian and Asian North American women are formed into one methodological and discursive mode after long years of study in the system, but this same system, with an often insincere nod towards political correctness, pressures us to expound in an altogether different mode. Now, I know that my continual self-reflection on what it means to be an Asian North American woman has been an extraordinarily enriching one. But I resent having to produce it on demand in a white male religious and academic context—a context populated by men who have not made that oftentimes painful journey into self-reflection and discovery themselves. How many men do you know who were asked to expound on the white male German reading of a religious text during a job interview or in a theological debate? And yet we Asian and Asian North American women have to do it all the time in the classroom, in the guild, and in the pulpit.

I come to the point in my remarks, where I might be really straining this metaphor, so if I hear any groans out there, I will know when to quit. The "natives" whom the missionaries tried to convert, so the story goes, favored a plurality of sexual positions rather than the one endorsed by the missionaries. One of my sources dryly remarked that the missionary position was unknown and unmissed in many cultures. Missionaries in Asia had to labor in a very religiously pluralistic context in which they definitely were in the minority. They encountered and conflicted with a number of indigenous religions, such as Buddhism, Taoism, Hinduism, Shinto, and Confucianism. These all had their own theological *Weltanschauung* (oops, blame this on my nine years of doctoral study), scriptures, ritual practices, and zealous clergy intent on preserving their own religious hegemony over their "flock." The absolutist claims of missionaries to the "Truth" antagonized Asian religious systems, especially when missionaries vilified these systems as heathen and demonic. One of the methodological issues Asian women theologians face as they try to get up from down under is how to dialogue with these indigenous Asian religions in developing distinctively Asian Christian theologies, ministries, and hermeneutics. How can they learn from these other religions? What can Asian religions learn from them? What forms will Asian theology, ministry, and hermeneutics take? In whatever forms, one cannot label them "syncretistic," which implies a pure Christianity (usually a Western one) that has become polluted by the Asian context. A specifically Asian Christianity is one that undergoes a process of convergence with and differentiation from Western Christianity, in dialogue with Asian indigenous religions.

Besides coping with religious pluralism, Asian and Asian North American women must reckon with ethnic pluralism as well. One of the reasons why it is difficult for us to deliver *the* Asian or *the* Asian North American position on theological or ministerial matters is precisely because of our ethnic plurality. We must negotiate national and cultural differences among the many diverse populations that fall under the category Asian: Chinese, Japanese, Korean, Pacific Islander, Taiwanese Malaysian, Filipina, etc. (and my apologies to those who are subsumed under the "et cetera"). Those of us here who are Asian North American must distinguish among generations, between Asian immigrants and North American–born Asians, between those of us who grew up in an Asian-identified community like Toronto's Chinatown and those for whom an Asian North American critical mass was absent. Asian North American women must deal with strong regional differences among us. An Asian Quebequois has a different worldview than an Asian Manitoban. An Asian American Southern woman is a completely different breed from an Asian American Midwestern female. (My cousin is an Asian American Southern belle living in Savannah, Georgia. My aunt used to send me my cousin's dresses when she outgrew them, and I definitely looked ridiculous in Southern frills and ruffles.)

I have used the metaphor of the missionary position to epitomize the current position of Asian and Asian North American women in theology and ministry. The metaphor embodies cultural beliefs that society, guild, and church have of us as humble and submissive women. It succinctly describes our invisibility in theology and ministry and exemplifies our theological formation into a specifically male, Western mode. It may seem that the religious, ethnic, and regional differences among us obstruct us as we try to work our way up from the missionary position. Yet this is our challenge in developing an Asian or Asian North American female way of doing theology and ministry. I see hope for the future in the fact that we are here at this gathering in solidarity with one another even in our diversity. Whatever the future holds, I know that we Asian and Asian North American women will not take this lying down.

5

Yin/Yang Is Not Me

An Exploration into an Asian American Biblical Hermeneutics[1]

I AM GRATEFUL TO Mary Foskett and Jeffrey Kuan for this opportunity to explore the contours and seams of Asian American biblical interpretation, something that I have wanted to do since delving into the politics of national identity as an Asian American woman for an AAR Women and Religion session back in 1994.[2] Over ten years have elapsed since that presentation. In many ways what follows is a very personal account of my efforts to theorize and problematize Asian American biblical hermeneutics since then. All theories, whether consciously or (more often) not, arise from the diverse experiences and social locations of their theorizers. I will thus use two stories as springboards into a discussion of an Asian American biblical hermeneutics.

Anecdote One

When I had my first job interviews just after graduate school in the early 1980s, my (primarily male) interviewers wanted to know if there was a difference in my interpretation of the biblical text as a woman. The presumption was, of course, that their (male) way of interpreting the Bible

---

1. Originally published in Yee, "Yin/Yang Is Not Me." A draft was presented at the 2003 annual meeting of the Society of Biblical Literature, Atlanta.

2. Yee, "Inculturation and Diversity."

was the "traditional" (read: real) way, and then there was the "woman's way." During job interviews in the 1990s, however, when feminism became more established in the guild, my interviewers would turn to my race/ethnicity and whether or not it made any difference in my biblical interpretations. This usually happened at the awkward moment when people could think of no other questions regarding my scholarship. They could always ask me something about my race/ethnicity. I do remember that I resented such questions more than those based on gender, because I at least knew that the white women in the group might know something of what I was talking about with respect to gender. I recall one occasion when I commented obliquely on the appropriateness of such questioning, that a white German male would never be asked in an interview, "What does a white German male interpretation of the biblical text look like?" I did not get that job.

I remember feeling pressed to conform to some nebulous ideal of an Asian American woman, to perform according to some preconceived script of what an Asian American woman should be. Whatever I said would not have been understood. Although I look Chinese, I do not have the usual markers of Asianness.[3] I cannot draw on immigrant experience, since I am a third-generation Chinese American. Unlike Maxine Hong Kingston's, my mother never told me Chinese legends of ghosts and woman warriors,[4] probably because she didn't know about these herself as a second-generation Chinese American. Although I grew up in a Chinese speaking household, my parents deliberately did not teach me to speak Chinese. So I do not have a Chinese accent. I did not live in Chicago's Chinatown, but in the gang-ridden Blackstone Ranger territory of Chicago's South Side. My cultural formation was not among other Chinese Americans, but among African American and Puerto Rican slum dwellers, like my family and me. My parents were zealous Roman Catholics, not practicing the traditional Asian religions, Buddhism, Taoism, and Confucianism. *So Yin/Yang is not me.* Except for my face and name, none of the usual ethnic markers of being Asian fit me, yet white society compels me, however well-intended, to explain how my Asian Americanness makes me different. And this particular volume asks me to discuss Asian American Biblical Hermeneutics as an Asian North American woman.

---

3. Some of what follows is explored more fully in Yee, "Inculturation and Diversity," 108–12.

4. Kingston, *The Woman Warrior*.

A book by Rey Chow helped me immensely in understanding my antipathy against racial/ethnic pigeon-holing by white society. According to Chow, ethnic persons become like animals in the zoo, under the gaze of the present politics of ethnicity in capitalist liberalism.[5] Chow distinguishes three levels of mimeticism or imitation in postcolonial cultural politics. At the first level, the colonized *had* to imitate the white man, whose language, culture, and values were considered superior, while her own were regarded as inferior. At the second level of mimeticism, the colonized *wants* to imitate white society. In contrast to the *imperative* of being white (ontologically unattainable by a non-white) is now the desire to be white. What results is a more fluid, unstable form of mimeticism where the colonized subject simultaneously wishes to be like the colonizer but hates him at the same time.[6]

By concentrating on whiteness as the original superior, Chow thinks that cultural theorists have neglected a third level of imitation, in which the ethnic person is expected by white culture to resemble what is recognizably ethnic. Instead of imitating white society, the ethnic person is now obliged to conform to a stereotypical construction of ethnicity. Chow calls this a "coercive mimeticism," in which racial/ethnic persons are expected to resemble and replicate certain socially endorsed preconceptions about them, and in doing so, authenticate the familiar descriptions of them as ethnics.[7] She describes the dilemma of the racial/ethnic scholar thusly:

> If an ethnic critic should simply ignore her own ethnic history and become immersed in white culture, she would, needless to say, be deemed a turncoat (one that forgets her origins). But if she should choose, instead, to mimic and perform her own ethnicity in her work—that is, to respond to the hailing, "Hey, you!" that is issued from various directions in the outside world—she would still be considered a turncoat, this time because she is too eagerly pandering to the orientalist tastes of Westerners. Her only viable option seems to be that of reproducing a specific version of herself—and her ethnicity—that has, somehow, already been endorsed and approved by the specialists of her culture. It is at this juncture that coercive mimeticism acquires additional

---

5. Chow, *The Protestant Ethnic*, 95–87.
6. Chow, *The Protestant Ethnic*, 104–5.
7. Chow, *The Protestant Ethnic*, 107.

significance as an institutionalized mechanism of knowledge production and dissemination..."[8]

Chow helped me see that in those job interviews, I was like a caged animal, bred in captivity, under voyeuristic scrutiny, expected to respond and behave according to hidden parameters of an ostensibly recognizable Asian American female identity. On the one hand, Orientalist boundaries were defined by my white interrogators, male and female. On the other hand, there is an added institutional script, one that I am still trying to decipher, that constructs ethnicity "that has, somehow, already been endorsed and approved by the specialists of [my] culture."[9] Negotiating the coercive mimeticism of these cultural "specialists" is another constraint that I labor under. For example, Chow describes the disciplinary conflicts within Asian Studies and between Asian Studies and Asian American Studies. In the former, certain Western sinologists (who may not be Asian themselves) privilege *ancient* Chinese literary works as more "authentically" Chinese than those of modern Chinese writers, whom, they feel, have become too "Westernized." By privileging knowledge of the ancient Chinese *language* as a marker of authenticity, many of these sinologists also regard Asian American studies disparagingly, because Chinese American writers in this discipline use English as their preferred mode of expression.[10]

In Henry Yu's provocative investigation of the Chicago school of white sociologists who devoted their efforts to the "Oriental Problem," race was a theatrical drama for their discipline to examine.

> The job of the exotic, unknown ethnics was to play their roles on stage for the edification of the audience. Race was a performance, complete with masks and costumes and uniforms. What was most interesting to the audience was what was exotic. Elaborate costumes, funny accents, and fantastic tales of exotic origins were part of the proper role for Orientals in the playhouse of America. Who wanted to see a play about Orientals in which all the actors wore three-piece suits and acted exactly like white people?[11]

8. Chow, *The Protestant Ethnic*, 117.

9. Chow, *The Protestant Ethnic*, 117.

10. Chow, *The Protestant Ethnic*, 123–27. Also Chow, *Writing Diaspora*, 1–26, where she lays out the problem of white male Western Orientalists describing the "disease of modern Chinese poetry."

11. Yu, *Thinking Orientals*, 163.

Yu will go on to say, however, that the white sociologists really did want to see the performance of ordinary Americans in Oriental drag: "As an audience, they still demanded the exotic costumes, but in the end they preferred to see the mundane acts of everyday life....What made such a performance racial was the necessity of acting like everyone else, except with the constant constraint of not being like everyone else."[12] Whether in a zoo or on stage, the metaphor of being on racial display foregrounds the power differential between the racial-ethnic individual and the Anglo-establishment. As my mind tries to navigate individual and institutional minefields to determine what it means to be an Asian American biblical scholar in a predominantly white guild, I recall the scene at the zoo in the film, *Harry Potter and the Sorcerer's Stone*. The Muggle Dursleys are banging on the window cage and yelling at the snake to move. When the snake refuses to respond, Dudley declares it to be "boring."

Anecdote Two

The problematics of an Asian American identity became quite evident for me during August 2003 when, as a Visiting Professor at the Chinese University of Hong Kong, I applied for my Hong Kong I.D. card. On the application form, I put down "Chinese American," for "Nationality," an identity I claim in the States. However, the immigration officer said that I could only be one or the other. I had to choose between being "Chinese" or being "American." I could not be both. Since I had been waiting two hours to see this officer, this was not the time or the place to enter into a discourse about dominant and minority cultures in the United States. I had to choose, and I chose "American." The few weeks I had spent in Hong Kong up to that point reinforced my choice. I may look Chinese, but in Hong Kong I am as American as the white tourists there. The major difference is that Hong Kongers do not speak Cantonese to these tourists, as they always do to me. These tourists also do not suffer the embarrassment that I feel when I must say that I do not speak the language.

Is my identity "Asian American" only in the US context and "American" in the Hong Kong context where I taught for the year? Am I simply an "American" when I am in Hong Kong, becoming an "Asian American" again when I return to the States? And how does this slippage of identity

12. Yu, *Thinking Orientals*, 163–64.

affect my interpretation of the biblical text? Is my interpretation of the Bible different in each context? *Time* magazine devoted a recent special Asian issue to Asian Americans journeying to their ethnic homelands. In the issue, Chinese American writer Gish Jen recalls a crisis of identity similar to mine, but in reverse. When her sister became ill during the family's first trip to China in 1979, the local officials refused to recognize her as a "real" American. Thus, she was not eligible for the best hospital in town which was reserved for white foreigners. Jen and her family were considered Overseas Chinese and were put in a completely substandard hospital, filled with trash. The doctor there carried the sister on his back because the hospital had no elevator.

In a Chinese context, Jen and I experienced in different ways the struggle to claim a Chinese American identity as a "real" American identity. Although our Chinese officials would not accept a pluralistic notion of an American identity, definitions of identity among the Chinese themselves are clearly unstable. Jen relates: "A few years ago in Hong Kong, for example, I had heard Chinese intellectuals question whether anyone was really Chinese anymore. After all, they joked, the Chinese in Hong Kong were so British, the Chinese in Taiwan so Japanese, the Chinese on the mainland so communist."[13] Does it follow then that Chinese in America are no longer Chinese, but American, I ask myself? With shifting notions of Chinese identity, coupled with the plurality, heterogeneity, and hybridity of Asian American identity,[14] is it any wonder that I find an Asian American biblical hermeneutics elusive?

These anecdotes reveal that, in America and in Hong Kong, I am an ethnic foreigner. I remain an oddity in both contexts, and my identity and my biblical hermeneutics are shaped as such.[15] The mere fact of being a woman does not mean an individual is a feminist. In the same way, I know that my being a Chinese American woman does not automatically

---

13. Jen, "Racial Profiling," 68. See also the remarks in Chow, *The Protestant Ethnic*, 28–30 on the "Westernized" Chinese, for whom it is impossible to assume an unmediated access to Chinese culture.

14. Explored fully in Lowe, "Heterogeneity, Hybridity, Multiplicity."

15. According to Tuan, *Forever Foreigners or Honorary Whites*, 8. Black Americans experience *racialization* processes differently. For Asians, the stain of foreignness further compounds racial marginalization: "Blacks may be many things in the minds of whites, but foreign is not one of them." White society usually does not ask African Americans, "Where are you from?" as it repeatedly does Asian Americans. Regarding Asian Americans as permanent outsiders or foreigners in America, see also Wu, *Yellow*, 79–129; Chuh, *Imagine Otherwise*, 20.

mean that my interpretations of the Bible are from an Asian American advocacy stance. So in what consists my Asian Americanness, and how does this identity affect my biblical interpretation? Does "Asian American" refer to my ethnicity as a biblical scholar or to the thematic content of my biblical interpretation?[16] If it refers primarily to content, can a non-Asian create an Asian American reading of the biblical text? Conversely, would all of my previous published work not be regarded as Asian American because it did not deal specifically with an Asian American subject matter?

Toward an Asian American Biblical Hermeneutics

In 1926 W. E. B. Du Bois sketched the following criteria to determine an authentic Black theatre:

> The plays of a real Negro theatre must be: 1. *About us.* That is they must have plots which reveal Negro life as it is. 2. *By us.* That is they must be written by Negro authors who understand from birth and continual association just what it means to be a Negro today. 3. *For us.* That is, the theater must cater primarily to Negro audiences and be supported and sustained by their entertainment and approval. 4. *Near us.* The theater must be in a Negro neighborhood near the mass of ordinary Negro people.[17]

Can we apply these criteria in an analogous way to understand Asian American biblical interpretation?

The first criterion, that Asian American biblical interpretation should be *about* Asian Americans, might be difficult for the simple reason that the Bible is primarily *about* ancient Israel and the early Church. One could shift the emphasis from the biblical text to its cultural consumption in specific Asian American communities. This paradigm change is the guiding principle behind Vincent L. Wimbush's outstanding collection of essays dealing with the numerous and eclectic ways in which African American communities engaged the Bible.[18] Asian American interaction with the biblical text is historically not as extensive or as rich as in African American communities. However, the recent *Semeia* volume on *The Bible in Asian America*, edited by Benny Liew and myself (vol. 90/91

---

16 The question posed in Ling, "Emerging Canons," 195–96 in a literary context.
17. Du Bois, "Krigwa Players Little Negro Theater," 134.
18. Wimbush, *African Americans and the Bible*.

[2002]), provides an excellent beginning in discovering the importance of the Bible in various Asian American contexts and how Asian Americans read themselves into the text.[19]

By underscoring the racial/ethnic individual as the subject (*about us*), one of the values of this criterion is that it attempts to counteract racist biblical interpretations by white society, such as "slaves should be obedient to their masters," and the conversion of the "heathen Chinee"[20] with its attendant colonialism. In a similar vein, early feminists sought to discover or recover positive images of women to counterbalance sexist portrayals. Highlighting positive images to counter negative ones, however, is methodologically limited, because it is prompted largely by what the white male world thinks, believes, or constructs about Asian Americans. The danger here is allowing the primary focus to be the white male superior that Chow cautioned against for cultural studies.[21] Biblical interpretation *about* Asian Americans should be guided by the positive *and* negative engagement of these communities with the biblical text, and not solely by the negative use of these texts by white male society against Americans of Asian descent.

The second criterion, that Asian American biblical hermeneutics should be *by us*, written by Asian American authors who "understand from birth and continual association" what it means to be Asian American today, is a problematic one. Who is the "us" who are deemed "Asian American"? The term Asian American emerged during the 1960s as a political category. On the one hand, it was meant to unify culturally different Asian groups with their varied US histories of immigration and racial inequities. On the other hand, by claiming an authentic *American* identity, it tried to repudiate the collapsing of these numerous and diverse groups monolithically known as "Orientals" and "perpetual foreigners."[22] Earlier definitions of "Asian American" based on birth, ethnicity of descent, or cultural tradition have been criticized for being too essentialist, failing to account for historical, economic, and political structures and

---

19. See also, Liew, "Reading with Yin Yang Eyes"; Liew, "More than Personal Encounters"; Kim, "Reading the Bible as Asian Americans"; Kuan, "My Journey into Diasporic Hermeneutics"; Kuan, "Diasporic Readings of a Diasporic Text"; Yee, "Inculturation and Diversity."

20. Harte, *The Heathen Chinee*.

21. Chow, *The Protestant Ethnic*, 106.

22. Lowe, "Heterogeneity, Hybridity, Multiplicity"; Kang, *Compositional Subject*, 5; Chuh, *Imagine Otherwise*, 20.

conditions that are fused with ethnic identities.[23] These circumstances are too varied to insist on a pan-Asian American identity based solely on ethnic or cultural origins. No one experience binds Asian Americans together. We have nothing in common that resembles the history of slavery that African Americans share. Moreover, African Americans do not understand their identities in terms of their African origins. They do not refer to themselves as Ghanan American, Senegalian American, Nigerian American, much less their tribal origins as Mandingo American, Ashanti American, or Yoruban American. Asian Americans, however, often highlight their ethnic identities as Chinese American, Japanese American, Korean American, and so forth, because of the unique histories of these groups and their interaction in the United States. During World War II, for example, Chinese Americans consciously differentiated themselves from Japanese Americans, so that they would not be interred with them or otherwise subjected to anti-Japanese racism.

In contrast to an identity rooted in some essentialized past or fixed cultural heritage, the tendency now among Asian American theorists is to characterize Asian American identity through the lenses of heterogeneity, hybridity, and multiplicity. In an important essay, Lisa Lowe describes heterogeneity as the differences among Asian American groups with respect to national origin, immigration histories, class backgrounds, generational and gender specific attitudes, and so forth. Hybridity results from the accommodation and negotiation of these groups in and among various relations of unequal power. Multiplicity specifies the various ways in which ethnic subjects are positioned across and within different axes of power.[24] Ethnic identity could thus be inherited and invented at the same time, involving both personal exchanges and social construction.[25] Such an understanding of identity underscores the continuous interplay of history, culture, and power in the mutable act of defining. "Identities are the names we give to the different ways we are positioned by, and position ourselves within, the narratives of the past."[26]

An Asian American biblical hermeneutics *by us* would therefore be created by ethnic Asian individuals who, at some point in their histories in the US, have consciously adopted an Asian American advocacy stance.

23. Xing, *Asian America through the Lens*, 20–39; Lowe, "Heterogeneity, Hybridity, Multiplicity," 427.
24. Lowe, "Heterogeneity, Hybridity, Multiplicity," 428–29.
25. Xing, *Asian America through the Lens*, 140–43.
26. Hall, "Cultural Identity and Diaspora," 394.

"Asian American" becomes the name one gives to his or her specific positioning by and within the narratives of the "past" in the United States. The question shifts here from "being" to "becoming," from "Who is an Asian American?" to "What are the different ways of becoming Asian American?"[27] What are the personal, interpersonal, cultural, and systemic influences that allow, trigger, or compel one of Asian descent in the US to become an Asian American and appropriate this nomenclature intentionally for herself? I will describe my own process of becoming one shortly.

If one follows Du Bois's reasoning, an Asian American biblical hermeneutics *for us* must cater primarily to Asian American audiences and be supported and sustained by their entertainment and approval. Du Bois's argument, however, relates to African American theatre, in which "catering" to a particular "audience" for "entertainment and approval" would be appropriate. Such features do not fit the context of an Asian American biblical hermeneutics. A hermeneutics *for us* does not "cater" to Asian American communities, but rather interprets the biblical texts on their behalf. These communities are not like theatrical audiences who come to see a play, but places in which the Bible has a powerful prescriptive influence, for better or for worse, in the lives of their citizens. The purpose of an Asian American biblical hermeneutics is not to entertain or seek the approval of these communities. Such a hermeneutics may, in fact, critique the ways in which Asian Americans use the Bible to legitimate sexism, racism, or heterosexism in their congregations. Such a hermeneutics may edify, strengthen, and empower Asian American communities. It also may take an oppositional, prophetic role in condemning any biblically-based histories or actualities of injustice or oppression within them.

According to Du Bois's fourth and final criterion, a "real Negro theatre" must be *near us*, i.e., located in a Negro neighborhood near the ordinary Negro people. This criterion highlights the praxis face of an Asian American biblical hermeneutics. Contrary to the distancing and disinterested training of most biblical scholars in the ivory tower, an Asian American biblical hermeneutics demands that interpretation be *near us*. An Asian American biblical scholar combines theory and practice from a specific and *interested* position in studying the biblical text. We read our

---

27. See Xing, *Asian America through the Lens*, 147, on the ways in which "becoming" an Asian American is reflected in Asian American filmmaking. See also Fenton, *Ethnicity*, 180, on the "contexts of ethnicity."

own history, experiences, and stories as Asian Americans into the biblical story, as well as liberate ourselves from that story, when it becomes a source of injustice.

My Asian American Condition

I now wish to examine my own process of becoming an Asian American by outlining, for the sake of argument, what is Asian about me and what is American, the two prongs of my hyphenated condition.[28] Let us start first with the Asian part. Aside from the fact that I look Asian (which Hong Kongers do recognize), how am I culturally Asian?

Essential to my own self-understanding is the fact that, during my formative years, my grasp of what is Asian has been mediated, for the most part, by American Orientalism: the American representation of Asia, as a geographically remote, foreign land filled with exotic and suspicious cultural practices. This land is thought to be discovered, described, and dominated by the United States.[29] Since I have only recently gone to Hong Kong (which is itself markedly distinct from mainland China and Taiwan), my early contact with what is Chinese and Asian has been through Charlie Chan and Pearl Buck[30] movies, in which the main characters were played by white actors with scotch-taped eyes. Think John Wayne as Genghis Khan: "I feel this tartar woman is for me. My blood says take her!"

Every Saturday morning, I was enthralled by reruns of *Flash Gordon*, with Ming the Merciless from the planet Mongo. Not knowing who she was or what she represented, I adopted the nickname Dragon Lady in college because of its Chinese connotations. I even named my used Plymouth Duster Dusty Dragon because of this nickname and the fact that it

---

28. My description, "hyphenated condition," is rhetorical. Within Asian American studies are discussions whether or not to use the hyphen in "Asian(-)American": Eng, *Racial Castration*, 211–25. Kang, *Compositional Subject*, 2, prefers the slash, Asian/American woman, as a "diacritically awkward shorthand for the cultural, economic, and geopolitical pressures on the continental (Asian), the national (American), and the racial-ethnic (Asian American) as they come to bear on an implicitly more solid gendered ontology (woman)."

29. For studies of this phenomenon, see Ma, *The Deathly Embrace*; Yu, *Thinking Orientals*; Lee, *Orientals*; Yoshihara, *Embracing the East*; Espiritu, "Ideological Racism and Cultural Resistance"; Zia, "Gangsters, Gooks, Geisha, and Geeks."

30. See Yoshihara, "'Popular Expert on China,'" for an analysis of the Orientalist bias in Pearl Buck's *The Good Earth*.

was painted Earl Scheib green. Only many years later did I discover that Dragon Lady was a ruthless witch with a capital B with long fingernails.[31] I was captivated with the martial arts of Mrs. Peel in the TV series *The Avengers*, until after several rigorous years of karate and kung fu during graduate school, I realized that her flailing arms and legs were caricatures of real martial arts. As an avid reader of mysteries, I devoured all of the Judge Dee novels of Robert Van Gulik,[32] which, along with a Chinese detective, often featured his Orientalist etchings of half-naked Chinese females. I was fascinated by the pleasure pearls, one of the *harigata* (erotic toys), in the sexual arsenal of the Japanese geisha in James Clavell's *Shogun*.[33] And I am ashamed to say that I consumed arrogant, cheesy novels like Trevanian's *Shibumi*,[34] whose Western protagonist, steeped in the amatory arts of the Orient,[35] would punish a woman by giving her a sexual "high" that she would vainly try to replicate with ordinary men for the rest of her life.

I am one of those Asian Americans "who got their China and Japan from the radio, off the silver screen, from television, out of comic books, from the pushers of white American culture..."[36] Maxine Hong Kingston would interrogate me this way: "Chinese Americans, when you try to understand what things in you are Chinese, how do you separate what

---

31. Found in the comic strip *Terry and the Pirates*. For a discussion, see Ma, *The Deathly Embrace*, 12–20. This icon has been recouped by some Asian American feminists. See Shah, *Dragon Ladies*.

32. E.g., *The Chinese Maze Murders, The Chinese Nail Murders, The Emperor's Pearl, The Red Pavilion*. His classic Orientalist work on Chinese eroticism, van Gulik, *Sexual Life in Ancient China*, is critiqued in Furth, "Rethinking Van Gulik."

33. Clavell, *Shogun*, 692–96. This string of four round beads of white jade was pushed into the anus and pulled out by one's partner at the moment of "Clouds and Rain" (read: orgasm). For an analysis and critique of the American exoticization of Asian women, see Uchida, "The Orientalization of Asian Women." The Asian-Woman Fetish of white men has been explored in the novel by Yoshikawa, *One Hundred and One Ways*. One Hundred and One ways refers to the number of ways a geisha was supposedly able to "unlock [men's] bodies with a groan" (9).

34 Trevanian, *Shibumi*. Another novel of the same ilk is Lustbader, *The Ninja: A Novel*.

35. Evidently the highest level of erotic proficiency involves the use of razor-sharp knives in vulnerable places. In a textual note, Trevanian wrote that he felt it was irresponsible for him to describe the procedure in detail, lest some mere mortals attempt it.

36. From the introduction to Chin, *Aiiieeeee!*, xi–xii; See also Marchetti, *Romance and the "Yellow Peril"*; Feng, *Screening Asian Americans*; Xing, *Asian America through the Lens*, 53–86; Hamamoto, *Monitored Peril*.

is peculiar to childhood, to poverty, insanities, one family, your mother who marked your growing with stories, from what is Chinese? What is Chinese tradition and what is the movies?"[37]

As I turn to the "American" prong of my hyphenated condition, things become even more complicated. Who I am as an American is directly affected by my Asian ethnicity. What reminds me every day of my Asian identity are my name and my face. Something you hear, my name Yee, and something you see, my Chinese face. The historical responses of American white society to markers like my name and face has been *racism*. I have experienced this racism in its violent forms as a child growing up and in more subtle forms of American Orientalism, which I have consumed—a murky brew of both external and internalized oppression. What defines Asian Americanness, for me, are not essentialist categories marking what is authentically Asian and what is American. Rather, it is the historical and cultural experiences of personal and collective racism of the dominant white society in America, perpetrated against Americans of Asian descent. This racism runs the gamut from the predacious Yellow Peril to the Model Minority success story. Its history has been documented in a number of studies.[38]

Pyke and Johnson contributed extensive studies of the external racism of white society and its correlation with the internalized oppression of Asian American women.[39] Attempting to integrate gender with the study of race, Pyke and Johnson found that Asian American women used the term "American" as a code for "white" in describing their self-understanding as female. Many of these women claimed that they were not Asian at all, because they rejected the controlling images of Asian women as meek and submissive. Asian cultures were deemed bastions of patriarchy, from which they escaped by denying any affiliation with them. They regarded themselves as American, identifying with the hegemonic femininity of white American society. They constructed white femininity as monolithically self-confident, independent, and successful, traits that ironically replicated white hegemonic masculinity.[40]

---

37. Kingston, *The Woman Warrior*, 6. For a helpful sixty-minute video of clips of Hollywood depictions of Asians, see Gee, *Slaying the Dragon*.

38. Takaki, *Strangers from a Different Shore*; Daniels, *Prisoners Without Trial*; Chan, *Entry Denied*; Okihiro, *Margins and Mainstreams*; Zia, *Asian American Dreams*:

39. Pyke and Johnson, "Asian American Women."

40. Pyke and Johnson, "Asian American Women," 50–51.

One of the challenges in counteracting the external racism against and the internalized oppression of Asian Americans is making "whiteness" visible "as a culturally constructed ethnic identity, historically contingent upon the disavowal and violent denial of difference."[41] Instead of admitting its own sociohistorical production, whiteness sets itself up as *the* universal norm, disparaging all Others as pitiful aberrations. Those who are white often fail to see how their racial position (pre)determines the social realities of which they are a part. "When Americans with the privileges of being white deny the relevance of race in their own lives, it is functionally equal to preserving the historical inequities in American society that have been built on racial exclusion."[42]

If they do acknowledge their ethnicity, as the Irish on St. Patrick's Day or the Germans during Oktoberfest, they have the luxury of choice to claim this identity and select which parts of it to incorporate into their lives. For the rest of the year, they can be indifferent to their ethnic identity.[43] Asian and African Americans, however, do not have choice in the matter. They cannot escape the material indicators of race. Race for them is "skin-deep," and they must continue to live in a society that has historically and systemically marginalized them because of the color of their skin or the shape of their eyes.

Because whiteness is not named and remains hidden, white society places the burden of accounting for racial difference upon the racial-ethnic individuals themselves.[44] The unhyphenated American (read: white) is unconsciously assumed to have no race. It is those Other Americans—Asian, African, Native, and Hispanic—who must defend their racial differences in this society. Because their own racial makeup was unacknowledged, my ostensibly "colorless" interviewers, to whom I referred at the beginning, asked that I expound on the ways my Asian American identity affects and influences my biblical interpretation. Because whiteness currently functions incognito, we can go only so far in developing an Asian American biblical hermeneutics. Because our hermeneutics does not develop in a vacuum but is conducted within larger white institutional—and often racist—contexts, it is vital that we Asian American biblical

---

41. Kobena Mercer cited in Eng, *Racial Castration*, 138. See also Yu, *Thinking Orientals*, 201.

42. Yu, *Thinking Orientals*, 199.

43. See Tuan, *Forever Foreigners*, 5–8, 21–22; and Yu, *Thinking Orientals*, 202 on ethnicity as a matter of choice for whites.

44. Eng, *Racial Castration*, 141–42.

scholars make whiteness transparent as a culturally-constructed and racialized category. I related at the beginning of this essay about how white society compels me, however kindheartedly, to tell them how my Asian Americanness makes *me* different. I think the time has come for white men and women to reflect critically and honestly on how their whiteness makes *them* different. How their whiteness accords them privilege and access to resources that they withhold from those who are "not their kind." How their whiteness has been made the unacknowledged norm of what it means to be human. How their whiteness has brought hardship and misery to millions. Critical White Studies is a field in its infancy,[45] but we Asian Americans, who live and work in the belly of the beast, should keep tabs on the developments in this field, as we create our own Asian American biblical hermeneutics.

An Asian American Reading of Judges 4–5

I now turn the discussion to how would I interrogate the biblical text from an Asian American perspective. I have chosen the story of Jael in Judges 4–5, as an experiment for such cross-examination. With an Asian American appraisal of Judges 4–5, I return full circle back to Jael. I had studied her text in a previous investigation of woman warriors in ancient Israel.[46] When I wrote this article over ten years ago, I remember entitling Jael as a woman warrior, because of Maxine Hong Kingston's memoir, *The Woman Warrior*. I had bought this book when it first came out in 1976, because I was attracted by the concept of a powerful Chinese woman, embodied in the woman warrior. Because of space constraints, I can only offer some of the questions I would ask of Judges 4–5 as an Asian American biblical scholar.

---

45. See Delgado and Stefancic, eds., *Critical White Studies*; Hill, *Whiteness: A Critical Reader*; Frankenberg, ed., *Displacing Whiteness*; Berger, *White Lies*; Kincheloe et al., *White Reign*; Jacobson, *Whiteness of a Different Color*; Ferber, *White Man Falling*; Lipsitz, *The Possessive Investment in Whiteness*; Stokes, *The Color of Sex*; Levine-Rasky, *Working through Whiteness*; Waren and Back, *Out of Whiteness*; Hobgood, *Dismantling Privilege*; Brodkin, *How Jews Became White Folks*; Newman, *White Women's Rights*; Wiegman, "Whiteness Studies"; Marcus, *Hearts of Darkness*; Guglielmo and Salerno, eds., *Are Italians White?*; Heneghan, *Whitewashing America*.

46. Yee, "'By the Hand of a Woman.'"

Jael was outside the mainstream of Israelite society, as a woman and probably a foreigner, a Kenite.⁴⁷ As my surname Yee is a marker of my ethnicity, I will inquire first into the etymology of Jael's name to see if it bears on her Kenite origins or her characterization. I will inquire into the nature of her ethnicity: Was Jael a foreigner (non-Israelite) like her husband, Heber the Kenite? Was Jael a Kenite like her husband? What was the nature of Kenite/Hebrew ethnic, political and/or economic relations? Was Jael's ethnicity different from Deborah the prophet? What was Deborah's ethnicity? How does Jael's ethnicity influence her status as a Woman Warrior? What is the nature of her class status? Jael's story is a site of struggle for Israel's identity. In the book of Judges, foreigners are represented as a snare or trap. How then does Jael as an ethnic foreigner serve the ideological interests of the biblical author? Does the fact that Jael has her own tent have ethnic significance? Baruch Halpern argues that the Kenites were fifth columnists in ancient Canaan, working for the invading Israelites.⁴⁸ Are there intertextual connections between Judges 4–5 and alleged Japanese American fifth columnists during World War II, or are they both propaganda, serving political interests?⁴⁹ How does gender intersect with ethnicity and ethnic Otherness in the woman warrior? For example, the Chinese woman warrior, Fa Mulan, used deception and *disguised her gender* to become a military hero for her country against *foreign* invaders. Jael also used deception but *exploited her gender* as a *foreign* woman to become an Israelite military hero. What happened to Jael's ethnicity in the later retelling of her story? Are there any racist sentiments in these retellings? These are just some of the questions I would ask, as I consciously read Judges 4–5 from an Asian American perspective.⁵⁰

Conclusion

I have raised more problems and questions in theorizing about an Asian American biblical hermeneutic than I have laid out the parameters of

---

47. Pending further study, I am assuming that Yael is a Kenite, although the only mention of ethnicity is with her husband, Heber the Kenite.

48 Halpern, "Sisera and Old Lace."

49. Daniels, *Prisoners Without Trial*, 24–25, 36–38; Wu, *Yellow*, 95–103.

50. Chapter 6 of this book, on "The Woman Warrior Revisited," attempts to wrestle later with these earlier questions regarding Yael.

one. I began my article with two personal anecdotes that have highlighted these difficulties. On the one hand, we face personal and institutional pressures to conform to some recognizable Asian American identity. On the other hand, mutable notions of both Asian and Asian American identities make an Asian American biblical hermeneutics a hard one to pin down. If we apply Du Bois's criteria, "about us," as a way to conceive our biblical hermeneutics, we shift our point of departure from the biblical text to Asian American communities absorbed in the text, both positively and negatively. An Asian American biblical hermeneutics "by us" also shifts the identity question from "Who is an Asian American?" to "What are the different ways of becoming an Asian American?" An Asian American biblical hermeneutics is fashioned by an American of Asian descent who has intentionally adopted a stance of Asian American advocacy. An Asian American biblical hermeneutics "for us" will interpret the biblical text on behalf of Asian American communities, motivating and enlightening them, as well as critiquing and admonishing them. An Asian American biblical hermeneutics "near us" reminds us of praxis: as Asian American biblical scholars we need to keep our fingers on the pulse of what is going on in Asian America, religiously and socially. In all of these endeavors, we must keep in mind that we do not interpret in a vacuum but must negotiate a white hegemonic guild. Making whiteness visible is one of our challenges in creating our own biblical hermeneutics.

Works Cited

Berger, Maurice. *White Lies: Race and the Myths of Whiteness*. New York: Farrar, Straus & Giroux, 1999.

Brodkin, Karen. *How Jews Became White Folks: And What That Says about Race in America*. New Brunswick, NJ: Rutgers University Press, 1999.

Chan, Sucheng. *Entry Denied: Exclusion and the Chinese Community in America, 1882–1943*. Asian American History and Culture. Philadelphia: Temple University, 1991.

Chin, Frank. *Aiiieeeee! An Anthology of Asian American Writers*. New York: Mentor, 1974.

Chow, Rey. *The Protestant Ethnic and the Spirit of Capitalism*. New York: Columbia University Press, 2002.

———. *Writing Diaspora: Tactics of Intervention in Contemporary Cultural Studies*. Arts and Politics of the Everyday. Bloomington: Indiana University Press, 1993.

Chuh, Kandice. *Imagine Otherwise: On Asian Americanist Critique*. Durham: Duke University Press, 2003.

Clavell, James. *Shogun*. New York: Dell, 1975.

Daniels, Roger. *Prisoners without Trial: Japanese Americans in World War II*. A Critical Issue. New York: Hill & Wang, 1993.

Delgado, Richard, and Jean Stefancic. *Critical White Studies: Looking behind the Mirror*. Philadelphia: Temple University Press, 1997.
Du Bois, W. E. B. "Krigwa Players Little Negro Theater." *The Crisis* 32 (1926) 134.
Eng, David L. *Racial Castration: Managing Masculinity in Asian America*. Perverse Modernities. Durham: Duke University Press, 2001.
Espiritu, Yen Le. "Ideological Racism and Cultural Resistance." In *Asian American Women and Men*, 86–107. Gender Lens 1. Thousand Oaks, CA: Sage, 1997.
Feng, Peter X. *Screening Asian Americans*. Rutgers Depth of Field Series. New Brunswick, NJ: Rutgers University, 2002.
Fenton, Steve. *Ethnicity*. Key Concepts. Cambridge: Polity, 2003.
Ferber, Abby L. *White Man Falling: Race, Gender, and White Supremacy*. Lanham, MD: Rowman & Littlefield, 1998.
Frankenberg, Ruth, ed. *Displacing Whiteness: Essays in Social and Cultural Criticism*. Durham: Duke University Press, 1997.
Furth, Charlotte. "Rethinking Van Gulik: Sexuality and Reproduction in Traditional Chinese Medicine." In *Engendering China: Women, Culture, and the State*, edited by Christina K. Gilmartin et al., 125–46. Harvard Contemporary China Series 10. Cambridge: Harvard University Press, 1994.
Gee, Deborah. *Slaying the Dragon*. San Francisco: NAATA Distribution, 1995.
Guglielmo, Jennifer, and Salvatore Salerno, eds. *Are Italians White? How Race Is Made in America*. New York: Routledge, 2003.
Gulik, Robert Hans van. *Sexual Life in Ancient China: A Preliminary Survey of Chinese Sex and Society from ca. 1500 B.C. till 1644 A.D.* Sinica Leidensia 57. Leiden: Brill, 1961.
Hall, Stuart. "Cultural Identity and Diaspora." In *Colonial Discourse and Post-Colonial Theory: A Reader*, edited and introduced by Patrick Williams and Laura Chrisman, 392–401. New York: Columbia University Press, 1994.
Halpern, Baruch. "Sisera and Old Lace: The Case of Deborah and Yael." In *The First Historians: The Hebrew Bible and History*, 76–103. San Francisco: Harper & Row, 1988.
Hamamoto, Darrell Y. *Monitored Peril: Asian Americans and the Politics of TV Representation*. Minneapolis: University of Minnesota Press, 1994.
Harte, F. Bret. *The Heathen Chinee*. Chicago, IL: Western News, 1870.
Heneghan, Bridget T. *Whitewashing America: Material Culture and Race in the Antebellum Imagination*. Jackson: University Press of Mississippi, 2003.
Hill, Mike. *Whiteness: A Critical Reader*. New York: New York University Press, 1997.
Hobgood, Mary E. *Dismantling Privilege: An Ethics of Accountability*. Cleveland: Pilgrim, 2000.
Jacobson, Matthew Frye. *Whiteness of a Different Color: European Immigrants and the Alchemy of Race*. Cambridge: Harvard University Press, 1998.
Jen, Gish. "Racial Profiling." *Time* (Asian ed.), August 18–25, 2003, 68–69.
Kang, Laura Hyun Yi. *Compositional Subjects: Enfiguring Asian/American Women*. Durham: Duke University Press, 2002.
Kim, Chan-Hie. "Reading the Bible as Asian Americans." In *The New Interpreter's Bible*, edited by Leander E. Keck, 1:161–66. 13 vols. Nashville: Abingdon, 1994.
Kincheloe, Joe L., et al. *White Reign: Deploying Whiteness in America*. New York: St. Martin's, 1998.

Kingston, Maxine Hong. *The Woman Warrior: Memoirs of a Girlhood among Ghosts.* New York: Vintage, 1976.

Kuan, Jeffrey Kah-jin. "Diasporic Readings of a Diasporic Text: Identity Politics and Race Relations and the Book of Esther." In *Interpreting beyond Borders*, edited by Fernando F. Segovia, 161–73. Bible and Postcolonialism 3. Sheffield: Sheffield Academic, 2000.

———. "My Journey into Diasporic Hermeneutics." *Union Seminary Quarterly Review* 56 (2002) 50–54.

Lee, Robert G. *Orientals: Asian Americans in Popular Culture.* Asian American History and Culture. Philadelphia: Temple University Press, 1999.

Levine-Rasky, Cynthia. *Working through Whiteness: International Perspectives.* Interruptions—Border Testimony(ies) and Critical Discourse/s. Albany: State University of New York Press, 2002.

Liew, Tat-Siong Benny. "More than Personal Encounters: Identity, Community, and Interpretation." *Union Seminary Quarterly Review* 56 (2002) 41–44.

———. "Reading with Yin Yang Eyes: Negotiating the Ideological Dilemma of a Chinese American Biblical Hermeneutics." *BibInt* 9 (2001) 309–35.

Ling, Amy. "'Emerging Canons' of Asian American Literature and Art." In *Asian Americans: Comparative and Global Perspectives*, edited by Shirley Hune et al., 191–97. Pullman: Washington State University Press, 1991.

Lipsitz, George. *The Possessive Investment in Whiteness: How White People Profit from Identity Politics.* Philadelphia: Temple University Press, 1998.

Lowe, Lisa. "Heterogeneity, Hybridity, Multiplicity: Marking Asian American Difference." In *Asian American Studies: A Reader*, edited by Jean Yu-Wen Shen Wu and Min Song, 423–42. New Brunswick, NJ: Rutgers University Press, 2000.

Lustbader, Eric Van. *The Ninja: A Novel.* New York: Fawcett Crest, 1980.

Ma, Sheng-Mei. *The Deathly Embrace: Orientalism and Asian American Identity.* Minneapolis: University of Minnesota Press, 2000.

Marchetti, Gina. *Romance and the "Yellow Peril": Race, Sex, and Discursive Strategies in Hollywood.* Berkeley: University of California Press, 1993.

Marcus, Jane. *Hearts of Darkness: White Women Write Race.* New Brunswick, NJ: Rutgers University, 2003.

Newman, Louise Michele. *White Women's Rights: The Racial Origins of Feminism in the United States.* New York: Oxford University Press, 1999.

Okihiro, Gary Y. *Margins and Mainstreams: Asians in American History and Culture.* Seattle: University of Washington Press, 1994.

Pyke, Karen D., and Denise L. Johnson. "Asian American Women and Racialized Femininities: 'Doing' Gender across Cultural Worlds." *Gender & Society* 17/1 (2003) 33–53.

Shah, Sonia. *Dragon Ladies: Asian American Feminists Breathe Fire.* Boston: South End, 1997.

Stokes, Mason. *The Color of Sex: Whiteness, Heterosexuality, and the Fictions of White Supremacy.* New Americanists. Durham: Duke University Press, 2001.

Takaki, Ronald. *Strangers from a Different Shore: A History of Asian Americans.* Updated and rev. ed. New York: Back Bay, 1998.

Trevanian. *Shibumi: A Novel.* New York: Ballantine, 1979.

Tuan, Mia. *Forever Foreigners or Honorary Whites: The Asian Ethnic Experience Today.* New Brunswick, NJ: Rutgers University Press, 1998.

Uchida, Aki. "The Orientalization of Asian Women in America." *Women's Studies International Forum* 21 (1998) 161–74.

Waren, Vron, and Les Back. *Out of Whiteness: Color, Politics, and Culture*. Chicago: University of Chicago Press, 2002.

Wiegman, Robyn. "Whiteness Studies and the Paradox of Particularity." *Boundary 2* 26/3 (1999) 115–50.

Wimbush, Vincent L. *African Americans and the Bible: Sacred Texts and Social Textures*. New York: Continuum, 2000.

Wu, Frank H. *Yellow: Race in America beyond Black and White*. New York: Basic Books, 2002.

Xing, Jun. *Asian America through the Lens: History, Representations, and Identity*. Critical Perspectives on Asian Pacific Americans 3. Walnut Creek, CA: Alta Mira, 1998.

Yee, Gale A. "'By the Hand of a Woman': The Biblical Metaphor of the Woman Warrior." *Semeia* 61 (1993) 99–132.

———. "Inculturation and Diversity in the Politics of National Identity." *JAAAT* 2 (1997) 108–12.

———. "Yin/Yang Is Not Me: An Exploration into an Asian American Biblical Hermeneutics." In *Ways of Being, Ways of Reading: Asian-American Biblical Interpretation*, edited by Mary F. Foskett and Jeffrey K. Kuan, 152–63. St. Louis: Chalice, 2006.

Yoshihara, Mari. *Embracing the East: White Women and American Orientalism*. New York: Oxford University Press, 2002.

———. "'Popular Expert on China': Authority and Gender in Pearl S. Buck's *The Good Earth*." In *Embracing the East: White Women and American Orientalism*, 149–69. New York: Oxford University Press, 2003.

Yoshikawa, Mako. *One Hundred and One Ways*. New York: Bantam, 1999.

Yu, Henry. *Thinking Orientals: Migration, Contact, and Exoticism in Modern America*. Oxford: Oxford University Press, 2001.

Zia, Helen. *Asian American Dreams: The Emergence of an American People*. New York: Farrar, Straus & Giroux, 2000.

———. "Gangsters, Gooks, Geisha, and Geeks." In *Asian American Dreams: The Emergence of an American People*, 109–35. New York: Farrar, Straus & Giroux, 2000.

6

"She Stood in Tears amid the Alien Corn"

Ruth, the Perpetual Foreigner and Model Minority[1]

ONE OF THE JOYS of reading a biblical text from my own social location was learning about the history of my people here in the States. I immersed myself into the vast field of Asian American Studies. Even as it was an immensely satisfying experience, especially as I inserted my family's story into the larger narrative of the Chinese in America, it was also sobering. Our immigration history is one of bitter hardship and oppression. As I looked for a biblical text to explore through Asian American eyes, I found one that readily lent itself to such a reading. One can safely say that, of the books of the Hebrew Bible, the book of Ruth has captured the attention of many scholars interested in feminist and multicultural interpretations of the text.

---

1. Originally published in Yee, "'She Stood in Tears amid the Alien Corn,'" (2009). Citing John Keats, "Ode to a Nightingale," st. 6.

The book conjoins issues of gender,[2] sexuality,[3] race/ethnicity, immigration,[4] nationality, assimilation, and class[5] in tantalizing ways that allow different folk to read their own stories into the multivalent narrative of Ruth and Naomi. It is particularly apt for the purposes of this volume on minority criticism that the book of Ruth is the only biblical text bearing the name of a female gentile,[6] a non-Jew, and a foreigner. The multicultural perspectives on the book of Ruth are a veritable global village: African-South African female,[7] South African Indian female,[8] Botswana female,[9] Kenyan female,[10] Mexican American male,[11] Costa Rican female,[12] Cuban American male,[13] Hindu Indo-Guyanese female,[14] Latin American female,[15] Brazilian male,[16] Palestinian female,[17] Hong Kong Chinese male[18] and female,[19] Taiwanese female,[20] mainland (PRC)

---

2. The feminist bibliography on Ruth is large. For good starting points see Brenner, ed., *A Feminist Companion to Ruth*; Brenner, ed., *Ruth and Esther*; Levine, "Ruth"; Kates and Reimer, eds., *Reading Ruth*. One of the earliest feminist commentaries makes Ruth into a protoliberated woman who works for a living: "Ruth said to Naomi, I must not sit here with folded hands, nor spend my time in visiting neighbors, nor in such of amusement, but I must go forth to work, to provide food and clothes, and leave thee to rest ... It was evident that Ruth believed in the dignity of labor and of self-support." Stanton, *The Woman's Bible*, 39.

3. Although this essay focuses primarily on race/ethnicity, I want to acknowledge the various readings of the homoeroticism in the book of Ruth: Duncan, "The Book of Ruth"; Alpert, "Finding Our Past"; Jordan, "Ruth and Naomi"; Exum, "Is This Naomi?"; Brenner, "The Three of Us."

4. Honig, "Ruth, the Model Emigrée."

5. Boer, "Terry Eagleton: The Class Struggles of Ruth."

6. Bearing the title of a male Gentile is the book of Job.

7. Masenya, "NGWETSI. (BRIDE)"; Masenya, "Ruth."

8. Nadar, "A South African Indian Womanist Reading of the Character of Ruth."

9. Dube, "The Unpublished Letters"; Dube, "Divining Ruth."

10. Kanyoro, "Biblical Hermeneutics."

11. Maldonado, "Reading Malinche Reading Ruth."

12. Foulkes, "The Book of Ruth"; Nayap-Pot, "Life in the Midst of Death."

13. De La Torre, "Cubans in Babylon"; García-Treto, "Mixed Messages."

14. Gossai, "Recasting Identity in Ruth."

15. Cavalcanti, "The Prophetic Ministry of Women."

16. Mesters, *Rute: Una Historia Da Biblia*.

17. Raheb, "Women in Contemporary Palestinian Society."

18. Lee, "Two Stories of Loyalty."

19. Kwok, "Finding a Home for Ruth"; Wong, "History, Identity and a Community."

20. Chu, "Returning Home."

Chinese female,[21] Thai and Philippine females,[22] New Zealand *Pakeha* (non-Maori) female,[23] Native American female,[24] African American Womanist,[25] European female immigrants,[26] German rural women,[27] Eastern European foreign workers in Israel,[28] and African women suffering from HIV/AIDS.[29]

In this essay, I enter into this global conversation by reading the book of Ruth as an Asian American biblical scholar of Chinese descent. I argue that the construction of Asian Americans historically as the "perpetual foreigner" and "model minority" can shed light on the various, often conflicting interpretations and readings about Ruth the Moabite. The portrayal of Ruth as the model emigrée is similar to the construction of Asian Americans as the model minority. Their depictions in both cases are used for propagandistic purposes, casting them simultaneously as the perpetual foreigner in the lands in which they live.

The Asian American as the Perpetual Foreigner

Asian American racialization involves two specific and related stereotypical configurations. The first is that of the perpetual foreigner,[30] which lurks behind the seemingly harmless question white people constantly ask Asian Americans, "Where are you from?"[31] Notice that this question is usually not asked of African Americans. When I tell whites that I am from Chicago, they are not satisfied. Predictably, they follow up with, "Where are you *really* from?" Sometimes I inform them directly that I am

---

21. Kuo, "Ruth the Moabitess."

22. Gallares, *Images of Faith*, 104–11; see also Sakenfeld, "Ruth and Naomi"; Sakenfeld, "The Story of Ruth."

23. McKinlay, "A Son Is Born to Naomi"; McKinlay, "Reading Rahab and Ruth"; Dawson, "The Power of Women's Friendship."

24. Donaldson, "The Sign of Orpah."

25. Weems, *Just a Sister Away*, 23–36; Kirk-Duggan, "Black Mother Women and Daughters"; Travis, "Love Your Mother"; Williams, "Breaking and Bonding."

26. Erbele-Küster, "Immigration and Gender Issues."

27. Silber, "Ruth and Naomi."

28. Brenner, "Ruth as a Foreign Worker."

29. Van Dyk and van Dyk, "HIV/AIDS in Africa."

30. Tuan, *Forever Foreigners*; Ancheta, *Race, Rights, and the Asian American Experience*; Wu, *Yellow*, 79–129; Bow, "Making Sense of Screaming," 489.

31. See Ang, "On Not Speaking Chinese," for the Chinese Dutch equivalent.

a Chinese American. At other times, I cheekily play with and deflect their interrogation: I now live in Boston, I was born in Ohio; and I have lived in Canada and in Minnesota. The dance of the seven veils performed by white America to uncover my ethnicity is symptomatic of their assumption that I do not really belong in this country.

Asian American intellectuals have criticized the US discourse on race as being circumscribed by the conflicts between Blacks and whites.[32] They point out that in the Black/white binary, the experiences of Asian Americans (as well as Latino/a and Arab Americans) fall through the cracks, since racial bigotry can vary qualitatively among different racial and ethnic groups. Asian Americans experience the process of racialization differently than African Americans.[33] Although both groups have suffered horrendously under white racism, the markers for determining the Other rest on different axes. For African Americans, the axis is color, white versus Black. For Asian (and Latino/a and Arab) Americans, it is citizenship, American versus foreigner[34]

Because of the focus on racial color (being Black), as well as a shared history of slavery, African Americans do not identify themselves by their national origins, such as Nigerian American, or Ghanan American, much less by their African tribal origins, such as Mandingo American or Ashanti American.[35] In contrast, Asian Americans hail from ethnically and culturally distinct Asian nations and have different immigration histories to and ethnic conflicts with white America. They therefore consistently describe themselves in terms of their national or ethnic origins: Chinese American, Japanese American, Korean American, and so forth. With respect to citizenship in the US, these ethnic demarcations have often been a matter of great importance in the conflicted history of US–Asian relations. During World War II, Chinese Americans consciously distinguished themselves from Japanese Americans to prevent being interred with them.

---

32. Wu, *Yellow*, 79–129; Ancheta, *Race, Rights, and the Asian American Experience*, 1–18.

33. I am using as a springboard here the discussion of racial formation in Omi and Winant, *Racial Formation in the United States*, 52–76. For them, racialization is the extension of racial meaning to a relationship, social practice, or group.

34. Ancheta, *Race, Rights, and the Asian American Experience*; Tuan, *Forever Foreigners*, 8; Miller, *The Unwelcome Immigrant*.

35. Ebron and Tsing, "From Allegories of Identity," 131; Bruner, "Tourism in Ghana."

Institutional and cultural racism found in the legal system, government policy, and so forth, has traditionally constructed what it means to be American and hold power in terms of white, male, European descent—particularly Anglo-Saxon Protestant descent—to the exclusion of Other groups. After long and difficult struggles, women and Blacks were enfranchised as American citizens with the right to vote. Evinced by the ubiquitous experience of being asked "Where are you from?" Asian Americans have not been fully assimilated into the collective consciousness of what it means to be American.[36] Even though many, like my family, have been here for generations, the perception of being aliens in their own land is one that Asian Americans find difficult to shake off. They continue to be seen as more Asian than American.

The notion of Asian Americans as the perpetual foreigner intensifies during certain overlapping periods of economic, military and political conflicts in US–Asia relations. The US government and businesses exploited Chinese peasants as cheap labor at various points of American history (e.g., building the transcontinental railroad, replacing Blacks on Southern plantations after emancipation, as strikebreakers for New England textile mills).[37] Incensed by the competition, however, whites violently harassed and oftentimes killed Chinese laborers and their families. They eventually lobbied Congress to pass the Chinese Exclusion Act in 1882, barring Chinese from entering the US and becoming citizens. This act was not repealed until December 17, 1943, when the US wanted the Chinese as allies during World War II against Japanese aggression. Nevertheless, Chinese Americans were still racialized as the foreign Asian enemy.

Collapsing diverse Asian groups into the foreign Other, white Americans did not always distinguish Chinese Americans from the Japanese (during WWII), the Koreans (during the Korean War) and Vietnamese (during the Vietnam War). In 1982, the economic downturn in the Detroit automobile industry fueled the rage of two white men who killed the Chinese American Vincent Chin, scapegoating Chin as one of

---

36. Brought home in a very public way during two winter Olympics when Chinese American skater Michelle Kwan failed to win gold. The MSNBC headline in 1998 read "American beats Kwan," when Kwan finished second to teammate Tara Lipinski. In 2002, the *Seattle Times* described Kwan's loss to teammate Sarah Hughes, "American outshines Kwan, Slutskaya in skating surprise."

37. For histories, see Chang, *The Chinese in America*; Takaki, *Strangers from a Different Shore*; Takaki, *A Different Mirror*.

the Japanese auto makers who cost them their jobs.[38] During the Cold War, the US recruited Chinese scientists and engineers to strengthen American defense systems, only to nurse suspicions later that some Chinese were passing nuclear secrets to mainland China. The unfounded accusations against the Taiwanese American Wen Ho Lee during the late 1990s continue to demonstrate that simply looking like the enemy means that you are.[39] The Chinese American architect, Maya Lin, who won the national contest to design the Vietnam Memorial, was condemned as a "gook" (a derogatory term for the Vietnamese) by US veterans. Chinese American identity is thus inescapably linked with other Asian ethnic and national identities for whom it is mistaken.

The perpetual foreigner syndrome takes on a different permutation nowadays in the politics of US multiculturalism, which "in its reliance on symbolic representations of diversity, only serves to oversimplify and essentialize the diversity of racial and ethnic groups in the United States."[40] Chinese Americans are expected to put their Chinese "culture" on display. This culture becomes objectified and measurable, taking the form, for example, of speaking and writing Chinese, using chopsticks, immersing oneself in the *Analects* by Confucius, celebrating Chinese New Year, enjoying Jackie Chan movies, and perhaps even taking kung fu lessons.[41] Chinese American females might feel compelled to "go native" and slip their heftier American bodies into *cheongsams*, those form-fitting Suzy Wong–type dresses with the slit up the side.

When such traits of Chineseness become essentialized as visible hallmarks of authenticity, Chinese Americans are put in a double bind. As perpetual foreigners they are tagged as being not American enough. Alternatively, they are expected to exhibit on demand their knowledge and culture of China, about which many, whose families have lived in the US for generations, know little. The commodification of Chinese identity in US multicultural politics presumes that this identity is "out there," just waiting to be discovered.

When placed on a continuum of being more or less authentically Chinese, many American-born Chinese sometimes experience

---

38. Zia, *Asian American Dreams*, 55–81.
39. Chang, *The Chinese in America*, 236–60, 359–64.
40. Louie, *Chineseness across Borders*, 97.
41. Except for reading *The Analects*, I have dabbled in all of the above.

ambivalence in the presence of those who seem to be "more" Chinese, e.g., those who have a Chinese accent or have recently come from China.

> While on the one hand Chinese Americans, under assimilationist models, should identify with their U.S. roots, the realities of racial politics cause them to remain perpetual foreigners. Chinese Americans have always been told that "home" is in the United States but that their "roots," and therefore a missing piece of their identity is somewhere in China.[42]

Eventually, some American-born Chinese, such as myself, might actually visit China to find that missing piece that will ostensibly transform one into an "authentic" Chinese. Actually finding that piece is another matter. Although the stigma of perpetual foreigner assumes that I do not belong in the US, I discovered that I did not belong in China either, as my recent year-long experience teaching in Hong Kong starkly revealed.[43]

I faced several challenges during my time in Hong Kong that I did not have to face in my twenty years of undergraduate and graduate teaching in the US. In the first place, there were the obvious personal and cultural dislocations that I experienced as a Chinese American, who had never been West of San Francisco, going ashore in a Hong Kong Chinese context. (Asian Americans often refer to newly arrived immigrant Asians as FOBs or Fresh off the Boats. In a sense I was the FOB counterpart in Hong Kong, although it would be more accurate to say that I was a FOP, Fresh off the Plane.) Second was a linguistic dislocation, since my three weeks of Mandarin study (which was not good to begin with) were completely forgotten in the largely Cantonese-speaking culture. I taught in English, a dislocation for my students. There was also a gender dislocation. The Department of Religion at the Chinese University of Hong Kong was primarily composed of men. Only one other female colleague, untenured, taught in the department, while more than half of the faculty in my home institution, the Episcopal Divinity School, are female and all tenured. Finally, there were what I can only describe as ideological dislocations in that I came as a feminist, with strong social views on racism, class exploitation, American imperialism and colonialism, and fundamentalistic readings of the biblical text. All of these strong positions are formed by and in reaction to my US context. For a third-generation Chinese American who grew up in the urban slums of Chicago's South

---

42. Louie, *Chineseness across Borders*, 104.
43. Yee, "Yin/Yang Is not Me."

Side,[44] Asian forms of theologizing, such as Waterbuffalo Theology,[45] seemed to come from another planet and were just as alien. Minimally knowing the language, the history, and the culture in Hong Kong made me like Ruth the Moabite, a woman "who stood in tears amid the alien corn."

My experience of being a foreigner both in the US and in China is typical of many American-born Chinese who visit China in search of their "roots." Just as Chinese Americans are not American enough for whites in the US, they are not culturally Chinese enough with respect to China.[46]

The Asian American as the Model Minority

Besides being pigeonholed as the perpetual foreigner, Asian Americans simultaneously labor under the model minority stereotype.[47] After a century of blatant racial discrimination and slander,[48] Asian Americans are singled out as a group that has successfully assimilated into American society, becoming financially well-off and achieving the American Dream. This stereotype is often part and parcel of those essentialist traits that "real" Chinese individuals are assumed to have. Traditional Chinese values and attributes are said to include respect for elders, strong family ties, intellectually gifted, hard work ethic, a focus on higher education, a striving to achieve, mathematical and scientific ability, and so forth.

---

44. Yee, "Inculturation and Diversity."

45. Koyama, *Waterbuffalo Theology*; Koyama, "Waterbuffalo Theology," 1998.

46. See especially Louie, *Chineseness across Borders*, who examines issues of Chinese identity through an in-depth ethnographic study of the In Search of Roots program, sponsored by the People's Republic of China (PRC) and certain Chinese American organizations. The intent of program is to bring young Chinese Americans to the villages of their ancestors to learn about the greatness of Chinese "culture." The underlying motive of the PRC is to encourage Chinese American economic investment in China, their true "homeland." Louie draws conclusions for Chinese identity from the PRC perspective, especially in its agenda for the In Search of Roots program and how this agenda is negotiated and often subverted by the Chinese American students who participate in it. Also, Ang, "On Not Speaking Chinese," 2–3.

47. Wu, *Yellow*, 39–77; Lee, *Orientals*, 145–79; Osajima, "Asian Americans as the Model Minority"; Cho, "Converging Stereotypes."

48. In the popular media, see the fears about the "Yellow Peril," Fu Manchu and Dragon Lady, and Ming the Merciless from the planet Mongo, documented in Lee, *Orientals*, 106–44.

My experiences as a model minority were much more conflicted. For example, when my family moved from the inner-city to a white neighborhood, the Catholic grade school I attended had "homogeneous" groupings. In descending order, Group One comprised the most intelligent and talented, and Group Four was regarded as the "dumb-dumb" group. I was put in the latter. Even at the young age of ten, I saw that the individuals in Group One were all white, and that Group Four contained the racial and ethnic students and those whites who were regarded as "trash." With respect to the assumption that Asians are good in math, I withdrew from college algebra three times before I flunked the course and had to change my major from Psychology to English Literature because there was no way I could pass the required Statistics course. When I took the GRE I barely made it on the scale for mathematical ability. In the range of 300–800, I received something like 320.

The model minority stereotype is a gross generalization of disparate Asian immigrant populations that vary in terms of ethnicity, immigration history, linguistic facility, education, and economic class.[49] Camouflaged by the notion of model minority are the unexpressed questions, "Model of what" and a "Model for whom?"[50] On the one hand, the phrase "model minority" could imply that Asian Americans are exemplary, despite the fact that they happen to be "colored," and as such, still inferior to the dominant white society. This understanding is hardly flattering to Asian Americans. On the other hand, the phrase could mean that Asian Americans are exemplary and other racial and ethnics groups should take after them. The model minority stereotype then becomes more of a critique and a denigration of other racial groups, rather than a compliment to Asian Americans.

It is no accident that articles hailing Asian Americans as the "super-minority" and the "whiz kids" emerged particularly during the Cold War of the 1950s and the racial conflicts of the 1960s:

> The narrative of Asian ethnic assimilation fit the requirements of Cold War containment perfectly. Three specters haunted Cold War America in the 1950s: the red menace of communism, the black menace of race mixing, and the white menace of homosexuality. On the international front, the narrative of ethnic assimilation sent a message to the Third World, especially to Asia where the United States was engaged in increasingly fierce

49. Cheng and Yang, "The 'Model Minority' Deconstructed."
50. Wu, *Yellow*, 59.

struggles with nationalist and communist insurgencies, that the United States was a liberal democratic state where people of color could enjoy equal rights and upward mobility. On the home front, it sent a message to "Negroes and other minorities" that accommodation would be rewarded while militancy would be contained or crushed.[51]

Asian Americans are held up as living proof that racial minorities can succeed in America presumably by the sweat of their brow, and not by civil rights demonstrations or protests. Using the model minority stereotype as a weapon, whites tell Blacks and Latinos/as that "Asian Americans do not 'whine' about racial discrimination; they only try harder."[52] The supposed accomplishments of Asian Americans divert attention away from the fact that racial discrimination is a structural feature of US society, produced by centuries of systematic exclusion, exploitation, and disregard of racially defined minorities.[53] Blame for any social disparities falls on the other racial minorities, who "whine" about racial discrimination. White construction of the model minority stereotype has as its antithesis their racist construction of other groups, such as Blacks, as the "deficient" or "depraved" minority.

The model minority stereotype buttresses the dominant ideology of the US as a just and fair society, in which all its citizens compete on a level playing field. All foreign immigrants and racial minorities who have worked hard and played by the rules can be readily assimilated and succeed economically. White America judged and rewarded Asian Americans not by the color of their skin but by the content of their character.[54] Significantly, some Asian American students have espoused the stereotype as a means of upward mobility and white approval. These students are primarily immigrants who have bought into the ideology of white America as the land of opportunity and dismissed any racial episodes as the isolated acts of single individuals. American-born Asians, however, are more likely to be wary of the model minority stereotype and view any racial incidents as part of a larger social problem.[55]

---

51. Lee, *Orientals*, 146.
52. Wu, *Yellow*, 44.
53. Omi and Winant, *Racial Formation in the United States*, 69.
54. My apologies to Dr. Martin Luther King Jr.
55. Tuan, *Forever Foreigners*, 8.

Following the model minority stereotype can backfire on Asian Americans.[56] The perception of Asian American success in higher education often rebounds in anti-Asian attitudes. White students become threatened by and resent the growing number of Asian students in classrooms. They fear that so-called hordes of Asian students distort the grading curve, and many refuse to register for sections containing a large Asian critical mass. The zero-sum perception that Asian American gains denote white American losses often results in violence, as the Detroit death of Vincent Chin (1982) demonstrates. The Michigan Congressman John Dingell angrily accused "little yellow men" for the economic hardships of Detroit automakers, rather than placing the blame on the fact that domestic cars are not as skillfully made or as fuel efficient as Japanese imports.[57]

The perpetual foreigner and the model minority stereotypes work in tandem to construct contradictory images of Asian Americans in general and Chinese Americans in particular. As perpetual foreigners, they become a secondary caste that can be exploited and used. They are perceived as aliens in their own land, even though their citizenship often goes back several generations. When they ostensibly excel as model minorities through industry and entrepreneurial talents, they become a threat to be contained or destroyed. These two stereotypes make more complex the nature of US race relations, which have usually operated under a black/white binary. Rather than functioning on the color axis, racial discrimination against Asian Americans operates on the axis of citizenship, casting Asian Americans as the perpetual foreigner. Colluding with this stereotype is the pigeonholing of Asian Americans as the model minority, which at times benefits them compared to other ethnic groups while simultaneously obscuring the countless ways in which they are marginalized and victimized by racism. It is through these two lenses that I view the book of Ruth.

The Book of Ruth

The social matrixes in the book of Ruth are rich. They include male/female, husband/wife, mother/son, mother-in-law/daughter-in-law, owner/overseer/laborers, mother's house/father's house, native resident/

56. Wu, *Yellow*, 67–77.
57. Zia, *Asian American Dreams*, 58.

foreigner, and so forth. These relations are forged through marriage, friendship, widowhood, sexual attraction, economic and labor arrangements, immigration, and political amity or enmity. As the wealth of global interpretations of Ruth attests, the story is a "mine or mosaic of social relations, where readers can take their pick."[58] With the plurality of different readers comes a plurality of differing, often antithetical, interpretations. Juxtaposed to the more positive readings of the book, as an enchanting bucolic story about female empowerment and romantic heterosexual love, are others that see a more ambiguous and unsettling narrative.[59] I follow the lead of other people of color and allow the ambiguity of the text to favor a reading against the grain.[60] The usual optimistic and romantic readings of Ruth obscure issues of ethnicity, economic exploitation, and racist attitudes about the sexuality of foreigners that are evident in the text. Refracting the story of Ruth through the prism of the Asian American experience, I argue that, in its own way, the ideology of the text constructs Ruth the Moabite as a model minority and perpetual foreigner.

Gēr and Nokrîyâ in Ruth

The book of Ruth utilizes two words to describe foreigners, *gēr* and *nokrîyâ*.[61] A *gēr* is a foreigner who has immigrated into and taken up residence in a society, in which she or he has neither familial nor tribal associations. Although granted some protection under the Holiness Code (HC) and Deuteronomic Code (DC), the *gēr* is not a full-fledged member of the Israelite community, but, rather, someone of different and lower status. Ruth is not called a *gēr*. A term from the same root (*gur*) is

58. Dube, "Divining Ruth," 68.

59. Van Dyk and van Dyk, "HIV/AIDS in Africa," 15–24 classify these differing readings under four categories: (1) reading with the grain of the text (positive), (2) a romantic reading (even more positive), (3) a feminist perspective (against the grain), (4) "a man, trapped by the slyness of two women." See also Masenya, "NGWETSI. (BRIDE)," 82–85.

60. Maldonado, "Reading Malinche Reading Ruth"; Donaldson, "The Sign of Orpah"; Kwok, "Finding a Home for Ruth"; García-Treto, "Mixed Messages"; Wong, "History, Identity and a Community"; see also Fewell and Gunn, *Compromising Redemption*; Levine, "Ruth"; Linafelt and Beal, *Ruth and Esther*.

61. See Houten, *The Alien in Israelite Law*; Rendtorff, "The *Ger* in the Priestly Laws"; Snijders, "The Meaning of *Zar*"; Bennett, *Injustice Made Legal*; Begg, "Foreigner"; Spencer, "Sojourner."

used to describe Elimelech's sojourn to Moab with his family (Ruth 1:1). However, because Ruth takes advantage of the laws about gleaning for the poor, the *gēr*, and the widow (Lev 19:9–10; 23:22; Deut 24:19–22), the text implies that Ruth is a *gēr*.

When Ruth encounters Boaz's kindness for the first time, she falls on her face and exclaims: "Why have I found favor in your sight, that you should take notice of me, when I am a *nokrîyâ*?" (Ruth 2:10). The text has Ruth acknowledge in direct speech her status as a foreigner in Judah. The connotation of *nokrî* is generally negative, highlighting the person's otherness and separateness from the dominant culture.[62] We will see that the negativity of the *nokrî* is particularly underscored by the fact that Ruth was a Moabite, one of Israel's traditional hated enemies. If Ruth was written during the time of Ezra and Nehemiah, the use of *nokrîyâ* in the mouth of Ruth is significant. Intermarriage between the exiles and foreign women (*nāšîm nokrîyôt*. Ezra 10:2, 10; Neh 13:26) was severely condemned. Note that the nemesis of Lady Wisdom is the Foreign Woman[63] in the book of Proverbs, whose author shares Ezra's and Nehemiah's Persian-period ideologies.[64] Some interpret the marriage of Boaz to the *nokrîyâ* Ruth as a critique of Ezra's and Nehemiah's policies against foreign marriages.[65] Others argue for an earlier context for the composition of Ruth, perhaps as an apology for David to remove the taint of Moabite descent.[66] I maintain, however, that whatever the date, the negative connotations of Ruth's foreignness implied in *nokrîyâ* are not completely erased in the book.

Ruth as a Model Minority

In the construction of Ruth as the model minority, her Moabite ancestry is of prime importance. Ruth is not simply from any foreign nation, but from Moab, whose entanglements with Israel have been antagonistic. According to Gen 19:37, the Moabites were the spawn of a drunken

---

62. Rendtorff, "The *Ger* in the Priestly Laws," 77; Begg, "Foreigner," 829.

63. *'iššâ zārâ* which parallels *nokrîyâ* in Prov 2:16, 5:20 and 7:5. Cf. also 5:3 in which *nokrîyâ* parallels *ēšet râ*, evil woman, in 6:24, and *zônâ*, harlot, in 23:27.

64. Yee, "The Other Woman in Proverbs."

65. LaCocque, *Ruth*; Matthews, *Judges and Ruth*; Bush, *Ruth, Esther*. See overviews in Larkin, *Ruth and Esther*; Sakenfeld, *Ruth*, 1–5.

66. Gow, *The Book of Ruth*.

incestuous encounter between Lot and his eldest daughter. Numbers 25:1–3 blames the idolatry of Israelite men, who "yoked" themselves to the Baal of Peor, on the bewitching sexuality of Moabite women. The seer Balaam, hired by the king of Moab to curse the Israelites, ends up blessing them and cursing Moab instead (Numbers 22–24). Moab, along with Ammon, refused to offer bread (*leḥem*) and water on Israel's journey from Egypt and was thus denied admittance to the assembly of God, even down to the tenth generation (Deut 23:3–4). The irony is that Elimelech and his family must emigrate from Bethlehem (House of Bread) to Moab because of a famine in Judah.[67] But this flight comes at a great cost: the patriarch and his two sons die in Moab, leaving three impoverished widows and a threatened patriline.

The deeper the enmity between Moab and Israel, the greater the valor in Ruth's resolve to embrace the latter and its God. Her rejection of Moab and its negative links with Israel transforms her into the Jewish convert par excellence. In rabbinic interpretation, Ruth was the daughter of a Moabite king when she rejected her homeland and its false deities "to become a God-fearing Jewess—loyal daughter-in-law, modest bride, renowned ancestress of Israel's great king David."[68] Ruth's *ḥesed* (generosity, compassion and love) toward her mother-in-law in accompanying Naomi to a strange land and in supporting her by gleaning is recognized by Ruth's future husband and provider. Boaz exclaims that the Israelite God will fully reward Ruth, under whose wings she has sought refuge (2:11–12). If the book was written as an apology for the Moabite ancestry in David's line (cf. 1 Sam 22:3–4), Ruth the faithful convert purges the line of any foreign stain.

Indeed, Ruth is not only the model convert, but also an exemplar for the Jewish people. According to André C. LaCocque, "[Ruth's] 'heroism' is to become more of a Judean than those who are Judean by birth! Retrospectively, one can say that her fidelity toward the people and their God provides a lesson to those who should have been her teachers."[69] LaCocque further adds that the central theological message of the book

---

67. Moab had reasonably good agricultural land, which was productive even when other parts of Palestine were hit by famine. According to 2 Kgs 3:4, King Mesha of Moab bred sheep and used to deliver one hundred thousand lambs and the wool of one hundred thousand rams to the king of Israel. See Miller, "Ancient Moab."

68. Darr, *Far More Precious Than Jewels*, 72; Caspi and Havrelock, *Women on the Biblical Road*, 85.

69. LaCocque, *Ruth*, 24–25.

is the meaning of *ḥesed*, which Ruth epitomizes for the people: "A non-Judean shows the way to the Judeans, precisely in an era where the respect for the letter had become the very condition of membership in the Second Temple community."[70]

In her article, "Ruth, the Model Emigrée," Bonnie Honig criticizes readings that turn the book into "a kind of nationalist narrative that Ruth's story does not only nor unambivalently support."[71] She outlines the two problems for the present discussion that inhere in the concept of the model emigrée. According to Honig, dominant readings of Ruth fall into two categories that correspond to the two major responses to immigrants. On the one hand, immigrants are welcomed for what they can bring to a nation, whether it is diversity, talents, energy, novel cuisines, or a rekindled sense of national pride that had attracted the immigrants to us in the first place. On the other hand, immigrants are dreaded because of what they will do to us (burden our welfare system, weaken our common heritage, and so forth).[72] Ruth's decision to leave her natal land for Israel reconfirms Israel's identity as the Chosen People, a people worthy of being chosen. Nevertheless, Ruth's relocation does not mean that Israel is now is > a borderless land, embracing all foreigners, even the hated Moabites. "Israel is open only to the Moabite who is exceptionally virtuous, to Ruth but not Orpah."[73]

The construction of Ruth as the model emigrée is similar to the model minority stereotype of Asian Americans. Ruth is held up for propagandistic purposes, either to expunge any contamination of Moabite descent for David or to critique Ezra and Nehemiah's policies against intermarriage. She thus reveals what a virtuous foreigner can teach the nation. As model minorities, Asian Americans supposedly exemplify traditional values, such as respect for elders, industry and hard-work, and family loyalty. Similarly, Ruth incarnates the quality of *ḥesed* in her overwhelming devotion to her mother-in-law, her willingness to support her by diligently gleaning in a strange man's field, not resting "even for a moment" (2:7), and in her conversion to another God. As Ruth the Moabite teaches Judeans the meaning of *ḥesed*, Asian Americans educate Others on how to be "good" minorities who know their place in a white

---

70. LaCocque, *Ruth*, 28.
71. Honig, "Ruth, the Model Emigrée," 51.
72. Honig, "Ruth, the Model Emigrée," 54.
73. Honig, "Ruth, the Model Emigrée," 55–56.

society. Nevertheless, just as Asian Americans remain perpetual foreigners in the land of their birth, Ruth's disappearance in chapter 4 after the birth of her son leads one to question whether Ruth has been successfully assimilated as a foreigner into Judean society or, ultimately, abandoned once she preserves the male lineage.[74]

Ruth the Perpetual Foreigner

The flip side of the model minority stereotype for Asian Americans is that of the perpetual foreigner. This Janus-like phenomenon is also apparent in the book of Ruth. Just as Asian Americans are consistently perceived as being more Asian than American by the dominant white society, so is Ruth continually called Ruth the Moabite, rather than Israelite, even after her immigration (1:22; 2:2, 6, 21: 4:5, 10). Ruth seems to lose this qualifier after she finally gives birth to a son (4:13), but it comes at the cost of not being recognized as his mother (4:17).[75] Naomi's ultimate incorporation back into the community is manifested by her displacement of Ruth as Obed's mother. This displacement implies that the revitalization of this community and the continuation of the patriline towards David's monarchy depend not only on Ruth's exemplary character but also on her marginalization as a foreigner.[76]

As Chinese Americans were economically exploited in the US for cheap labor, particularly during the 1800 and early 1900s, so is Ruth's foreign labor exploited by both Naomi and Boaz. Jack M. Sasson[77] and Athalya Brenner[78] argue that 1:16–17, which is usually read as Ruth's tender pledge to Naomi, is actually a verbal contract in which Ruth submits her person to the wishes of her mother-in-law. The "love" that Ruth has for Naomi (4:15) can connote the relationship between an inferior to

---

74. Levine, "Ruth," 85.

75. Although space constraints limit my discussion, issues of surrogate motherhood and its exploitation of poor and ethnic women loom here, as they do in the Sarah and Hagar story of Genesis 16. Also on the horizon is the practice of white Americans adopting female Chinese babies abandoned at birth. It remains to be seen whether or not these babies will be fully accepted as "Americans" or also tagged as perpetual foreigners in spite of having white adoptive parents.

76. Honig, "Ruth, the Model Emigrée," 73–74.

77. Sasson, *Ruth*, 124.

78. Brenner, "Ruth as a Foreign Worker."

her or his superior, such as the one between a vassal and his lord.[79] This interpretation would explain, for example, why Ruth alone goes out to glean, and why she easily acquiesces to Naomi's dangerous proposal to seduce Boaz on the threshing floor. She might have had little choice in the matter.

Issues of class, especially as they intersect with ethnicity and gender in Ruth, are also underscored in a perceptive analysis by Roland Boer. In Marxist fashion, Boer notices who owns the means of production, namely, the land, and who actually works it in the book of Ruth. The economic gulf between Boaz, as owner of the land, and Ruth, as foreign gleaner of the land's leftovers, is wide. For Boaz does not work in the fields as do his reapers or his overseer, but, rather, he commands them. "In other words, he lives off the surplus labour of those who do work."[80] His seeming munificence towards Ruth (2:8–9, 14–16) is that of one who has more than enough already. He can afford to dole out a little something for Ruth. In this regard, Boaz's injunction to Ruth not to work in another man's field (2:8) may be motivated more by economic rather than personal interests in her. Boaz has already been told that Ruth "has been on her feet from early this morning until now, without resting even for a moment" (2:7). She continues the grueling work of gleaning until evening and then she beats out an *ephah* of barley (2:17), which weighs somewhere between 30–50 pounds.[81] Boaz knows good foreign help when he sees it, and his so-called generosity can be read as offering inducements to keep Ruth's productiveness for his own benefit. Although Boaz does not acquire economic capital from Ruth's labor, he certainly reaps much social capital and prestige in the Israelite community as a benefactor of widows. We will see shortly that Boaz will eventually acquire land as economic capital through Ruth's person. Ruth continues to toil in his field "until the end of the barley and wheat harvests" (2:23). Boer quips, "This is hardly benevolence, but more like pure exploitation."[82]

Naomi does not work in the fields either. She too lives off the labor of Ruth the foreigner, whose actions she directs: urging Ruth to continue the non-stop work of gleaning, instructing her to make herself attractive to seduce a man in the middle of the night, and ultimately taking Ruth's

---

79. Thompson, "Israel's 'Lovers'"; Ackerman, "The Personal Is Political"; Cf. Dube, "Divining Ruth," 77.
80. Boer, "Terry Eagleton: The Class Struggles of Ruth," 79–80.
81. Bush, *Ruth, Esther*, 133.
82. Boer, "Terry Eagleton: The Class Struggles of Ruth," 83.

child as her own. Some justify Naomi's absence in the field to her old age or that she still grieves the loss of her husband and sons. Others think she is hard at work in the invisible domestic sphere, while Ruth works outside the home. However, within the economics of the text, Naomi is more aligned with Boaz than with Ruth, especially when kinship intersects with ownership of the means of production. As related kin, Naomi and Boaz are complicit regarding "that piece of land" (4:3) that belonged to Naomi's husband, Elimelech. Another kinsman has a better claim to redeem this land, but Boaz is able to trump this claim by means of Ruth's body. "On the day you acquire the field from the hand of Naomi, you are also acquiring Ruth the Moabite, the widow of the dead man, to maintain the dead man's name on his inheritance" (4:5). Because of kinship with Boaz and by strategically using Ruth to preserve the lineage of her husband, Naomi ultimately dislocates Ruth as Obed's mother.

Marxist feminists have often noted the deficiency in Marxist theory in not fully incorporating into its theorizing on class women's productive labor and their reproductive (or sexual) labor in the continuation of the species.[83] These labors interconnect most clearly in the person of Ruth. Exhausting herself by working the land for Boaz and Naomi, Ruth also becomes the reproductive means by which Boaz and Naomi profit economically. In Boaz's case, Ruth becomes the stumbling block that prevents the land from falling into the hands of Mr. So-and-So, who cannot marry Ruth and beget a son through her without jeopardizing his own inheritance (4:6). Through Ruth, Boaz is thus able to enlarge his landholdings. And it is Ruth's birth labors in producing a son that secure Boaz's patriline and Naomi's economic place in the community.

Other aspects of Ruth's sexual exploitation in the text work hand-in-hand with Ruth's foreignness. Foreign women in the Hebrew Bible have a long tradition of erotic allure and sexual insatiability. Witness Madame Potiphar, Delilah, the queen of Sheba, Solomon's foreign wives, Jezebel, the whore of Babylon, and the Foreign Woman in Proverbs. These women bring about the downfall of men through their sexuality. Asian American women also suffer under similar exoticization by white American males in the images of Suzy Wong, Madame Butterfly, the submissive lotus blossom, the seductive geisha, the Mongol slave girl, and the treacherous Dragon Lady.[84] Catering to the sexual fantasies of white men, the

---

83. Hartmann, "The Unhappy Marriage"; Barrett, *Women's Oppression Today*, 8–41.

84. Uchida, "The Orientalization of Asian Women"; Yoshikawa, *One Hundred and*

flourishing global trafficking of Asian women's bodies is built on such stereotypes.[85] Male domination and colonial supremacy coalesce here in the sexual depiction and exploitation of the foreign woman.

Lingering over Ruth is the notorious tradition of the Moabites as the perverse progeny of incest, whose women sexually seduced the Israelites away from YHWH (Num 25:1–3). Ruth is particularly vulnerable to sexual harassment and violence in the fields by the male farmhands, who may regard her as "easy," because she is a Moabite, one of "those" women.[86] To protect his industrious worker and keep her working in his field, Boaz shields Ruth from these "attentions," by ordering his men to keep their hands to themselves (2:9).

The reputed carnality of foreign women injects greater ambivalence into the narrative of Ruth and Boaz on the threshing floor (Ruth 3). Biblical commentaries are rife with speculation on whether Ruth and Boaz "did it" that night. If intertextual parallels are drawn between Lot's daughters (Genesis 19), and Tamar (Genesis 38), Ruth did indeed "do it" with Boaz.[87] All three stories involve a threat to the patriline because of the death of a male. The fiancés of Lot's daughters are killed in the destruction of Sodom. God slays Er and Onan, leaving Judah's lineage in jeopardy. Elimelech and his sons die in Moab. In all three stories, women take the initiative to restore and continue the lineage. Further, foreignness is attached to all three. Lot's daughters become the progenitors of the Moabites and Ammonites. Tamar is most likely a Canaanite, and Ruth is a Moabite. All three adopt sexually unorthodox means to achieve their purposes. Lot's daughters collude in an incestuous encounter with their father. Tamar pretends to be a hooker at the side of the road. Ruth marshals her charms to seduce Boaz on the threshing floor. All three take advantage of the men's inebriation from too much wine.[88] Certainly, Lot's daughters and Tamar succeed in having sex with their targeted males, becoming pregnant with sons as a result. If the story of Ruth follows the same literary pattern, Ruth and Boaz consummated their union on the threshing floor, issuing in the birth of David's grandfather.

One Ways.
    85. Brock and Thistlethwaite, *Casting Stones*.
    86. Carasik, "Ruth 2,7"; Shepherd, "Violence in the Fields?"
    87. Fisch, "Ruth"; Fuchs, "Structure, Motifs and Ideological Functions"; Wolde, "Intertextuality: Ruth in Dialogue."
    88. Wine is implied in Gen 28:12–13, since it is the festive time of sheep shearing.

Whether Ruth and Boaz had sex that fateful night should not distract us from the economic urgency that compelled Ruth the foreigner to go to the threshing floor in the first place. Here, I am in complete agreement with Katherine Doob Sakenfeld (who does not think the couple "did it") that:

> No woman should have to do something so socially unacceptable in Israelite culture as to approach a man in the dark of night, at risk of discovery and public humiliation, and possibly severe legal penalties in order to put food on her family's table for the longer term. This is not a slightly adventurous tryst. It is a desperate act by a desperate person.[89]

While some white feminists may be appalled at the notion that the key to a woman's happiness is the Cinderella story of finding and seducing a rich man who will become her patron, for many destitute women in the Third World such a hope is often one of the few options available.[90] Sakenfeld relates a story about a young, impoverished Filipina who was recruited to go to a wealthy foreign country as a "dancer." In response to her pastor's suspicions that she was destined for the Asian sex trade, the girl pointed to the book of Ruth: "Ruth put herself forward attractively to a rich man in hopes that he would marry her and take care of her family. I am doing the same. Hopefully a rich man from that country will choose me to marry and will look after me and my family. God made things turn out right for Ruth and God will take care of me too."[91] The adverse consequences of global capitalism were brought home to me recently in Hong Kong, where it is not uncommon for Filipina domestic help (whose working conditions are often deplorable) to seduce the male head of household and sometimes engineer a divorce in order to better her situation. In these cases, as in the book of Ruth, economic survival often forces impoverished women to acts they would never do otherwise, literally spending their lives "in tears amid the alien corn."

Conclusion

Seen through the eyes of the dual Asian American experiences of being a model minority and perpetual foreigner, the book of Ruth holds in

---

89. Sakenfeld, "At the Threshing Floor," 174.
90. Kanyoro, "Biblical Hermeneutics," 373.
91. Sakenfeld, "The Story of Ruth," 221.

dialectical tension the positive and the more ambivalent interpretations of the story. On the one hand, the book of Ruth is a (fairy)tale about a devoted widow who rejects her homeland and her idols to accompany her mother-in-law to a new country. In this scenario, Ruth becomes a model emigrée *(gēr)*—a model convert—who teaches the Chosen People the true meaning of God's covenantal *ḥesed*. She is an exemplar of female empowerment, initiative, hard work, family loyalty, and upward mobility. And to top things off, she does get the guy in the end.

On the other hand, Ruth is also the perpetual foreigner—a *nokrîyâ*—whose consistent label of Moabite implies that she, not unlike Asian Americans in the US, is not fully assimilated in the text's consciousness of what it means to be Israelite. Ruth's foreignness is the linchpin in the economics of the text. It sets her apart from those characters who do not work in the book, but who appropriate her labor and her body. Chinese American labor contributed to the building of a nation, but their efforts went unacknowledged.[92] So also does Ruth's labor in the field and especially in giving birth to Obed play a major role in strengthening the Davidic line and the formation of the state, but she too disappears at the end. The insidious economic picture that surfaces in the book of Ruth is that the Israelites—in the persons of Naomi and Boaz—are those who do not work, who exploit and live off the surplus labor of the foreign Other. Naomi assimilates into the world of Israelite men, the landowners who possess the means of production, while the foreign female worker, Ruth, vanishes when her body is exhausted. Ruth's story thus becomes an indictment for those of us who live in the First World who exploit the cheap labor of developing countries and poor immigrants from these countries who come to the First World looking for jobs.

Works Cited

Ackerman, Susan. "The Personal Is Political: Covenantal and Affectionate Love (*'aheb, 'ahaba*) in the Hebrew Bible." *VT* 52 (2002) 437–58.

Alpert, Rebecca. "Finding Our Past: A Lesbian Interpretation of the Book of Ruth." In *Reading Ruth: Contemporary Women Reclaim a Sacred Story*, edited by Judith A. Kates and Gail Twersky Reimer, 91–96. New York: Ballantine, 1996.

Ancheta, Angelo N. *Race, Rights, and the Asian American Experience*. New Brunswick, NJ: Rutgers University Press, 2000.

---

92. Cf. the famous picture of the white men posing at the completion of the transcontinental railroad, with not a Chinese face in sight.

Ang, Ien. "On not Speaking Chinese: Postmodern Ethnicity and the Politics of Diaspora." *New Formations* 24 (1994) 1–18.
Barrett, Michèle. *Women's Oppression Today: The Marxist/Feminist Encounter.* Rev. ed. London: Verso, 1988.
Begg, Christopher T. "Foreigner." In *ABD* 2 (1992) 829–30.
Bennett, Harold V. *Injustice Made Legal: Deuteronomic Law and the Plight of Widows, Strangers, and Orphans in Ancient Israel.* The Bible in Its World. Grand Rapids: Eerdmans, 2002.
Boer, Roland. "Terry Eagleton: The Class Struggles of Ruth." In *Marxist Criticism of the Bible*, 65–86. London: T. & T. Clark, 2003.
Bow, Leslie. "Making Sense of Screaming: A Monkey's Companion." In *Screaming Monkeys: Critiques of Asian American Images*, edited by M. Evelina Galang et al. 87–97. Minneapolis: Coffee House, 2003.
Brenner, Athalya, ed. *A Feminist Companion to Ruth.* FCB 3. Sheffield: Sheffield Academic, 1993.
———, ed. *Ruth and Esther: A Feminist Companion to the Bible.* FCB, 2nd ser., 3. Sheffield: Sheffield Academic, 1999.
———. "Ruth as a Foreign Worker and the Politics of Exogamy." In *Ruth and Esther: A Feminist Companion to the Bible*, edited by Athalya Brenner, 158–62. FCB, 2nd ser., 3. Sheffield: Sheffield Academic, 1999.
———. "The Three of Us: Ruth, Orpah, Naomi." In *I Am . . . Biblical Women Tell Their Own Stories*, 99–119. Minneapolis: Fortress, 2005.
Brock, Rita Nakashima, and Susan Brooks Thistlethwaite. *Casting Stones: Prostitution and Liberation in Asia and the United States.* Minneapolis: Fortress, 1996.
Bruner, Edward M. "Tourism in Ghana: The Representation of Slavery and the Return of the Black Diaspora." *American Anthropologist* 98 (1996) 290–304.
Bush, Frederic W. *Ruth, Esther.* Word Biblical Commentary 9. Waco: Word, 1996.
Carasik, Michael. "Ruth 2,7: Why the Overseer Was Embarrassed." *ZAW* 107 (1995) 493–94.
Caspi, Mishael Maswari, and Rachel S. Havrelock. *Women on the Biblical Road: Ruth, Naomi, and the Female Journey.* Lanham, MD: University Press of America, 1996.
Cavalcanti, Tereza. "The Prophetic Ministry of Women in the Hebrew Bible." In *Through Her Eyes: Women's Theology from Latin America*, edited by Elsa Tamez, 118–39. Maryknoll, NY: Orbis, 1989.
Chang, Iris. *The Chinese in America: A Narrative History.* New York: Viking, 2003.
Cheng, Lucie, and Philip Q. Yang. "The 'Model Minority' Deconstructed." In *Contemporary Asian America: A Multidisciplinary Reader*, edited by Min Zhou and James V. Gatewood, 459–82. New York: New York University Press, 2000.
Cho, Sumi K. "Converging Stereotypes in Racialized Sexual Harassment: Where the Model Minority Meets Suzie Wong." In *Critical Race Feminism: A Reader*, edited by Adrien Katherine Wing, 203–20. Critical America. New York: New York University Press, 1997.
Chu, Julie Li-Chuan. "Returning Home: The Inspiration of the Role Dedifferentiation in the Book of Ruth for Taiwanese Women." *Semeia* 78 (1997) 47–53.
Darr, Katheryn Pfisterer. *Far More Precious Than Jewels: Perspectives on Biblical Women.* Gender and the Biblical Tradition. Louisville: Westminster John Knox, 1991.
Dawson, Jenny. "The Power of Women's Friendship." *In God's Image* 20/1 (2001) 39–40.

De La Torre, Miguel A. "Cubans in Babylon: Exodus and Exile." In *Religion, Culture, and Tradition in the Caribbean*, edited by Hemchand Gossai and Nathaniel Samuel Murrell, 73–91. New York: St. Martin's, 2000.

Donaldson, Laura E. "The Sign of Orpah: Reading Ruth through Native Eyes." In *Ruth and Esther: A Feminist Companion to the Bible*, edited by Athalya Brenner, 130–44. FCB, 2nd ser., 3. Sheffield: Sheffield Academic, 1999.

Dube, Musa W. "Divining Ruth for International Relations." In *Postmodern Interpretations of The Bible—A Reader*, edited by A. K. M. Adam, 67–80. St. Louis: Chalice, 2001.

———. "The Unpublished Letters of Orpah to Ruth." In *Ruth and Esther: A Feminist Companion to the Bible*, edited by Athalya Brenner, 145–50. FCB, 2nd ser., 3. Sheffield: Sheffield Academic, 1999.

Duncan, Celena M. "The Book of Ruth: On Boundaries, Love, and Truth." In *Take Back the Word: A Queer Reading of the Bible*, edited by Robert E. Goss and Mona West, 92–102. Cleveland: Pilgrim, 2000.

Dyk, Alta C. van, and Peet J. van Dyk. "HIV/AIDS in Africa: Suffering Women and the Theology of the Book of Ruth." *Old Testament Essays* 15 (2002) 209–24.

Ebron, Paulla, and Anna Lowenhaupt Tsing. "From Allegories of Identity to Sites of Dialogue." *Diaspora: A Journal of Transnational Studies* 4 (1995) 125–51.

Erbele-Küster, D. Dorothea. "Immigration and Gender Issues in the Book of Ruth." *Voices from the Third World* 25/1–2 (2002) 32–39.

Exum, J. Cheryl. "Is This Naomi?" In *Plotted, Shot, and Painted: Cultural Representations of Biblical Women*, 129–74. JSOTSup 215. Sheffield: Sheffield Academic, 1996.

Fewell, Danna Nolan, and David M. Gunn. *Compromising Redemption: Relating Characters in the Book of Ruth*. Literary Currents in Biblical Interpretation. Louisville: Westminster John Knox, 1990.

Fisch, Harold. "Ruth and the Structure of Covenant History." *VT* 32 (1982) 425–37.

Foulkes, Irene. "The Book of Ruth and a Group of Prostitutes in Costa Rica." In *Feminist Interpretation of the Bible and the Hermeneutics of Liberation*, edited by Silvia Schroer and Sophia Bietenhard, 86–87. JSOTSup 374. London: Sheffield Academic, 2003.

Fuchs, Esther. "Structure, Motifs and Ideological Functions of the Biblical Temptation Scene." *Biblicon* 2 (1997) 51–60.

Gallares, Judette A. *Images of Faith: Spirituality of Women in the Old Testament*. Maryknoll, NY: Orbis, 1994.

García-Treto, Francisco. "Mixed Messages: Encountering Mestizaje in the Old Testament." *Princeton Seminary Bulletin* 22/2 (2001) 150–71.

Gossai, Hemchand. "Recasting Identity in Ruth and Hindu Indo-Guyanese Women." In *Religion, Culture, and Tradition in the Caribbean*, edited by Hemchand Gossai and Nathaniel Samuel Murrell, 167–79. New York: St. Martin's, 2000. http://catdir.loc.gov/catdir/toc/holo51/00023368.html/.

Gow, Murray D. *The Book of Ruth: Its Structure, Theme and Purpose*. Leicester, UK: Apollos, 1992.

Hartmann, Heidi. "The Unhappy Marriage of Marxism and Feminism: Towards a More Progressive Union." In *The Second Wave: A Reader in Feminist Theory*, edited by Linda Nicholson, 97–122. New York: Routledge, 1997.

Honig, Bonnie. "Ruth, the Model Emigrée: Mourning and the Symbolic Politics of Immigration." In *Ruth and Esther: A Feminist Companion to the Bible*, edited by Athalya Brenner, 50–74. FCB, 2nd ser., 3. Sheffield: Sheffield Academic, 1999.

Houten, Christiana van. *The Alien in Israelite Law*. JSOTSup 107. Sheffield: JSOT Press, 1983.

Jordan, June. "Ruth and Naomi, David and Jonathan: One Love." In *Out of the Garden: Women Writers on the Bible*, 82–87. Columbine, NY: Fawcett, 1994.

Kanyoro, Musimi R. A. "Biblical Hermeneutics: Ancient Palestine and the Contemporary World." *Review & Expositor* 94 (1997) 363–78.

Kates, Judith A., and Gail Twersky Reimer, eds. *Reading Ruth: Contemporary Women Reclaim a Sacred Story*. New York: Ballantine, 1994.

Kirk-Duggan, Cheryl A. "Black Mother Women and Daughters: Signifying Female-Divine Relationships in the Hebrew Bible and African-American Mother-Daughter Short Stories." In *Ruth and Esther*, edited by Athalya Brenner, 192–210. FCB, 2nd. ser., 3. Sheffield: Sheffield Academic, 1999.

Koyama, Kosuke. *Waterbuffalo Theology*. Maryknoll, NY: Orbis, 1974.

———. "Waterbuffalo Theology—After 25 Years." *PTCA Bulletin* 11.2 (1998) 5–9.

Kuo, Sui May. "Ruth the Moabitess." *In God's Image* 13/1 (1994) 53–56.

Kwok, Pui-Lan. "Finding a Home for Ruth: Gender, Sexuality, and the Politics of Otherness." In *Postcolonial Imagination and Feminist Theology*, 100–121. Louisville: Westminster John Knox, 2005.

LaCocque, André C. *Ruth*. Translated by K. C. Hanson. Continental Commentary. Minneapolis: Fortress, 2004.

Larkin, Katrina J. A. *Ruth and Esther*. Old Testament Guides. Sheffield: Sheffield Academic, 1996.

Lee, Peter K. H. "Two Stories of Loyalty." *Ching Feng* 32/1 (1989) 24–40.

Lee, Robert G. *Orientals: Asian Americans in Popular Culture*. Asian American History and Culture. Philadelphia: Temple University Press, 1999.

Levine, Amy-Jill. "Ruth." In *Women's Bible Commentary*, edited by Carol A. Newsom and Sharon H. Ringe, 84–90. Expanded ed. Louisville: Westminster John Knox, 1998.

Linafelt, Tod, and Timothy K. Beal. *Ruth and Esther*. Berit Olam. Collegeville, MN: Liturgical, 1999.

Louie, Andrea. *Chineseness across Borders: Renegotiating Chinese Identities in China and the United States*. Durham: Duke University Press, 2004.

Maldonado, Robert D. "Reading Malinche Reading Ruth: Toward a Hermeneutics of Betrayal." *Semeia* 72 (1995) 91–109.

Masenya, Madipoane. "Ruth." In *Global Bible Commentary*, edited by Daniel Patte, 86–91. Nashville: Abingdon, 2004.

Masenya, Madipoane J. "NGWETSI. (BRIDE). The Naomi-Ruth Story from an African-South African Woman's Perspective." *JFSR* 14/2 (1998) 81–90.

Matthews, Victor H. *Judges and Ruth*. New Cambridge Bible Commentary. Cambridge: Cambridge University Press, 2004.

McKinlay, Judith E. "A Son Is Born to Naomi: A Harvest for Israel." In *Ruth and Esther: A Feminist Companion to the Bible*, edited by Athalya Brenner, 151–57. FCB, 2nd ser., 3. Sheffield: Sheffield Academic, 1999.

———. "Reading Rahab and Ruth." In *Reframing Her: Biblical Women in Postcolonial Focus*, 37–56. Bible in the Modern World 1. Sheffield: Sheffield Phoenix, 2004.

Mesters, Carlos. *Rute: Una Historia Da Biblia*. Sao Paolo: Paulinas, 1985.
Miller, Max. "Ancient Moab Still Largely Unknown." *Biblical Archaeologist* 60 (1997) 194–204.
Miller, Stuart Creighton. *The Unwelcome Immigrant: The American Image of the Chinese, 1785–1882*. Berkeley: University of California Press, 1974.
Nadar, Sarojini. "A South African Indian Womanist Reading of the Character of Ruth." In *Other Ways of Reading: African Women and the Bible*, edited by Musa W. Dube, 159–75. Global Perspectives on Biblical Scholarship 2. Atlanta: Society of Biblical Literature, 2001.
Nayap-Pot, Dalila. "Life in the Midst of Death: Naomi, Ruth and the Plight of Indigenous Women." In *Vernacular Hermeneutics*, edited by R. S. Sugirtharajah, 52–65. Bible and Postcolonialism 2. Sheffield: Sheffield Academic, 1999.
Omi, Michael, and Howard Winant. *Racial Formation in the United States: From the 1960s to the 1990s*. Critical Social Thought. New York: Routledge, 1994.
Osajima, Keith Hiroshi. "Asian Americans as the Model Minority: An Analysis of the Popular Press Image in the 1960s and 1980s." In *Contemporary Asian America: A Multidisciplinary Reader*, edited by Min Zhou and James V. Gatewood, 449–58. New York: New York University Press, 2000.
Raheb, Viola. "Women in Contemporary Palestinian Society: A Contextual Reading of the Book of Ruth." In *Feminist Interpretation of the Bible and the Hermeneutics of Liberation*, 87–93. JSOTSup 374. London: Sheffield Academic, 2003.
Rendtorff, Rolf. "The *Ger* in the Priestly Laws of the Pentateuch." In *Ethnicity and the Bible*, edited by Mark G. Brett, 77–88. Biblical Interpretation Series 19. Leiden: Brill, 1996.
Sakenfeld, Katharine Doob. "At the Threshing Floor: Sex, Reader Response, and a Hermeneutic of Survival." *Old Testament Essays* 15 (2002) 164–78.
———. *Ruth*. Interpretation. Louisville: John Knox, 1999.
———. "Ruth and Naomi: Economic Survival and Family Values." In *Just Wives? Stories of Power and Survival in the Old Testament and Today*, 27–48. Louisville: Westminster John Knox, 2003.
———. "The Story of Ruth: Economic Survival." In *Realia Dei. Essays in Archaeology and Biblical Interpretation in Honor of Edward F. Campbell, Jr. at His Retirement*, edited by Prescott H. Williams and Theodore Hiebert, 215–27. Scholars Press Homage Series 23. Atlanta: Scholars, 1999.
Sasson, Jack M. *Ruth: A New Translation with a Philological Commentary and a Formalist-Folklorist Interpretation*. Biblical Seminar. Sheffield: Sheffield Academic, 1989.
Shepherd, David. "Violence in the Fields? Translating, Reading, and Revising in Ruth 2." *CBQ* 63 (2001) 444–63.
Silber, Ursula. "Ruth and Naomi: Two Biblical Figures Revived among Rural Women in Germany." In *Ruth and Esther: A Feminist Companion to the Bible*, edited by Athalya Brenner, 93–109. FCB, 2nd ser., 3. Sheffield: Sheffield Academic, 1999.
Snijders, L. A. "The Meaning of Zar in the Old Testament." *Oudtestamentische Studien* 10 (1954) 1–154.
Spencer, John R. "Sojourner." In *ABD* 6 (1992) 103–4.
Stanton, Elizabeth Cady. *The Woman's Bible*. Edited by Maurene Fitzgerald. Boston: Northeastern University Press, 1993.

Takaki, Ronald. *A Different Mirror: A History of Multicultural America.* Boston: Little, Brown, 1993.

———. *Strangers from a Different Shore: A History of Asian Americans.* Updated and rev. ed. New York: Back Bay, 1998.

Thompson, J. A. "Israel's 'Lovers.'" *VT* 27 (1977) 475–81.

Travis, Irene S. "Love Your Mother: A Lesbian Womanist Reading of Scripture." In *Take Back the Word: A Queer Reading of the Bible,* edited by Robert E. Goss and Mona West, 35–42. Cleveland: Pilgrim, 2000.

Tuan, Mia. *Forever Foreigners or Honorary Whites: The Asian Ethnic Experience Today.* New Brunswick, NJ: Rutgers University, 1998.

Uchida, Aki. "The Orientalization of Asian Women in America." *Women's Studies International Forum* 21 (1998) 161–74.

Weems, Renita J. *Just a Sister Away: Womanist Vision of Women's Relationships in the Bible.* San Diego: Lura Media, 1988.

Williams, Dolores S. "Breaking and Bonding." *Daughters of Sarah* 15/3 (2000) 10–14.

Wong, Angela Wai Ching. "History, Identity and a Community of *Hesed*: A Biblical Reflection on Ruth 1:1–17." *Asian Journal of Theology* 13 (1999) 3–13.

Wu, Frank H. *Yellow: Race in America beyond Black and White.* New York: Basic Books, 2002.

Yee, Gale A. "Inculturation and Diversity in the Politics of National Identity." *JAAAT* 2 (1997) 108–12.

———. "The Other Woman in Proverbs: My Man's Not Home—He Took His Moneybag with Him." In *Poor Banished Children of Eve: Woman as Evil in the Hebrew Bible,* 135–58. Minneapolis: Fortress, 2003.

———. "'She Stood in Tears amid the Alien Corn': Ruth, the Perpetual Foreigner and Model Minority." In *They Were All Together in One Place? Toward Minority Biblical Criticism,* edited by Randall C. Bailey et al., 119–40. Semeia Studies 57. Atlanta: Society of Biblical Literature, 2009.

———. "Yin/Yang Is Not Me: An Exploration into an Asian American Biblical Hermeneutics." In *Ways of Being, Ways of Reading: Asian-American Biblical Interpretation,* edited by Mary F. Foskett and Jeffrey K. Kuan, 152–63. St. Louis: Chalice, 2006.

van Wolde, Ellen. "Intertextuality: Ruth in Dialogue with Tamar." In *A Feminist Companion to Reading the Bible: Approaches, Methods and Strategies,* edited by Athalya Brenner and Carole Fontaine, 426–51. FCB 11. Sheffield: Sheffield Academic, 1997.

Yoshikawa, Mako. *One Hundred and One Ways.* New York: Bantam, 1999.

Zia, Helen. *Asian American Dreams: The Emergence of an American People.* New York: Farrar, Straus & Giroux, 2000.

7

Racial Melancholia and the Book of Ruth[1]

ASIAN AMERICANS HAVE COME to occupy a peculiar place in the North American racial imaginary, signifying approbation and revulsion in the Janus-like stereotype of the "model minority" and the "perpetual foreigner." This essay is a continuation of my work on Ruth as a model minority and perpetual foreigner,[2] by exploring the psychic dimensions of her perpetual foreignness through the lens of racial melancholia. Freud describes melancholia as a psychic condition of loss, the state or feeling of grief when deprived of someone or something of value. In melancholia, that loss cannot be named and thus cannot be mourned properly.[3] Unlike mourning, in which one is eventually able to relinquish or "let go of" the lost person, value, or object, in melancholia one is unable to "get over" the loss and invest energies in new persons or objects. Instead, that loss becomes incorporated into one's ego or sense of self, and that self becomes haunted by it.[4] "The melancholic assumes the emptiness of the lost object or ideal, identifies with this emptiness, and thus participates in his or her own self-denigration and ruination of self-esteem."[5]

---

1. Originally published as Yee, "Racial Melancholia," 2018. A shorter version was read at the 2016 International Meeting of the Society of Biblical Literature in Seoul, Korea.
2. Yee, "'She Stood in Tears.'"
3. Freud, "Mourning and Melancholia," 245.
4. Cf. Cheng, "The Melancholy of Race," 50–53.
5. Eng and Han, "A Dialogue on Racial Melancholia," 343–46.

In analyzing the tangled psychical webs of Asian American racialization, Asian American cultural critics have applied the notion of racial melancholia.[6] Racial melancholia is the psychic condition of loss experienced by racialized groups living in a white dominant society. This condition implicates both white and racialized entities, though in different ways. According to Cheng,

> [R]acial melancholia affects both dominant white culture and racial other; indeed, racial melancholia describes the dynamics that constitute their mutual definition through exclusion. The terms thus denote a complex process of racial rejection and desire on the parts of whites and nonwhites that expresses itself in abject and manic forms. On the one side, white American identity and its authority is secured through the melancholic introjection of racial others that it can neither fully relinquish nor accommodate and whose ghostly presence nonetheless guarantees its centrality. On the other side, the racial other (the so-called melancholic object) also suffers from racial melancholia whereby his or her racial identity is imaginatively reinforced through the introjection of a lost, never-possible perfection, an inarticulable loss that comes to inform the individual's sense of his or her own subjectivity.[7]

In other words, white culture unconsciously defines itself against the racial other while simultaneously denying any substantive social links with that other. The racial other, in turn, is unconsciously unable to "get over" the lost and unobtainable ideal of whiteness in the process of assimilation. This phenomenon can be compared to the postcolonial concept of mimicry in which the colonizer desires a "reformed recognizable Other, *as a subject of a difference that is almost the same, but not quite.*"[8] Asian Americans become almost, but not quite "white" in US society: the model minority but also the perpetual foreigner. The etiology of racial melancholia for Asian Americans can be traced to historical forms of institutionalized racism and economic exploitation by white America and the attempts of Asian American subjects to negotiate the conflicted histories

---

6. Chang, "'I Cannot Find Her'"; Cheng, *The Melancholy of Race*; Parikh, "Blue Hawaii"; Shiu, "On Loss."

7. Cheng, *The Melancholy of Race*, xi. Cf. the studies of white melancholia by Hübinette and Räterlinck, "Race Performativity"; Hübinette, "Swedish Antiracism"; Hübinette and Lundström, "Three Phases of Hegemonic Whiteness."

8. Bhabha, *The Location of Culture*, 122, *italics* in original; see also Eng and Han, "A Dialogue on Racial Melancholia," 349; Cheng, *The Melancholy of Race*, 79–80.

of Asian immigration and assimilation in the United States.[9] Because of these histories, racial melancholia is not simply an individual condition of loss, but one that characterizes Asian American ethnic groups because of institutionalized racist exclusions by white society. Their psychic racial melancholia arises from a discernible political and material base.[10]

White society incurs a "loss" when it demeans the racial other and internalizes this demeaned object. It can then split off these problematic aspects of its racist self and project them upon the racial other. Such splitting allows white society to project an idealized image of itself and use its location in networks of power to make this idealization appear real.[11] This white melancholia will take the form of a misremembering of this history of legalized racial exclusions.

> Because the American history of exclusions, imperialism, and colonization runs so diametrically opposed to the equally and particularly American narrative of liberty and individualism, cultural memory in America poses a continuously vexing problem: how to remember those transgressions without impeding the ethos of progress? How to bury the remnants of denigration and disgust created in the name of progress and the formation of an "American identity."[12]

This white misremembering is evident the famous pictures of white men posing at the completion of the transcontinental railroad with not a Chinese face in sight,[13] even though this great national achievement was built by cheap Chinese labor.[14]

The book of Ruth depicts both Ruth and Naomi as racial/ethnic melancholics in a dialectical relationship with each other: Ruth as the melancholic object and Naomi as the melancholic subject. Ruth is described as a melancholic object by the nineteenth-century English Romantic poet, John Keats, in the penultimate stanza of his "Ode to a Nightingale." Keats imagines that the nightingale's immortal soothing song, even

---

9. Chang, *The Chinese in America*; Takaki, *Strangers from a Different Shore*.

10. Eng and Han, "A Dialogue on Racial Melancholia," 355–56.

11. Flax, "What Is the Subject?," 916.

12. Cheng, *The Melancholy of Race*, 50–51.

13. http://thewildgeese.irish/profiles/blogs/transcontinental-railroad-in-united-states and http://bloximages.chicago2.vip.townnews.com/missoulian.com/content/tncms/assets/v3/editorial/2/28/22825e1b-5eef-5a97-87b5-732d7eec4d3d/22825e1b-5eef-5a97-87b5-732d7eec4d3d.image.jpg.

14. Chang, *The Chinese in America*, 53–54.

"found a path/through the sad heart of Ruth, when, sick for home,/She stood in tears amid the alien corn" (v. 65).[15] In the biblical text, the person of Ruth the Moabite experiences many losses. First of all, there is the loss of her Judean husband in Moab. We are not even told the name of this husband (Mahlon) until the very last chapter (4:10). There is the loss of her father-in-law Elimelech and that of her brother-in-law Chilion. There is the permanent loss of her homeland Moab, her nationality, her citizenship, and her native language. There is the loss of "her people" in order to become part of Naomi's people. There is the loss of her native deity, probably Chemosh, for Naomi's God (1:14–16). There is her anguished parting from her sister-in-law Orpah, who, according to Honig,[16] embodies all that Moab represents for Ruth. And the final culmination of her losses: the relinquishment of her newborn son Obed over to Naomi (4:17). Although there are expressions of sorrow and weeping by Naomi, Ruth, and Orpah at their leave-taking (1:9, 14), the narrative expresses Ruth's grieving or mourning in none of the other losses just described.[17] As instances of racial melancholia, these losses are inferred in the text, but are not named and therefore not mourned properly. They become a living list of inarticulated grief in the story and are a constituent part of her racial/ethnic identity as a Moabite immigrant in the book. This internalized grief and the ambivalence in the narrative regarding Ruth's Moabite status and its and her disappearance at the end of the book can be argued as an example of what Asian American critics deem as racial melancholia, experienced in the negotiation and assimilation of foreign immigrants into another society.

According to Frymer-Kensky, the book of Ruth answers three questions.[18] When I read these questions, the Marxist literary critic in me automatically interprets them ideologically, assuming "If the text of Ruth was the answer, what was/were the question/s?" What were the social problems, contradictions, conflicts, etc. that the text was trying to re/

---

15. See https://en.wikipedia.org/wiki/Ode_to_a_Nightingale for lyrics.

16. Honig, "Ruth, the Model Emigrée," 71.

17. According Hawkins, the tearful scene of Ruth in the fields of "alien corn" envisaged by Keats is nowhere to be found in the biblical text. He also notes that these verses are the only two times Ruth is said to weep in the book. Hawkins, "Ruth Amid the Gentiles," 76.

18. Frymer-Kensky, *Reading the Women*, 255; Koosed, *Gleaning Ruth*, 13.

solve?[19] The narrative's "answers" provided the ideological solutions to these questions:

- "Should the returnees from Babylon be able to recuperate their former lands?" (Yes, property should revert to its original owners.)
- "What is the status of foreigners, especially foreign spouses, accompanying the returnees?" (They should be welcomed and assimilated into the community.)
- "What should be the relationship between the returnees and those who remained in the land?" (Along with the assimilated foreigners, the returnees and the remainees should strive together to insure a prosperous future for Israel.)

Indeed, the story of Naomi the returnee, Ruth the foreigner, and Boaz (the kinsman already in the land) seems to be an allegory of the larger Israelite narrative of exile, return, and restoration.[20] The story makes use of the traditions of the female ancestors of Israel's past (Rachel, Leah, and Tamar; 4:11-12) and male genealogies leading up to David (4:17-22), in such a way that "the ancestry story and the genealogy of the great king of Israel's past point the way toward the nation's glorious future."[21]

This positive interpretation of the book belies the fact that relations among the returnees, remainees, and foreigners during the Persian period were quite conflicted.[22] Koosed and Schipper argue that, if not read alongside select passages in Genesis, Numbers, and Deuteronomy, reading Ruth alone fails to present the negative assessment of Moabites as foreigners.[23] However, the materialist and ideological critic in me cannot ignore the general and literary modes of production that produced the book of Ruth.[24] At its deeper level, the book can be considered an ideological misremembering of the conflicted relations among the returnees, the remainees, and foreigners during the Persian period, in order (1) to anchor the present *golah* community in the past great traditions of the patriarchs and matriarchs and their God YHWH (Ruth 1:16; 4:11-12);

---

19. Cf. Yee, *Poor Banished Children of Eve*, 25-26.
20. Frymer-Kensky, *Reading the Women*, 254.
21. Frymer-Kensky, 256.
22. Yee, *Poor Banished Children of Eve*, 140-46.
23. Koosed, *Gleaning Ruth*, 106; Schipper, *Ruth: A New Translation*, 38.
24. Yee, *Poor Banished Children of Eve*, 18-28.

(2) to legitimate the recovery of their lost land and restore their privileged position within it; and (3) to provide a rationale for the fact that the ancestress of Judah's greatest king happens to be one of those "difficult" foreigners, a Moabite (Ruth 1:4, 22; 2:2, 6, 21; 4:5, 10).

What is Israelite in this text cannot simultaneously escape its double: What is Moabite? The Hebrew Bible frequently depicts Moab as Israel's enemy.[25] Moreover, the sexual relations and intermarriages between Israelite men and Moabite women has led Israel into idolatry,[26] and has influenced scholars to read the book of Ruth against the background of these foreign alliances particularly during the time of Ezra and Nehemiah.[27] Complicating matters is the fact that the biblical traditions describe Israel and Moab as sharing a patrilineal closeness in that the Moabites are the descendants of Abraham's nephew Lot, according to Gen 19:30–37. That the birth of Moab was the result of incest between Lot and his daughter should not be regarded as a disparagement of his descendants in Genesis 19. There is no condemnation of Moab's mother for her action. Indeed, believing with her sister that there were no men left in the world, she had sex with her father "to preserve offspring through our father" (Gen 19:32). Her unconventional sexual efforts thus insured the continued lineage of Abraham's brother Haran and his father Terah.[28] The danger of Ruth lies not in her as the "foreign" Other but in her alterity as the "familiar" Other "with its threat of assimilation."[29] "Unlike the trope of radical difference, common to racist, nationalist, and colonial discourse of the modern era, the Bible is concerned with drawing contrasts across a field of acknowledged similarity."[30] Differing from the struggles within the binary of the white/racialized minority in the US, the conflicted relations between the Israelites and Moabites were among blood relatives.[31]

---

25. Num 22–24 and Deut 23:3–6; Judg 3:12–30; 2 Sam 8:2; 2 Kgs 3:4–27; 13:20; 24:2; 1 Chr 18:2; the Mesha Inscription, *ANET*, 320–21; Isa 11:14; 15:1—16:14; Jer 9:25; 48:1–47; Amos 2:1–3. Regarding Ps 60:8, see Gillingham, "'Moab Is My Washpot.'"

26. Num 25:1–5; 1 Kgs 11:1–2, 7–8; Ezra 9:1–2; Neh 13:23–27.

27. Eskenazi and Frymer-Kensky, *Ruth*, xviii–xix; LaCocque, *Ruth*, 20–27.

28. Eskenazi and Frymer-Kensky, *Ruth*, 259–60; Schipper, *Ruth*, 41.

29. Routledge, *Moab in the Iron Age*, 42.

30. Routledge, *Moab in the Iron Age*, 44. Cf. also the critique of postcolonial readings of Ruth by Koosed, *Gleaning Ruth*, 28–29, 40–41.

31. Brenner, "Ruth," 85–86.

Submerged and misremembered in the book of Ruth is this history of conflicted Israelite and Moabite familial relations. Racial melancholia in Ruth results from an ever-deferred assimilation process arising from her alterity as a threatening familial Other. This alterity prevents her from being fully assimilated as Israelite. Her melancholia is the loss of ultimately becoming a true Israelite, which is reflected in the textual ambivalence already noted by scholars on the repeated references to her Moabite identity.[32] If she is integrated into Judean society, it will only be as "alien-kin." Although not explicitly described as a *gēr*, Ruth qualifies as a *gēr*, as resident alien who works under the authority of a wealthier clan member for wages, like Jacob under Laban (Gen 32:5). Moreover, as one who has also married into a Judahite clan, she is thus an "alien-kinswoman," a wage-earning laborer, a slave "in all but name."[33] A number of scholars, including yours truly, have already interpreted Ruth as an exploited worker.[34]

Racial melancholia and class become compounded with gender when one considers Ruth as an exploited *female* worker. Ruth thus becomes both a female Other as well as a familial Other. With memories of the Moabites as the product of incest (Gen 19:30–38) and the seduction of the Israelites away from YHWH by their women (Num 25:1–5; 1 Kgs 11:1–8; Ezra 9:1–2; Neh 13:23–27), non-normative sexuality clings to Ruth the Moabite, along with her class status and racialization. This can be seen in Boaz's and Naomi's concern that as a Moabite woman Ruth might be molested in the fields, if she does not stick close to the female reapers (Ruth 2:9, 22).[35] Non-normative sexuality is also evident in Ruth's unconventional seduction of Boaz on the threshing floor (Ruth 3). Intertextual parallels of irregular sexual relations in the stories of Lot's daughters (Genesis 19) and Tamar (Genesis 38) heighten sexuality in the encounter between Ruth and Boaz.[36] Ruth's racial melancholia thus becomes doubly apparent in Ruth as both a Moabite familial Other and

---

32. Eskenazi and Frymer-Kensky, *Ruth*, xlviii; Maldonado, "Reading Malinche Reading Ruth."

33. Schipper, *Ruth*, 48–49.

34. Yee, "'She Stood in Tears,'" 130–32; Brenner, "Ruth as a Foreign Worker," 158; Boer, "Terry Eagleton: The Class Struggles of Ruth," 65.

35. Shepherd, "Violence in the Fields?"; Linafelt and Beal, *Ruth and Esther*, 34–35; Carasik, "Ruth 2,7: Why the Overseer"; Fewell and Gunn, *Compromising Redemption*, 76, 122 n. 11.

36. Yee, "'She Stood in Tears,'" 132–33.

a female Other, which prevents her full assimilation in Judean society. Ruth neither achieves full Israelite identity nor recovers from a distorted and distorting racial/ethnic/sexual stereotype.

The price of Ruth's integration in the ideology of the book is the denigration and loss in her psychic self of her Moabite ethnicity and identity. Ruth's disappearance after she gives birth to Obed is the final consequence of being a racial melancholic object in the book.[37] Although not intended to be a remark on the psychic self-denigration that occurs in racial melancholia in the text's ideology, André LaCocque's statement is quite apt: "While the community around Ruth will not forget her Moabite identity, Ruth is willing to erase not only her ethnic roots, but also her very self."[38] This psychic erasure of herself is revealed in her expurgation from the narrative.

In order to better understand Ruth as a melancholic object, let us now compare her with Naomi, the melancholic subject. Israelite identity and its authority, embodied in the person of Naomi, is ensured through the melancholic introjection of Ruth the *Moabite foreigner*, which it cannot "fully relinquish and whose ghostly presence nonetheless guarantees its centrality."[39] White racial melancholia also experiences "loss," because

> teetering between the known and the unknown, the seen and the deliberately unseen, the racial other constitutes an oversight that is *consciously made unconscious—naturalized over time as absence, as complementary negative space*.[40]

The biblical narrative reflects the unconscious incorporation into its own psychic world the racialized characteristics of Ruth as "absence, as complementary negative space." This is especially evident when she disappears at the book's closure. The narrative defines Israelite identity against the Moabite Other, but, in an entangled sense, cannot deny the fact that they are linked as kin. Israelite identity cannot escape the fact that the Moabites are the "familiar" Other. Inasmuch as it tries to assimilate Ruth into the community, the narrative cannot shake off her Moabite-ness, which hovers in the text as a phantom in the multiple references to her ethnicity. Israelite identity cannot fully expunge the "familiar" Other.

---

37. Brenner, "Ruth," 84; Levine, "Ruth," 90.
38. LaCocque, *Ruth*, 23.
39. Cheng, *The Melancholy of Race*, xi.
40. Cheng, *The Melancholy of Race*, 16 (italics added).

What it does, however, is constrain and maintain that Other within existing structures that subordinate it. For Ruth, it subjects her in a triple subjection of her gender, ethnicity, and class, as an "alien-kinswoman" within Israelite society.

Naomi also suffers the loss of homeland in her sojourn to Moab because of the famine in Judah. She too loses her husband and two sons, just as Ruth loses her own husband, her father-in-law, and brother-in-law. However, in contrast to Ruth, Naomi, the melancholic subject, is given full expression of her grief in 1:20–21, blaming God for her losses: "I went away full, but the Lord has brought me back empty." Moreover, unlike Ruth, Naomi is able to "get over" her losses. She is reinstated in her homeland, able to recover her husband's property, and become incorporated back into her Israelite kin-group by taking Ruth's son into her own bosom and becoming his caregiver (4:16). The Moabite ancestry of their most famous monarch, David, presented a conundrum to the returning exiles. Because of the conflicted state of Israelite/Moabite relations, the narrative's depiction of its melancholic subject, Naomi, could not unproblematically present an optimistic picture of exiled elites returning to the land. Ruth therefore must be downgraded. Even though she is the agent of Naomi's restoration in Judah, Ruth herself does not obtain this full assimilation. As a racial melancholic object, Ruth's psychic self is split off, remaining the perpetual foreigner unable to "get-over" the loss of full integration into Israelite society.

Conclusion

Racial melancholia is the psychic condition of unarticulated loss experienced by racialized groups living in a dominant culture. Racialized objects are unable to "get over" the fact that they cannot be fully assimilated into that dominant culture because of institutionalized racism. The melancholic object identifies with this loss and internalizes this degraded racial sense of self projected by this racism. This paper argues that Ruth's unarticulated grief suffered from her numerous losses are internalized as racial melancholia in the book of Ruth. The book is a Persian period misremembering of the Israelite conflicts with the Moabites as the familial Other, their alien kin. The ideological purposes of the book are to secure the returning exiles in the traditions of the ancestors, legitimate the recovery of their lost lands and privilege, and to reckon with the Moabite ethnicity of David's great-ancestress. Although Ruth is the principal agent through whom the exiled Naomi is restored in the land and in her clan, her ideological status as both the familial and female Other makes it impossible for her to become fully Israelite herself. The internalized grief from this loss of Israelite identity is reflected in the narrative's ambivalence regarding her Moabite status and can be argued as an example of what Asian American critics identify as racial melancholia, experienced by Asian immigrants in their attempts to assimilate in the United States.

Works Cited

Bhabha, Homi K. *The Location of Culture*. With a new preface by the Author. London: Routledge, 1994.

Boer, Roland. "Terry Eagleton: The Class Struggles of Ruth." In *Marxist Criticism of the Bible*, 65–86. London: T. & T. Clark, 2003.

Brenner, Athalya. "Ruth as a Foreign Worker and the Politics of Exogamy." In *Ruth and Esther: A Feminist Companion to the Bible*, edited by Athalya Brenner, 158–62. FCB, 2nd ser., 3. Sheffield: Sheffield Academic, 1999.

———. "Ruth: The Art of Memorizing Territory and Religion." In *A Critical Engagement: Essays on the Hebrew Bible in Honour of J. Cheryl Exum*, edited by David J. A. Clines and Ellen van Wolde, 82–89. Hebrew Bible Monographs 38. Sheffield: Sheffield Phoenix, 2011.

Carasik, Michael. "Ruth 2,7: Why the Overseer Was Embarrassed." *ZAW* 107 (1995) 493–94.

Chang, Iris. *The Chinese in America: A Narrative History*. New York: Viking, 2003.

Chang, Juliana. "'I Cannot Find Her': The Oriental Feminine, Racial Melancholia, and Kimiko Hahn's *The Unbearable Heart*." *Meridians: Feminism, Race, Transnationalism* 4 (2004) 239–60.

Cheng, Anne Anlin. "The Melancholy of Race." *Kenyon Review* 19 (1997) 49–61.

———. *The Melancholy of Race: Psychoanalysis, Assimilation, and Hidden Grief*. Race and American Culture. New York: Oxford University Press, 2001.

Eng, David L., and Shinhee Han. "A Dialogue on Racial Melancholia." In *Loss: The Politics of Mourning*, edited by David L. Eng and David Kazanjian, 343–71. Berkeley: University of California Press, 2002.

Eskenazi, Tamara Cohn, and Tikva Frymer-Kensky. *Ruth: The Traditional Hebrew Text with the New JPS Translation and Commentary*. JPS Commentary. Philadelphia: Jewish Publication Society, 2011.

Fewell, Danna Nolan, and David M. Gunn. *Compromising Redemption: Relating Characters in the Book of Ruth*. Literary Currents in Biblical Interpretation. Louisville: Westminster John Knox, 1990.

Flax, Jane. "What Is the Subject? Review Essay on Psychoanalysis and Feminism in Postcolonial Time." *Signs: Journal of Women in Culture & Society* 29 (2004) 905–23.

Freud, Sigmund. "Mourning and Melancholia." In *The Standard Edition of the Complete Psychological Works of Sigmund Freud*, edited and translated by James Strachey, 14:243–58. 24 vols. London: Hogarth, 1953.

Frymer-Kensky, Tikva. *Reading the Women of the Bible*. New York: Schocken, 2002.

Gillingham, Susan. "'Moab Is My Washpot' (Ps 60:8 [MT 10]): Another Look at the MLF (Moabite Liberation Front)." In *Interested Readers: Essays on the Hebrew Bible in Honor of David J. A. Clines*, edited by James K. Aitken et al., 61–71. Atlanta: Society of Biblical Literature, 2013.

Hawkins, Peter S. "Ruth amid the Gentiles." In *Scrolls of Love: Ruth and the Song of Songs*, edited by Peter S. Hawkins and Lesleigh Cushing Stahlberg, 75–85. New York: Fordham University Press, 2006.

Honig, Bonnie. "Ruth, the Model Emigrée: Mourning and the Symbolic Politics of Immigration." In *Ruth and Esther: A Feminist Companion to the Bible*, edited by Athalya Brenner, 50–74. FCB, 2nd ser., 3. Sheffield: Sheffield Academic, 1999.

Hübinette, Tobias. "Swedish Antiracism and White Melancholia: Racial Words in a Post-Racial Society." *Ethnicity and Race in a Changing World: A Review Journal* 4 (2013) 24–33. https://doi.org/10.7227/ERCW.4.1.2.

Hübinette, Tobias, and Catrin Lundström. "Three Phases of Hegemonic Whiteness: Understanding Racial Temporalities in Sweden." *Social Identities* 20 (2014) 423–37. https://doi.org/10.1080/13504630.2015.1004827.

Hübinette, Tobias, and Lennart E. H. Räterlinck. "Race Performativity and Melancholic Whiteness in Contemporary Sweden." *Social Identities* 20 (2014) 501–14. https://doi.org/10.1080/13504630.2014.1003703.

Koosed, Jennifer L. *Gleaning Ruth: A Biblical Heroine and Her Afterlives*. Studies on Personalities of the Old Testament. Columbia: University of South Carolina Press, 2011.

LaCocque, André C. *Ruth*. Translated by K. C. Hanson. Continental Commentary. Minneapolis: Fortress, 2004.

Levine, Amy-Jill. "Ruth." In *Women's Bible Commentary*, edited by Carol A. Newsom and Sharon H. Ringe, 84–90. Expanded ed. Louisville: Westminster John Knox, 1998.

Linafelt, Tod, and Timothy K. Beal. *Ruth and Esther*. Berit Olam. Collegeville, MN: Liturgical, 1999.

Maldonado, Robert D. "Reading Malinche Reading Ruth: Toward a Hermeneutics of Betrayal." *Semeia* 72 (1995) 91–109.

Parikh, Crystal. "Blue Hawaii: Asian Hawaiian Cultural Production and Racial Melancholia." *Journal of Asian American Studies* 5 (2002) 199–216.

Routledge, Bruce. *Moab in the Iron Age: Hegemony, Polity, Archaeology*. Archaeology, Culture, and Society. Philadelphia: University of Pennsylvania Press, 2004.

Schipper, Jeremy. *Ruth: A New Translation with Introduction and Commentary*. Anchor Yale Bible 7D. New Haven: Yale University Press, 2016.

Shepherd, David. "Violence in the Fields? Translating, Reading, and Revising in Ruth 2." *CBQ* 63 (2001) 444–63.

Shiu, Anthony Sze-Fai. "On Loss: Anticipating a Future for Asian American Studies." *MELUS* 31 (2006) 3–33.

Takaki, Ronald. *Strangers from a Different Shore: A History of Asian Americans*. Updated and rev. ed. New York: Back Bay, 1998.

Yee, Gale A. *Poor Banished Children of Eve: Woman as Evil in the Hebrew Bible*. Minneapolis: Fortress, 2003.

———. "Racial Melancholia in the Book of Ruth." In *The Five Scrolls*, edited by Athalya Brenner-Idan et al., 61–70. Texts@Contexts. London: Bloomsbury T. & T. Clark, 2018.

———. "'She Stood in Tears Amid the Alien Corn': Ruth, the Perpetual Foreigner and Model Minority." In *They Were All Together in One Place? Toward Minority Biblical Criticism*, edited by Randall C. Bailey et al., 119–40. Semeia Studies 57. Atlanta: Society of Biblical Literature, 2009.

8

The Woman Warrior Revisited
Jael, Fa Mulan, and American Orientalism[1]

I PURCHASED THE PAPERBACK version of Maxine Hong Kingston's *The Woman Warrior* when it appeared in 1977. The irony is that I never read it until I had to teach it for a Women's Studies class in the late 1980s. Instead, it was the concept of a Chinese woman warrior that intrigued me as a Chinese American female: the ancient legend of a powerful woman who, like many in the US Women's Liberation Movement of the 1970s, defied the conventions of the weak, obedient womanhood of traditional Chinese patriarchy. She was for me a female counterpart of Superman who fought for truth, justice, but perhaps not for the "American Way." It was this concept of a female warrior that drew me to write on Jael in Judges 4 for a *Semeia* volume devoted to Women, War, and Metaphor.[2] My fascination with her continued as I speculated on what I would do for an Asian American reading of Judges 4–5.[3] This essay therefore offers me a welcomed opportunity to delve once more into the woman warrior motif through an intercontextual comparison between Jael[4] and Fa Mulan, the Chinese woman warrior who inspired Kingston's work. Intercontextual features can be found in their shared warriorhood, their respective ethnicities, their (trans)gendering, and the reception history

---

1. Originally published in Yee, "The Woman Warrior Revisited" (2013).
2. Yee, "'By the Hand of a Woman.'"
3. Yee, "Yin/Yang Is Not Me," 162–63.
4. The bibliography on Judges 4–5 is extensive. For research since 1990, see Mayfield, "The Accounts of Deborah."

of their narratives. Particularly with respect to Fa Mulan's reception history, I will focus on the American Orientalism that plays a significant part in the mass-marketed Disney production of *Mulan* (1998) and my own conceptualization of my ethnic heritage.

Warriorhood

Both Jael and Mulan can be considered warriors, although in differing ways. In my 1993 article on Judges 4, I argued that the social structure of premonarchic Israel offered possibilities for women to engage in informal wartime operations. Because the family household (*bēt 'āb*) was the basic socioeconomic unit and because women held critical leadership positions within this unit, albeit informal ones, women like Deborah had opportunities to emerge as leaders during times of war. Furthermore, if one extends the definition of warriorhood beyond those who fight on the battlefield to those who work in covert operations and intelligence, then Jael would be considered a warrior. Her assassination of Sisera, the enemy's top-ranking general, already classifies her as a warrior, more broadly defined. The fact that she uses trickery is no different from the guerilla tactics already employed by the Israelites.[5]

Defying stereotypes of women as victims of Chinese patriarchy are a significant number of myths of heroic Chinese women, of whom Fa Mulan is the most well-known.[6] Although originating between the fourth and sixth centuries CE, an anonymous folk-song, "The Ballad of Mulan," was published in a thirteenth-century anthology of lyrics, folk songs, and poems.[7] The song describes a young woman at a weaver's loom, anxious about her father's conscription into the khan's army, because he had no older son who could be drafted in his place. Mulan decides to purchase a horse and other equipment "to take my father's place to go on a military expedition."[8] Bidding farewell to her parents, she fights valiantly for twelve years alongside her fellow male warriors who take her to be one of them. When she is presented in the Emperor's court, she eschews a promotion in rank and honor, preferring a fast camel that would whisk her

---

5. Yee, "'By the Hand of a Woman,'" 109–12.

6. Dong, *Mulan's Legend and Legacy*, 9–50; Mann, "Myths of Asian Womanhood."

7. For an English translation of the poem, see *Yellow Bridge* (website), "Ode to Mulan."

8. Dong, *Mulan's Legend and Legacy*, 54.

back to her hometown. Upon her arrival, she enters her boudoir, removes her military attire, puts on a dress, fixes her hair, and applies makeup to her face. When she emerges as a lovely woman, her comrades, who evidently came home with her, are amazed: "We spent twelve years fighting together but didn't know that Mulan was a woman."[9]

Lest one regards Mulan as some protofeminist heroine, stories about Mulan and her kind were written and transmitted primarily to illustrate how Confucian patriarchy should function. Patriarchal Chinese values celebrated and hinged upon powerful women. Distinctive features of Confucian patriarchy are the separate realms of *yin/yang* cosmologies, the male with the public "outer" and the female, the domestic "inner."[10] Although Mulan transgresses these boundaries by her warriorhood, she adheres to the Confucian codes of duty, loyalty, and filial piety that did not threaten, but rather upheld, the dominant rule of men.[11] The poem opens with Mulan weaving at the loom in her house, a domestic task performed by women. The so-called masculine aspects of her life—her many years as a soldier—are simply compressed into a few lines. The poem focuses instead on the honors the Emperor bestows on her for her valor and her eventual return to the domestic sphere. After her turn as a loyal warrior for the empire, she resumes the traditional roles of daughter and potential wife/mother.

Tropes of inner/outer and domestic/public also figure in the story of Jael. Jael differs from Mulan in that she eliminates her enemy secretly: not on the open battlefield, but in the private sphere of her tent. Jael does not disguise her gender in her "combat" with Sisera, as Mulan does. In fact, she "performs" some of the traditional behaviors of her female gender.[12] She invites Sisera into her personal space, which some have likened to a womb.[13] Like a mother, she covers him with a rug, gives him milk to drink, and protects him from the dangers without (Judg. 4:18–20). Mulan displays her womanliness after her time in battle, when she returns to her family and reveals herself as a female before her fellow soldiers. Jael, on the other hand, exhibits her martial prowess only after she performs as

---

9. Dong, *Mulan's Legend and Legacy*, 55.
10. Mann, "Myths of Asian Womanhood," 842.
11. Dong, *Mulan's Legend and Legacy*, 13–15; Li, *Cross-Dressing in Chinese Opera*, 4–5.
12. Butler, *Gender Trouble*, 179.
13. Fewell and Gunn, "Controlling Perspectives," 393.

a traditional woman. Both heroines in their own different ways share the incongruity of being a female warrior in the male arena of war.

Ethnicity

In my 2006 article, "Yin/Yang is Not Me," I posed the following questions about Jael, inquiring into the nature of her ethnicity, as I contemplated my own as a Chinese American biblical scholar: Was Jael a foreigner (non-Israelite) like her husband, Heber the Kenite? Was Jael a Kenite like her husband? What was the nature of Kenite/Hebrew ethnic, political and/or economic relations? How does Jael's ethnicity influence her status as a woman warrior?[14] I return again to some of these questions, as I consider Jael's ethnicity from an Asian American perspective and compare it to Mulan's.

A major problem is that we cannot easily pinpoint Jael's ethnicity or even her marital status to a Kenite male. First of all, ambiguity surrounds the ethnicity of the Kenites themselves as kin-group relatives to Moses in Judges. According to Judg. 1:16, the descendants of the Kenite father-in-law of Moses—whom the LXX and Judg. 4:11 name Hobab—"went up with the people of Judah from the city of palms into the wilderness of Judah, which lies in the Negeb near Arad."[15] The text relates that these Kenite descendants settled with the Amalekites, raising the possibility of intermarriage between the two ethnic groups. Judg. 4:11 then explains how a group usually situated in the southern wilderness now resides in the far north: "Heber the Kenite had separated from the other Kenites, that is the descendants of Hobab the father-in-law of Moses, and had encamped as far away as Elon-bezanannim, which is near Kedesh." In Num. 10:29, Hobab is not Moses' father-in-law, but the son of Reuel the Midianite, not a Kenite (cf. Exod. 2:18). Another tradition names Moses' father-in-law Jethro, although still affirming the Midianite, rather than Kenite, connection (Exod. 3:1). Uncertainty regarding the name (Hobab/Reuel/Jethro) and ethnicity (Midianite/Kenite) of Moses' father-in-law and the possible Kenite/Amalekite intermingling complicates the ethnicity of the Kenite descendants described in Judges 4.[16]

---

14. Yee, "Yin/Yang Is Not Me," 162–63.

15. NRSV here and in further Bible citations.

16. Halpern, "Kenites," 20–21; Ackerman, *Warrior, Dancer, Seductress, Queen*, 94–95.

If we take *heber* as a proper name, Heber is the husband of Jael who belonged to a Kenite clan that had separated from the Kenites who settled in the south and had moved far north (Judg. 4:11). Because "there was peace between King Jabin of Hazor and the clan of Heber the Kenite," Sisera fled to the tent of Jael, wife (*'iššâ*) of Heber the Kenite (Judg. 4:17). This detail implies that the allegiance of Heber's northern clan to the Canaanites differed from the allegiance of the southern Kenites who were allied with the Israelites. However, if Heber's clan had friendly relations with Barak's Canaanite enemies, why did the Israelite leader respond freely to Jael's invitation, "Come, and I will show you the man whom you are seeking" (4:22)? "Would not the logic of the peace treaty suggest that this *Israelite* general should be wary of a *Canaanite* sympathizer?"[17] Boling remarks that it was providential that a Galilean Kenite chieftain had a loyal Yahwist wife.[18] However, this raises the question whether Jael was a Kenite convert to Yahweh or an Israelite Yahwist who married a Kenite, which may have lessened Barak's suspicions about entering her tent. The text is not clear regarding Jael's ethnicity or her religious and political alliances apart from her husband.

Furthermore, Heber the Kenite may not have been Jael's husband. If one does not read *heber* as a proper name but as an ethnic "group" or "clan," *heber haqqēnî* in 4:11, 17 could simply refer to the Kenite group or community. By moving north, this group had detached itself from the southern desert Kenites, who were distantly related to the Israelites through Moses' Midianite father-in-law Hobab. Jael would then be a woman (*'iššâ*) belonging to this indeterminate group of Kenite origin who had moved far north near Kedesh (4:11).[19] In this case, Jael would be a non-Israelite, an ethnic foreigner, from the Israelite perspective.[20]

The slipperiness in pinning down Jael's ethnicity and its geographical loci has some analogues with the Asian Fa Mulan. Mulan's tale probably originated from a non-Han ethnic tradition.[21] The poem resembles some of the folk songs about the heroic women of a foreign nomadic tribe known as the Xianbei who conquered and controlled northern China between 386 and 534 CE. Xianbei women were skilled in horseback riding

---

17. Ackerman, *Warrior, Dancer, Seductress, Queen*, 92.
18. Boling, *Judges*, 97.
19. Soggin, *Judges*, 65–66, 74–75; Halpern, "Kenites," 18.
20. Ackerman, *Warrior, Dancer, Seductress, Queen*, 99–100.
21. The Han was and is the largest ethnic group in China.

and in archery. If the "Ballad" came from a similar milieu, the martial features of these women would have been appropriated by the Han Chinese who infused them into their own heroine Fa Mulan. Thus, the character Mulan most likely had a foreign ethnic origin at the earliest stage of her literary history.[22] Nevertheless, because her story of gender defiance was so fascinating and engaging, various parts of China over the years wanted to claim her and incorporate her into their regional histories, augmenting the different traditions surrounding her.[23]

Jael's ethnicity also has intriguing analogues with the Asian American ethnic experience. Consider the description of Bobby, a resident of Koreatown in Los Angeles, in Karen Te Yamashita's imaginative and brilliant novel on the clash of cultures and hemispheres, *Tropic of Orange*:

> That's Bobby. If you know your Asians, you look at Bobby. You say, that's Vietnamese. That's what you say. Color's pallid. Kinda blue just beneath the skin. Little underweight. Korean's got rounder face. Chinese's taller. Japanese's dressed better. If you know your Asians. Turns out you'll be wrong. And you gonna be confused. Dude speaks Spanish. Comprende? So you figure it's one of those Japanese from Peru. Or maybe Korean from Brazil. Or Chinamex. Turns out Bobby's from Singapore. You say, okay, Indonesian. Malaysian. Wrong again. You say, look at his name. That's gotta be Vietnam. Ngu. Bobby Ngu. They all got Ngu names. Hey, it's not his real name. Real name's Li Kwan Yu. But don't tell nobody. Go figure. Bobby's Chinese. Chinese from Singapore with a Vietnam name speaking like a Mexican living in Koreatown. That's it.[24]

Here, stereotypes of Asian Americans are disrupted by reality, reflecting the diverse contexts of many Asian Americans.[25] Similarly, Jael's ethnicity has also been difficult to determine. She was part and parcel of that "mixed multitude" (cf. Exod. 12:38) that comprised early Israel: "a

---

22. Dong, *Mulan's Legend and Legacy*, 53; Lan, "The Female Individual and the Empire," 229–33.

23. Dong, *Mulan's Legend and Legacy*, 85–86.

24. Yamashita, *The Tropic of Orange*, 14–15.

25. I remember being in a diner in Chicago and saw my waitress and the cook arguing with each other. The waitress came over and told me that she and the cook had a bet with each other to identify which Native American tribe I belonged to. I don't remember the tribe, Apache, Sioux or whatever, but I had to disappoint both when I told them that I was Chinese. Furthermore, in this era of racial profiling, the Asian ethnic group most people think I'm from is Filipino/a.

collection of loosely organized and largely indigenous, tribal, and kin-based groups whose porous borders permitted penetration by smaller numbers from external groups."[26]

(Trans)Gendering

In my 1993 article, I maintained that the woman warrior occupies a structurally anomalous position in the human domain. She is neither male nor female as they are normally understood but shares features of both. She is a liminal figure and thus a threat to the dominant structures of power. In order to mitigate this threat, the author of Judges constructs Jael through syndromes—Shame and Sexual Voracity—that reinforce his androcentric interests. Jael primarily becomes a means to shame the men associated with her. She shames Sisera, because he suffers a humiliating death by the hand of a woman, and Barak, because he could not carry out Sisera's death himself. In keeping with the unbridled lust characterizing warrior queens, Jael lures Sisera to his death through her sexuality.[27] We have already seen the way the warrior woman Fa Mulan was portrayed in ways that bolstered Chinese patriarchy. Both women transgress the societal dictates of their gender, while still remaining paradoxically within their confines.

In the "Ballad of Mulan," Mulan violates gender norms through cross-dressing, disguising herself as a warrior by securing the accouterments of battle—a horse, saddle, bridle, and long horsewhip. It is here significant that "clothes do *not* make the man," but the supplies needed for military transport do. Clothing comes into play only when Mulan returns home and slips on a dress, highlighting her femininity and her return to the traditional order. Every development of her story over time and region will imprint upon her its own ideology of maleness and femaleness and the contradictions therein for a woman warrior. For example, in the sixteenth century play by Xu Wei, "Female Mulan Joins the Army Taking Her Father's Place," the heroine actually does dress in men's clothing, but paradoxically also has bound feet. Bound feet was a key signifier of femininity and the erotic of the time. The eroticism of bound feet emanates from the fact that men rarely see a bound foot without the

---

26. Killebrew, *Biblical Peoples and Ethnicity*, 184–85.
27. Yee, "'By the Hand of a Woman,'" 99–117.

white bandages covering it.[28] Thus when Mulan must loosen the bandages binding her feet as she dons her military uniform, especially the male footwear to accommodate these feet, it becomes an erotic moment. Mulan figures out a way to restore the damage to her "lotus feet" when she returns home to get married, all of which underscores the fact that Mulan does not deviate completely from the established male order.[29]

Gender contradictions become particularly apparent when Mulan's story is staged in Chinese opera, where even up to the twentieth century the most popular actors playing female leads were men.[30] The role of Mulan would be performed by a boy or a man, playing a woman who disguises herself as a man and then returns to being a woman. Shades of *Victor/Victoria* in reverse! Because the potential audience of Xu Wei's play is the male elite class, the addition of foot binding to Mulan's story takes on an (homo)erotic subtext, when a male actor plays a part of a woman unbinding her feet, while getting dressed as a man.[31] From the perspective of queer theory, Li expresses these contradictions in Chinese opera succinctly:

> The engendering of the spectacle and spectatorial gaze, and the circulation of the sexual and the homo/hetero-erotic in a multiple crisscrossing within and across the binary hierarchies of man/woman, sex/gender, (male) gaze and (female) object, erotic desire/object of desire—all subsumed within a heterosexual matrix.[32]

As we turn to Jael, one of the most provocative examinations of Jael's (trans)gendering to date is also a queer reading, one by Deryn Guest on Judges 4–5.[33] Guest rejects interpretations of Jael that persist in confining gender to the binaries male/female, masculine/feminine. As long as scholars remain within this closed dichotomous system, Jael's transgressive acts can only be seen as gender "reversal" that for Guest simply shifts the ground from one gender to the other. Guest prefers instead to resist, subvert, undo, and deconstruct these binaries to reveal them as social constructions (Guest 2011, 9). She finds my 1993 article on Jael

---

28. Jackson, *Splendid Slippers*, 103–22.
29. Dong, *Mulan's Legend and Legacy*, 66–72.
30. Li, *Cross-Dressing in Chinese Opera*.
31. Dong, *Mulan's Legend and Legacy*, 70–71.
32. Li, *Cross-Dressing in Chinese Opera*, 20.
33. Guest, "From Gender Reversal to Genderfuck."

to be the most promising study on which to build such a queer reading, because its focus on the liminality of Jael opens the way to gender destabilization (Guest 2011, 16–19). Nevertheless, she critiques my use of female pronouns to describe Jael, thus bypassing a syndrome that would have strengthened my argument for Jael's liminality, namely, the tomboy syndrome. This syndrome "catches the eye of a lesbian reader who can resonate with such preferences and the subsequent stigma" (Guest 2011, 16–17). According to Guest, *all* commentators have not been able to break through the male/female binary in consistently referring to Jael as female, because they fail to see, à la Judith Butler, that gender is a performance (Guest 2011, 20).

Along with Jael's transgressive warrior actions, Guest senses "gaydar bleeps" in Judges 4 that hint at Jael's genderqueerness: Jael's masculine name and the masculine imperative of Sisera's command to Jael to stand at the entrance of the tent (Guest 2011, 20–21). While several scholars, including myself, have described Jael's violent assassination of Sisera with a phallic tent peg as a reversal of male rape, Guest maintains that "Jael is not a *woman* warrior and equally Jael is not a *male* rapist . . . Jael is a figure who unsettles and destabilizes, whose performativity provides one of those unintelligible genders that give the lie to ideas of sex as abiding substance."[34] Jael's gender is not-man/not-woman.[35] Although ill at ease with the female pronouns in the following citation from Robyn Fleming, Guest thinks that Fleming comes close to explaining why Jael provokes such anxiety in her genderqueerness:

> Jael is almost the personification of gender blur, that force most threatening to the hierarchical structure of patriarchy. If you can't tell for sure which people are men, and which are women, how can power structures based on gender inequality be maintained? This then is the source of the phallocentric reader's unease about the character of Jael. The problem is not that she breaks with laws of hospitality, or even that she is a rapist, quite. The problem is that in doing those things, and in order to do those things, she destabilizes both her own gender construction and the gendered identities of others.[36]

---

34. Guest, "From Gender Reversal to Genderfuck," 26 (italics original).

35. Guest has explored this description of not-woman/not man with the butch lesbian experience in Guest, "Looking Lesbian," 254–58.

36. Fleming, "Jael's Gender," cited in Guest, "From Gender Reversal to Genderfuck," 29–30.

It is this gender blur, this gender confusion that aggravates and provokes the dominant structures of patriarchy in the Jael narrative.

As other regions and populations in China have wished to claim Mulan for their own, so does Guest desire to claim Jael for genderqueer readers who identify themselves as not-man/not-woman. "Jael seems to provide an unforeseen biblical character for those butch lesbians who desire to wear their genderqueerness with pride."[37] In commenting on Guest's article, Kamionkowski remarks that Guest's agenda is *"not just to break down heteronormative structures but to create a place for herself within biblical readings."*[38] Even in such a patriarchal text as the Bible, Guest is able to find something constructive in the person of Jael for those who occupy a space outside of heteronormativity.

Reception History

Because the woman warrior occupies such a liminal position, betwixt and between dominant conceptions of gender, my 1993 article discussed a number of different and contradictory ways in which Jael (and Deborah) have been taken up and represented in the course of their long reception history.[39] For example, in his first-century work, Pseudo-Philo depicts Sisera as a predatory collector of beautiful women as concubines in the spoils of war. For this reason, Deborah prophesies that "the arm of a weak woman would attack him and maidens would take his spoils and even he would fall into the hands of a woman" (*Bib. Ant.* 31:1).[40] Pseudo-Philo's Deborah becomes the champion of female honor that has been disgraced by Sisera. The vehicle of Sisera's demise is one of these women upon whom Sisera preys. Sexualizing the confrontation between Jael and Sisera, Pseudo-Philo describes Jael as "very beautiful in appearance." She "adorns herself" and goes out "to meet" Sisera to invite him back to her tent. Unlike Mulan who cross-dressed as a man, Jael highlights her femininity by getting dressed to kill in seductive attire. Upon seeing her bed festooned with roses, Sisera declares, "If I am saved, I will go to my mother, and Jael will be my wife." The net effect of Pseudo-Philo's sexual

---

37. Guest, "From Gender Reversal to Genderfuck," 31.

38. Kamionkowski, "Queer Theory and Historical-Critical Exegesis," 134 (italics original.

39. Yee, "'By the Hand of a Woman,'" 121–26.

40. Following Harrington, trans., "Pseudo-Philo: A New Translation," 296–377.

expansions is to make Jael an agent of revenge for the rape of women. Instead of seizing beautiful women as spoils for himself, Sisera becomes undone by one.

The study of the reception history on Jael has been enhanced by David Gunn's commentary on Judges.[41] Gunn examines ancient, medieval, modern, and contemporary religious and secular literature, paintings, engravings, and poems in their depictions of Jael. His study reinforces my own earlier conclusions regarding the contradictory interpretations of Jael from the earliest times, because of the liminal position she occupies as a woman warrior. On the one hand, she can foreshadow Jesus, the Church, or the Virgin Mary in that her assassination of Sisera anticipates Jesus', the Church's, and Mary's triumph over sin or the devil. On the other hand, she is the quintessential *femme fatale*, a mother-snake who lures one into her tent, soothes him into a false sense of security, and "slid like snake across the tent—struck twice—and stung him dead."[42] Jael has been a particular favorite in the visual arts,[43] music,[44] poetry,[45] film,[46] and children's literature.[47]

Lan Dong thoroughly documents the reception history of Fa Mulan, which she describes as a palimpsest, an evolving interplay of continuity and erasure in which Mulan's tale is written and rewritten into multiple layers that efface and erase previous versions.[48] Mulan is transformed from a foreign nomadic warrior into several iterations of an idealized Han Chinese heroic maiden. She becomes the avatar of Maxine Hong Kingston, the warrior avenger in Kingston's autobiography.[49] She morphs into several different incarnations in a number of American children's

---

41. Gunn, *Judges*, 53–92. In the Blackwell Bible Commentaries Series devoted to the reception history of the Bible.

42. Gunn, *Judges*, 77.

43. Bohn, "Death, Dispassion, and the Female Hero"; Haber, *Drawing on the Bible*, 87–92; Christiansen and Mann, "Jael and Sisera." A number of paintings about Jael can be viewed at http://www.biblical-art.com/biblicalsubject.asp?id_biblicalsubject=131&pagenum=1/. For art and music, see http://catholic-resources.org/Art/.

44. Leneman, "Re-Visioning a Biblical Story."

45. Robnolt, "Jael's Husband Returns from War."

46. Christianson, "The Big Sleep."

47. Bottigheimer, "Philogyny, Misogyny, and Erasure," 142–51.

48. Dong, *Mulan's Legend and Legacy*, 5.

49. Kingston, *The Woman Warrior*.

books, culminating in a major Disney animation, *Mulan*.[50] It is the Disney production of Mulan's story that interests me as an artifact of American Orientalism.

In my 2006 article, I examine my own process of becoming an Asian American, a totally different breed from one who is born and bred in Asia. Even though I look Chinese, I do not have the usual markers of Asianness. As a third generation Chinese American, I cannot draw on immigrant experience from a previous time in China. Unlike Maxine Hong Kingston's mother, my own never told me Chinese legends of ghosts and woman warriors, most likely because as a second generation Chinese American she didn't know any herself. Even though I was raised in a Chinese-speaking household, my parents did not teach their twelve children Chinese, so that we would assimilate more easily into American culture. I also suspect that they spoke Chinese whenever they didn't want us kids to understand what they were talking about. I did not grow up in Chinatown but in the slums of Blackstone Ranger Chicago, with Blacks and Puerto Ricans. My parents were devout Roman Catholics, who did not practice the traditional Asians religions: Buddhism, Taoism, and Confucianism. So, I can confidently declare that, with respect to my Chinese ethnicity, "Yin/Yang is not me."[51] I am a Chinese American inside and out.

Nevertheless, I've had to explore the Asian side of the hyphen in figuring out what an Asian American reading of the biblical text looked like. I discovered that during my formative years my understanding of Asian was refracted through the prism of American Orientalism: the representation of Asia as a geographically distant, foreign land filled with exotic and dubious characters and cultural practices that must be subdued and domesticated.[52] My early exposure to China and its culture was through Charlie Chan and Pearl Buck movies, where white actors played Chinese characters. My Chinese icons were Fu Manchu, Dragon Lady, and Ming the Merciless from the planet Mongo of the Flash Gordon TV series. I was mesmerized by the martial arts of Mrs. Peel in the TV series *The Avengers*, until after years of karate and kung fu myself, I realized that she knew very little about these skills. I actually enjoyed reading James Clavell's Asian Saga novels! I was one of those Chinese Americans "who got their

---

50. Madacy Entertainment Group 1999.
51. Yee, "Yin/Yang Is Not Me"; Yee, "Inculturation and Diversity."
52. Ma, *The Deathly Embrace*; Lee, *Orientals*; Okihiro, *Margins and Mainstreams*.

China and Japan from the radio, off the silver screen, from television, out of comic books, and from the pushers of white American culture..."[53] The Orientalist features of Disney's *Mulan* has already been examined at length.[54] Because of my own early racial formation, I want to explore the Americanization of Fa Mulan by Disney, and how it may affect the formation of racial and gender identity for young Chinese American females as they encounter this woman warrior of their ethnic heritage.

Disney's *Mulan* transforms the legend of our ancient Chinese heroine into a Western animated family feature film for a global market. Although she has Chinese features, Mulan seems to be a typical American teenager facing issues of identity and purpose. Like all Disney females, she sets out on a journey to discover her true self, one that involves plenty of adventure and a little romance. The cross-dressing aspect of the legend is particularly highlighted and conflated with the Confucian ideals regarding gender and family honor. In order to make a good impression on the matchmaker, Mulan is forced to undergo an extensive beauty treatment and complete clothing makeover. Playing during this makeover, the song "Honor to Us All" is replete with Chinese gender stereotypes:

> Men want girls with good taste,
> Calm,
> Obedient
> Who work fast-paced
> With good breeding
> And a tiny waist.
> You'll bring honor to us all.

After she blows her interview with the matchmaker, she expresses her search for identity in singing "Reflection":

> Who is this girl I see
> Staring straight
> Back at me?
> Why is my reflection someone
> I don't know?
> Somehow I cannot hide
> Who I am
> Though I've tried

---

53. Chin, *Aiiieeeee!*, xi–xii.

54. Dong, *Mulan's Legend and Legacy*, 159–87; Ma, "Mulan Disney"; Chan, "Disneyfying and Globalizing the Chinese Legend Mulan"; Wang and Yeh, "Globalization and Hybridization"; Tang, "A Cross-Cultural Perspective."

When will my reflection show
Who I am inside?

In contrast to the "Ballad of Mulan," Disney's Mulan makes a big display of seizing her father's sword, cutting off her hair, putting on her father's armor, and replacing her father's military summons with her decorative hair comb. The cross-dressing makes the transformation from female to male visually explicit.[55] Although Mulan struggles to play the part of a man, it is also clear that her male comrades fall short of the ideal manhood. General Li Shang, Mulan's potential love interest, scornfully sings at his troops:

You're a spineless, pale pathetic lot,
And you haven't got a clue
Somehow I'll make a man out of you.

The cross-dressing acquires a humorous reversal toward the end of the movie. In order to infiltrate the palace and save the Emperor from the evil clutches of Shan Yu, Mulan's comrades deck themselves in female clothing and pose as concubines.[56] While Shan Yu's thugs drool over and are beset by these cross-dressers, "I'll Make a Man Out of You" ironically plays in the background.

In contrast to other Disney films where the male hero rescues the female lead, Mulan actually saves Li Shang at several points in the film. She, not Li Shang, also dispatches the film's villain. In the slaying of Shan Yu, Mulan snaps open her fan (a feminine artifact) to catch and twist Shan Yu's sword (a masculine one) out of his hand. Reminiscent for me of Jael's killer tent peg, Shan Yu is then blown away by a giant phallic firecracker that hits him in his groin.

Plenty of academic articles exist that examine the influence of Disney on gender and race,[57] but none on the influence of Disney's Mulan on the racial formation of young Asian American girls specifically. I

---

55. A Disney movie poster, in dramatic Chinese red featuring Mulan in full military garb, astride a noble horse, with both staring fiercely as an unseen enemy, can be viewed at Wikipedia, s.v. "*Mulan* (1998 film)," https://en.wikipedia.org/wiki/Mulan_%281998_film%29. See also https://archive.nytimes.com/www.nytimes.com/imagepages/2006/03/19/arts/19solo_ready.html/. for a scene where Mulan leads a cavalry charge. Her love interest, Li Shange, is on the white horse to her left.

56. The cross-dressed concubines can be seen at https://www.fanpop.com/clubs/disney-princess/images/16075306/title/mulan-photo/.

57. Bell, et al., *From Mouse to Mermaid*; Brode, *Multiculturalism and the Mouse*; Ayers, *The Emperor's Old Groove*.

therefore combed the Web and blogs of Asian-Pacific Americans.[58] One in particular stands out, because it echoes some of the themes in Deryn Guest's queer study of Jael. Twenty-four-year-old Mimi Nguyen describes herself as a Vietnamese refugee-tomboy from "the swampy environs of a Midwestern small town."[59] As children, she and a fellow Latina migrant assimilated the identities of strong female icons, e.g., Bionic Woman and Wonder Woman, to help them survive as strangers in a strange land. However, all of these icons were "white as snow." Nguyen eventually finds her ethnic avatar in the Disney Mulan—"an Asian tomboy too butch for the bride gig"—and reads the film as gender subversion:

> What's amazing is the sly acknowledgement that gender norms are socially constructed—both masculinity and femininity are exposed as elaborate performances—while concurring that these same gender norms prove to be the source of much injustice. Never mind feudal China, it's a critique that resonates in contemporary U.S. society. So throw in lots of drag and transvestitism, "Mulan" becomes a veritable boiling pot of gender trouble.[60]

Nguyen tackles the question whether one should dismiss Disney's *Mulan* simply as a consumerist ploy to cash in on the global multicultural market or see it as a validation that Asian American has finally made it culturally on the big-screen. Nguyen opts for neither: "So let's get over the obvious, the bad dog/good dog scenario. We give too little credit to the power of the imagination if we believe either that until 'Mulan,' little Asian American girls floundered without inspiration or, on the other hand, that with 'Mulan,' little Asian American girls are ripe for conglomerate-sponsored consumer conformity."[61] Instead, for Nguyen there is a third space, a place in-between, where "we can juggle our critiques and our pleasures with the complexity of analysis they deserved," even though she

---

58. Among white audiences, Mulan seems to rate very highly. After researching many parents, dweeb posts an opinion on *fanpop!*, ranking the nine Disney princesses on terms of being good role models for young girls. Mulan was the number-one choice—"the ultimate Disney hero, male or female!"—and many responses to her blog concurred (dweeb, "Disney Princess.") For the opposite opinion, see Wilson, "Animated Children's Films: Mulan; The Twinkie Defense," who regards Disney's Mulan as a role model for a generation of "Twinkies," girls who are yellow (Asian) on the outside and white (American) on the inside, many of whom are adopted.

59. Nguyen, "Role Models: Mulan," 1.

60. Nguyen, "Role Models: Mulan," 2.

61. Nguyen, "Role Models: Mulan," 4.

acknowledges that she would have killed for a Mulan action figure when she was ten years old.[62]

And so would I!

Conclusion

Intercontextual overlaps exist between Jael of Judges 4 and the Chinese heroine Fa Mulan. Both women were warriors, one on the formal battlefield, the other in the informal arena of her tent. Their ethnic origins are a little suspect. Mulan may have been originally a non-Chinese heroine. We do not quite know Jael's ethnicity. Was she Israelite or Kenite? Both shared that slippery gendered space between male and female. As a result of this "gender blur," contradictory and conflicting interpretations of their narratives abound. Because of my own racial formation by American Orientalism, I was particularly focused on the representation of Fa Mulan by Disney, in which she becomes a spunky independent teen searching for her true self.

I have now come full circle in my study of Jael in Judges 4. This essay allowed me to catch-up on interesting research on Jael. But more importantly, it gave me a great excuse to examine contextually the Chinese woman-warrior Fa Mulan, something that I have been wanting to do since my 1993 article. And let's face it, since enjoying the Disney production *Mulan*, in spite of or maybe because of its American Orientalism. Perhaps if I had a Mulan action figure during my tender years, I would not have gravitated so readily to the woman-warrior Jael.

Postscript

I was fortunate to participate in the China study tour sponsored by my institution, Episcopal Divinity School, in May 2012. One of the stops was the important ancient capital city of Xi'an, where the Nestorian stele (781 CE) documents the presence of 150 years of Christianity in China. Also found in Xi'an are the famous terra cotta warriors of the first emperor of China, Qin Shi Huang. I took a detour to the exhibit and, in tourist mode, had the following picture taken to embody what Fa Mulan might have worn in one of her literary incarnations.

---

62. Nguyen, "Role Models: Mulan," 5.

Works Cited

Ackerman, Susan. *Warrior, Dancer, Seductress, Queen: Women in Judges and Biblical Israel.* Anchor Bible Reference Library. New York: Doubleday, 1998.

Ayers, Brenda. *The Emperor's Old Groove: Decolonizing Disney's Magic Kingdom.* New York: Lang, 2003.

Bell, Elizabeth, Lynda Haas, and Laura Sells. *From Mouse to Mermaid: The Politics of Film, Gender, and Culture.* Bloomington: Indiana University Press, 1995.

Bohn, Babette. "Death, Dispassion, and the Female Hero: Artemisia Gentileschi's Jael and Sisera." In *The Artemisia Files: Artemisia Gentileschi for Feminists and Other Thinking People,* edited by Mieke Bal, 107–27. Chicago: University of Chicago Press, 2005.

Boling, Robert G. *Judges: A New Translation with Introduction and Commentary.* AB 6A. Garden City, NY: Doubleday, 1975.

Bottigheimer, Ruth B. "Philogyny, Misogyny, and Erasure: Jael and Sisera." In *The Bible for Children from the Age of Gutenberg to the Present,* 142–51. New Haven: Yale University Press, 1996.

Brode, Douglas. *Multiculturalism and the Mouse: Race and Sex in Disney Entertainment.* Austin: University of Texas Press, 2005.

Butler, Judith. *Gender Trouble: Feminism and the Subversion of Identity.* Thinking Gender. London: Routledge, 1999.

Chan, Joseph M. "Disneyfying and Globalizing the Chinese Legend Mulan: A Study of Transculturation." In *In Search of Boundaries: Communication, Nation-States and Cultural Identities*, edited by Joseph M. Chan and Bryce T. McIntyre, 225–48. Advances in Communication and Culture. Westport, CT: Ablex, 2002.

Chin, Frank. *Aiiieeeee! An Anthology of Asian American Writers*. New York: Mentor, 1974.

Christiansen, Keith, and Judith Mann. "Jael and Sisera." In *Orazio and Artemisia Gentileschi*, 344–47. New York: Metropolitan Museum of Art, 2001.

Christianson, Eric S. "The Big Sleep: Strategic Ambiguity in Judges 4–5 and in Classic Film Noir." In *Images of the Word: Hollywood's Bible and Beyond*, 39–60. Semeia Studies 54. Atlanta: Society of Biblical Literature, 2008.

Dong, Lan. *Mulan's Legend and Legacy in China and the United States*. Philadelphia: Temple University Press, 2011.

dweeb. "Disney Princess Fan of the Month of April—Dweeb." *Fanpop*, 2009. https://www.fanpop.com/clubs/disney-princess/articles/54379/title/disney-princess-fan-month-april-dweeb.

Fewell, Danna Nolan, and David Miller Gunn. "Controlling Perspectives: Women, Men, and the Authority of Violence in Judges 4 & 5." *Journal of the American Academy of Religion* 58 (1990) 389–411.

Fleming, Robyn C. "Jael's Gender: A Story of Appropriation." November 9, 2005. https://revena.dreamwidth.org/128023.html#cutid1/.

Guest, Deryn. "From Gender Reversal to Genderfuck: Reading Jael through a Lesbian Lens." In *Bible Trouble: Queer Reading at the Boundaries of Biblical Scholarship*, edited by Teresa Hornsby and Ken Stone, 9–43. Semeia Studies 67. Atlanta: Society of Biblical Literature, 2011.

———. "Looking Lesbian at the Bathing Bathsheba." *BibInt* 16 (2008) 227–62.

Gunn, David M. *Judges*. Blackwell Bible Commentaries. Oxford: Blackwell, 2005.

Haber, Beth K. *Drawing on the Bible: Biblical Women in Art*. New York: Biblio, 1995.

Halpern, Baruch. "Kenites." In *ABD* 4 (1992) 17–22.

Harrington, D. J., trans. "Pseudo-Philo: A New Translation and Introduction." In *The Old Testament Pseudepigrapha*, edited by James H. Charlesworth, 2:296–377. 2 vols. Garden City. NY: Doubleday, 1985.

Jackson, Beverley. *Splendid Slippers: A Thousand Years of an Erotic Tradition*. Berkeley, CA: Ten Speed, 1997.

Kamionkowski, S. Tamar. "Queer Theory and Historical-Critical Exegesis: Queering Biblicists—A Response." In *Bible Trouble: Queer Reading at the Boundaries of Biblical Scholarship*, edited by Teresa Hornsby and Ken Stone, 131–36. Semeia Studies 67. Atlanta: Society of Biblical Literature, 2011.

Killebrew, Ann E. *Biblical Peoples and Ethnicity: An Archaeological Study of Egyptians, Canaanites, Philistines, and Early Israel 1300–1100 BCE*. Archaeology and Biblical Studies. Atlanta: Society of Biblical Literature, 2004.

Kingston, Maxine Hong. *The Woman Warrior: Memoirs of a Girlhood among Ghosts*. New York: Vintage, 1976.

Lan, Feng. "The Female Individual and the Empire: A Historicist Approach to Mulan and Kingston's Woman Warrior." *Comparative Literature* 55 (2003) 229–45.

Lee, Robert G. *Orientals: Asian Americans in Popular Culture*. Philadelphia: Temple University Press, 1999.

Leneman, Helen. "Re-Visioning a Biblical Story through Libretto and Music: Debora e Jaele by Ildebrando Pizzetti." *BibInt* 15 (2007) 428–63.

Li, Siu Leung. *Cross-Dressing in Chinese Opera*. Hong Kong: Hong Kong University Press, 2003.

Ma, Sheng-mei. "Mulan Disney, It's Like, Re-Orients: Consuming China and Animating Teen Dreams." In *The Emperor's Old Groove: Deconomizing Disney's Magic Kingdom*, edited by Brenda Ayres, 149–64. New York: Lang, 2003.

Ma, Sheng-Mei. *The Deathly Embrace: Orientalism and Asian American Identity*. Minneapolis: University of Minnesota Press, 2000.

Mann, Susan. "Myths of Asian Womanhood." *Journal of Asian Studies* 59 (2000) 835–62.

Mayfield, Tyler D. "The Accounts of Deborah (Judges 4–5) in Recent Research." *CBR* 7 (2009) 306–35.

Nguyen, Mimi. "Role Models: Mulan." *San Jose Mercury News*, July 5, 1998. http://www.theory.org.uk/ctr-rol2.htm/.

Okihiro, Gary Y. *Margins and Mainstreams: Asians in American History and Culture*. Seattle: University of Washington Press, 1994.

Robnolt, I'Laine. "Jael's Husband Returns from War after the Death of Sisera." *Daughters of Sarah* 21/3 (1995) 1.

Soggin, J. Alberto. *Judges: A Commentary*. OTL. Philadelphia: Westminster, 1981.

Tang, Jun. "A Cross-Cultural Perspective on Production and Reception of Disney's Mulan through Its Chinese Subtitles." *European Journal of English Studies* 12 (2008) 149–62.

Wang, Georgette, and Emilie Yueh-yu Yeh. "Globalization and Hybridization in Cultural Products: The Cases of *Mulan* and *Crouching Tiger, Hidden Dragon*." *International Journal of Cultural Studies* 8 (2005) 175–93.

Wilson, Karina. "Animated Children's Films: Mulan: The Twinkie Defense." *Bitch Flicks*, 2011. http://www.btchflcks.com/2011/11/animated-childrens-films-mulan-the-twinkie-defense.html/.

Yamashita, Karen Tei. *The Tropic of Orange*. Minneapolis: Coffee House, 1997.

Yee, Gale A. "'By the Hand of a Woman': The Biblical Metaphor of the Woman Warrior." *Semeia* 61 (1993) 99–132.

———. "Inculturation and Diversity in the Politics of National Identity." *JAAAT* 2 (1997) 108–12.

———. "The Woman Warrior Revisited: Jael, Fa Mulan, and American Orientalism." In *Joshua and Judges*, edited by Athalya Brenner and Gale A. Yee, 175–90. Texts@Contexts. Minneapolis: Fortress, 2013.

———. "Yin/Yang Is not Me: An Exploration into an Asian American Biblical Hermeneutics." In *Ways of Being, Ways of Reading: Asian-American Biblical Interpretation*, edited by Mary F. Foskett and Jeffrey K. Kuan, 152–63. St. Louis: Chalice, 2006.

Yellow Bridge (website). "Ode to Mulan." http://www.yellowbridge.com/onlinelit/mulan.php/.

9

Coveting the Vineyard

An Asian American Reading of 1 Kings 21

Disclaimer

WHEN I WAS ASKED to present a paper on an Asian American reading of 1 Kings 21, the Naboth Vineyard affair, I readily accepted.[1] I was already writing a commentary on 1 and 2 Kings, how hard could it be? However, when I actually started thinking about an actual Asian American reading of this passage, things became more problematic for me methodologically. My concerns definitely had implications on how we racial/ethnic scholars develop a minoritized criticism. I am therefore beginning this essay with a metacommentary on reading a scriptural passage from a racial and ethnic context.

I knew that I did not want to replicate the anachronistic Asian American attempt a few years ago in one of the SBL sessions, which unsuccessfully read the Sarah and Hagar story as examples of Asian American "Tiger Moms" and "Helicopter Moms."[2] At the start, I just could

---

1. This paper was originally presented in the "Minoritized Criticism and Biblical Interpretation" section at the 2013 Society of Biblical Literature (SBL) Annual Meeting in Baltimore. Different members of minoritized groups focused on 1 Kings 21 from their particular racial-ethnic contexts. It has been published in *Samuel, Kings, and Chronicles*, edited by Athalya Brenner-Idan and Archie C. C. Lee. 46–64. Texts@Contexts. New York: Bloomsbury, 2016.

2. "Tiger Mother/Mom" and "Helicopter Mom" are two Asian stereotypes of Chinese parenting. Tiger Moms are very strict in the upbringing of their children.

not conceptualize an Asian American reading of the Naboth vineyard story. In the first place, I could not separate the Asian American part of me from the feminist part, the historical-critical part, the literary-critical part, or the social-historian part in any analysis I would undertake. When I sat down to analyze the text, one idea would come to me, and I would throw it out as too historical-critical, not Asian American. Or another approach, and I would discard it as too literary-critical, because it might not be recognizable as an Asian American reading. I realized that I could not separate these parts of me, who I am, how I was trained, and my particular exegetical expertise in a number of methods to perform an Asian American reading. In true postcolonial form, I am a hybrid with all the nouns and adjectives we embody with regard to race, gender, class, and, I must add, exegetical training and knowhow. Whatever analysis I do will be an Asian American, feminist, middle-class, sociohistorical, literary-critical, and so forth, reading. This hybridity should be acknowledged in whatever reading we do as minoritized critics.

Second, I found being given the actual text to read from my Asian American perspective to be quite artificial. Although I understood the intent, namely, to experience how different racial and ethnic minorities approach the same text, I bristled at the thought of "forcing" an Asian American reading upon a particular text. Previous readings of the biblical text from my Asian American social location arose more organically, connecting more naturally with the complex aspects of my personal and societal experiences of being Asian American. Although there is comparative value of seeing different racial/ethnic readings of the same passage, I thought the process of imposing an Asian American reading on a text given to me was unnatural. As I talked with other presenters, I discovered that this feeling of artificiality was shared.

Who Is an Asian American?

Having said all this, I was eventually able to arrive at an analysis of 1 Kings 21 from an Asian American perspective.[3] Because 1 Kings 21 narrates the illegal appropriation of land by the royal court, I looked for parallels in

Helicopter Moms "hover" like helicopters over their children's experiences and education.

3. I am very grateful to Thomas Eoyang for his many suggestions for resources when I started investigating this Asian American reading, and to Margie Yamamoto for her own personal experiences of living in a Japanese internment camp as a child.

Asian American history in which the state or government illegitimately seized the land or property of Asian Americans. I saw several touchstones between 1 Kings 21 and the Japanese internment in so-called "evacuation camps" during World War II. One of the takeaways for me in researching this paper as a Chinese American is learning the terrible history of my Japanese American brothers and sisters. A number of different ethnic groups are awkwardly lumped under the umbrella term "Asia American": Chinese, Japanese, Korean, Filipino, Hmong, Thai, Vietnamese, Cambodian, Laotian, Burmese, Indian, and so forth. These groups have different immigration histories and experiences in coming to and living in the United States. When doing an Asian American reading, one's positionality within and in relation to these various groups needs to be considered.

The Case of Japanese Americans and 1 Kings 21

I grew up in a family where Japanese/Chinese relations were very conflicted. My maternal grandparents hated the Japanese after the destruction of their ancestral village in the Toishan district of southern China during the Sino-Japanese war of the late 1930s and early 1940s. The Toishan region was particularly hard hit by the Japanese.[4] One of the worst atrocities of that war was known as the "Rape of Nanking," during which the imperial Japanese army raped, tortured, and slaughtered hundreds of thousands of civilians in China's capital city, Nanjing, in December 1937.[5] After the Japanese bombing of Pearl Harbor on December 7, 1941, my maternal aunts and uncles who lived in Seattle's Chinatown and my mother who lived in Butte, Montana, all wore badges saying "I am Chinese," lest white people stigmatized them as the Japanese enemy. After decades of social, cultural, and institutional racism, the Chinese in the US were now seen as loyal, hardworking, honest allies, while the Japanese had become treacherous, warlike, and cruel.[6] My aunt reports that the Chinese wore these badges even after the Japanese were evacuated and told me that she wished she had saved them as historical family artifacts. Two other aunts on my mother's side had the audacity to marry Japanese men after World War II, breaking my grandparents' hearts.

---

4. Chang, *The Chinese in America*, 216.
5. Chang, *The Rape of Nanking*.
6. Takaki, *Strangers from a Different Shore*, 370–71; Lee, *Orientals*, 145–49.

The problem in comparing the Asian American experience with Ahab's land grab of Naboth's vineyard/property is the fact that for a good part of their early history in the US the Chinese and Japanese were not able to own land because of anti-immigrant and alien land laws. Particularly in the Western states where most immigrant Asians settled, laws were passed that declared that an applicant had to be eligible for naturalization in order to be qualified for property ownership. Because Asians were barred from becoming naturalized citizens, they were not eligible to own property. Significant is the fact that the 1870 Naturalization Act had removed the "white only" restriction on citizenship that had been in force since 1790 and had expanded naturalization rights to those of African descent. Those foreigners who were of neither white nor African descent were not eligible for citizenship, and therefore not eligible to own property. This became a legal way to limit the rights of Asian immigrants without specifying a particular racial group in the language of the law. The California Alien Land Law of 1913 did target Japanese immigrants specifically in response to anti-Japanese hysteria. Because they were barred from becoming citizens, they were ineligible to own land and also ineligible to hold long-term leases of agricultural land, which constituted much of their livelihood. Some Japanese found their way around this law by purchasing land through white intermediaries or in the names of their US-born citizen children.[7]

Before Pearl Harbor, President Franklin D. Roosevelt commissioned Chicago businessman Charles Munson to gather intelligence on the Japanese in the US to see if they were indeed a military threat. Munson's findings revealed no evidence of Japanese American disloyalty or threat of fifth-column sympathies among the *Issei* (first-generation Japanese immigrants) and the *Nisei* (their American-born children).[8] Munson quipped that perhaps the Japanese were "more in danger from the whites than the other way around."[9] However, his evidence and others were suppressed in favor of full-throttle, anti-Japanese hysteria and demands for Japanese evacuation and containment in the Western states.[10]

---

7. Lyon, "Alien Land Laws."
8. Kitagawa, *Issei and Nisei*.
9. Weglyn, "The Secret Munson Report."
10. Japanese Americans living in Hawaii were not interned, due to the resistance of General Delos Emmons, the military governor of Hawaii, and widespread local opposition to internment, particularly in the Hawaiian business community, who knew that evacuation of over one-third of Hawaii's population would decimate their labor

In response to the bombing of Pearl Harbor, Roosevelt signed Executive Order 9066[11] on February 19, 1942, authorizing military commanders to designate military areas from which any person could be excluded. Although the Japanese were not directly specified in Roosevelt's order, they were its principal targets. Roosevelt evidently had been considering the internment of Japanese five years before the attack on Pearl Harbor.[12]

Arguing that "military necessity" justified his racist actions, General John ("A Jap's a Jap") DeWitt then issued over one hundred military orders to remove and incarcerate over 110,000 civilians of Japanese ancestry living in the areas designated as Military Area 1 of Washington state, Oregon, California, and Arizona.[13] The amount of time for evacuation depended on where one lived. The Japanese residents of Terminal Island were informed on February 25, 1942, that they had forty-eight hours to leave the island. Terminal Island was located near an Army base and a Naval Station, so it was considered a high priority by the military to get them removed.[14] Those living in San Francisco were given a week to leave. They were to bring with them bedding, toilet articles, extra clothing, and eating implements for each member of the family.[15] They were then taken to ten incarceration camps primarily in remote desert areas, where they lived an isolated, highly regimented life surrounded by barbed wire and security towers.[16] Regarding this abhorrent part of US history, the report, *Personal Justice Denied*,[17] that summarized the finding of the 1980 Commission on Wartime Relocation and Internment of Citizens, concluded that the broad historical causes of the Japanese internment was not

---

force and destroy the island economy (Takaki 1998: 380–85)

11. http://www.ourdocuments.gov/doc.php?flash=false&doc=74&page=transcript.

12. See Robinson, *By Order of the President*; and Takaki, *Strangers from a Different Shore*, 390.

13. Smith, "Racial Nativism and the Origins of Japanese American Relocation," 82; see the map of the military areas and detention camps at http://www.historyonthenet.com/ww2/japan_internment_camps.htm/.

14. Margie Yamamoto in a personal communication.

15. See the exclusion poster at http://encyclopedia.densho.org/sources/en-denshopd-p25-00049-1/.

16. Ng, *Japanese American Internment*, 13–54; Daniels et al., eds., *Japanese Americans*.

17. US Commission on Wartime Relocation and Internment of Civilians (George Miller, chairman), *Personal Justice Denied*.

military necessity but "race prejudice, war hysteria and a failure of political leadership."

The "sons of Belial" falsely accused Naboth of cursing "God and king" (1 Kgs 21:10, 13), crimes which I interpret as blasphemy and treason. Patriotic Japanese Americans were falsely suspected of being traitors in sympathy with the war mongering Japanese emperor. The coastal areas of the Western states were deemed military zones that were vulnerable to Japanese attack, providing a rationale for Japanese American evacuation, even though there was no evidence of hostile or fifth-column activities among them. Moreover, it was also clear that white farmers wanted the Japanese Americans removed because they coveted their productive farmlands. The Grower-Shipper Vegetable Association was quoted saying in the *Saturday Evening Post*: "We've been charged with wanting to get rid of the Japs for selfish reasons. We might as well be honest. We do. It's a question of whether the white man lives on the Pacific Coast or the brown man . . . If all the Japs were removed tomorrow, we'd never miss them in two weeks, because the white farmers can take over and produce everything the Jap grows."[18]

Although 1 Kgs 21:2 expressly states that Ahab coveted Naboth's vineyard in Jezreel as a vegetable garden, 2 Kgs 9:21, 25 simply states "Naboth's property/portion" (*ḥelqat nābôt*), referring to Naboth's property in general. There are differences between these two accounts, which have occasioned much debate regarding the original story and its redactional history.[19] For example, in 1 Kings 21, Naboth's murder is accomplished through Jezebel's sly maneuverings, whereas these are not mentioned in 2 Kgs 9:21, 25–26, where only Ahab is accused. 2 Kings 9:26 cites the murder of Naboth's sons, while 1 Kings 21 does not. This difference in the perpetrator of the crime will be significant in the characterizations of Jezebel and Ahab, as we will see.

From a materialist perspective of ninth-century Israel, Ahab had good economic and military reasons for desiring this prime piece of real estate. The Jezreel Valley was known, first and foremost, as a rich agricultural region. Even in the Late Bronze Age, the annals of Thutmose III described a harvest of 207,300 [+] sacks of wheat, besides forage, from the areas around Megiddo.[20] A large spring ('Ein Jezreel) supplied a constant

18. Cited in Takaki, *Strangers from a Different Shore*, 398.

19. Cronauer, *The Stories about Naboth the Jezreelite*; Na'aman, "Naboth's Vineyard and the Foundation of Jezreel."

20. Wilson, "The Asiatic Campaigns of Thot-mose III," 238.

source of water. Furthermore, the area had access to the major highways of the time, such as the Via Maris (Way of the Sea) and one leading from Megiddo to Beth-Shean. The city also served as the northernmost point on the local highway, the Way of the Patriarchs that connected the northern valleys with the central mountain cities of Shechem, Samaria, Bethel, and Jerusalem.[21] These various routes suited Ahab's interests in maintaining good relations with his international trading partners. His marriage to Jezebel facilitated his economic and political alliances with Phoenicia, his neighboring partner to the north.

Besides being located in a rich agricultural area, Jezreel was also an important military center. The archaeology of the site reveals a large casement enclosure, similar to an Assyrian structure, Fort Shalmaneser, whose military function was well known. The chapters before and after this story deal with the Ahab's war with the Arameans (1 Kings 20, 22). Ahab most likely wanted Jezreel as an agricultural and military base to feed and house his sizeable cavalry and chariot units. Its location was ideal for assembling, outfitting, and dispatching troops to fight in Aram and in the Transjordan.[22] Barley, an important part of the diet of warhorses, was cultivated in the eastern part of the Valley of Jezreel.[23] Horses can consume ten times more grain than humans on a daily basis, even more during times of war, and this too needed to be extracted from the rural sectors, along with the huge food quotas for human tables (cf. 1 Kgs 4:27–28). According to the Kurkh Monolith, Ahab possessed enough horses (4,000–6,000) to pull two thousand chariots in a campaign against the Assyrian King Shalmaneser III.[24] His concern in 1 Kgs 18:5 to provide watering holes and grasses to keep his horses and mules alive, rather than provisioning his own starving people during the three-year drought, was thus quite plausible. What little arable land and water to be had during this drought was thus diverted from food production for the people to pastureland for Ahab's vast number of animals.

Therefore, in both the narrative of Naboth's vineyard and in the Japanese internment, "military necessity" and economic greed for agricultural land allegedly dictated the course of events: the unlawful seizure

---

21. Cline, *The Battles of Armageddon*; Grabbe, "The Kingdom of Israel from Omri to the Fall of Samaria"; Ebeling et al., "Jezreel Revealed in Laser Scans."
22. Aster, "The Function of the City of Jezreel," 37–39.
23. Ussishkin, "Samaria, Jezreel and Megiddo," 301–2.
24. Cantrell, *The Horsemen of Israel*, 36.

of land, on the one hand, and the criminal removal of people from the land, on the other.

I did not find any deliberate illegal confiscations of Japanese American land during their US internment that would have been comparable to Jezebel's illegal confiscation of Naboth's vineyard, primarily because Japanese Americans usually did not own land at the time.[25] However, upon entering World War II, the financial assets of many Japanese were frozen and taken over by the US government. Those who had money in Japanese-owned banks no longer had access to their funds. Business transactions between the two countries ceased, because the US was at war with Japan.[26] For the evacuation itself, a Civil Control Station supposedly provided "services with respect to the management, leasing, sale, storage or other disposition of most kinds of property including: real estate, business and professional equipment, buildings, household goods, boats, automobiles, livestock, etc."[27] Nevertheless, when the incarcerated returned to their property in 1945, they often were deprived of their possessions by being cheated out of them by the "friends" who held them, or forced to dispose of them cheaply to scavengers and speculators, or left with no alternative but to abandon them.[28]

Although the Supreme Court never ruled that the removal and incarceration of Japanese Americans was unconstitutional, historians and political analysts have described the violations that they believe have occurred.[29] A summary of constitutional rights violated can be found on the website of the Japanese American Citizens League (JACL).[30] According to Amendment XIV Section. 1, of the Bill of Rights:

---

25. However, I did discover that the Anglican Canadian diocese of New Westminster sold two churches in Vancouver of Japanese Canadian parishioners while they were interned. The Council of General Synod publicly acknowledged the racism and injustice to these parishioners only recently on March 14, 2013. See Sison, "Injustices toward Japanese Canadian Anglicans Acknowledged."

26. Ng, *Japanese American Internment*, 14.

27. See the exclusion poster at https://jacl.org/wordpress/wp-content/uploads/2015/01/Exclusion-Poster.pdf/.

28. Robinson, *By Order of the President*, 249; see also "Return to the West Coast," in *Densho Encyclopedia*; http://encyclopedia.densho.org/Return%20to%20West%20Coast/.

29. Yamamoto et al., *Race, Rights, and Reparations*.

30. Japanese American Citizens League, "Summary of Constitutional Rights Violated"; http://www.jacl.org/edu/SummaryofConstitutionalRightsViolated.pdf/.

> All persons born or naturalized in the United States and subject to the jurisdiction thereof are citizens of the United States and of the State wherein they reside. No State shall make or enforce any law, which shall abridge the privileges or immunities of citizens of the United States; nor shall any State deprive any person of life, liberty, or property, without due process of law; nor deny to any person within its jurisdiction the equal protection of the laws.[31]

Japanese Americans were singled out primarily on the basis of race and national ancestry with no due process under the law, and the government failed to compensate them for their loss of property when they were evacuated under such short notice. Only with the passage more than forty years later of the Civil Liberties Act of 1988 was there a national apology and a $20,000 compensation from the US government given to surviving Japanese American detainees for their traumatic ordeal.[32]

Furthermore, my former Chinese American colleague, Patrick Cheng, who is also a lawyer as well as a systematic theologian, directed me to a legal doctrine called "regulatory taking," defined by Wikipedia as "a situation in which a government regulates a property to such a degree that the regulation effectively amounts to an exercise of the government's eminent domain power without actually divesting the property's owner of title to the property."[33] In other words, the government does not have to physically seize property in order for it to be considered a taking. The article also goes on to say, "Governmental land-use regulations that deny the property owner any economically viable use are deemed a taking of the affected property."[34] I am not a lawyer, but it seems that a similar argument can be made that the internment deprived Japanese Americans of the economic use of their land or property by sequestering them from it, and that this action can be considered a governmental taking of property that required compensation. I therefore think that the illegal seizure of land and property by the governing bodies are commonalities in both the Naboth story of 1 Kings 21 and the Japanese American experience of internment.

---

31. http://www.ushistory.org/documents/amendments.htm/.

32. Ng, *Japanese American Internment*, 108–10.

33. Wikipedia, s.v. "Regulatory Taking," *http://en.wikipedia.org/wiki/Regulatory_taking/*.

34. Wikipedia, s.v. "Regulatory Taking," *http://en.wikipedia.org/wiki/Regulatory_taking/*.

Ahab and Jezebel

Besides reading 1 Kings 21 in light of the Japanese internment, the characters of Ahab and his queen, Jezebel, offer other avenues in which to pursue an Asian American reading of the passage. The demonization of Jezebel in 1 Kings 21 as a foreign woman has parallels with the "Dragon Lady" stereotype[35] that has plagued Asian American women. Likewise, the satirical disparagement of Ahab's manhood finds similar analogues in the construction of Asian and Asian American masculinity. We are introduced to Jezebel in 1 Kgs 16:31 as the daughter of King Ethbaal of the Sidonians who entered into a political marriage with Ahab, son of the powerful Israelite king Omri. Next, we discover her "killing off the prophets of the Lord," while four hundred and fifty prophets of Baal and four hundred prophets of the goddess Asherah ate at her table during Israel's divinely ordained three-year drought (18:4, 13, 19). The text implies that her group of foreign freeloaders enjoyed the rare consumption of food while the rest of the nation starved. After Elijah slaughtered the prophets of Baal following their encounter on Mount Carmel (18:40), Jezebel, speaking for the first time in the narrative, issued a death sentence against Elijah, who fled for his life. Jezebel probably did not intend to kill Elijah, which would have made him a martyr. Rather, her death threat was a clever tactic to make him flee, because this would have compromised his victory on Mount Carmel.[36] The portrayal of Jezebel delineated so far is of a ruthless, cunning, and idolatrous foreign queen.

With this characterization in mind, we thus arrive at the focus of this essay: 1 Kgs 21:1–16.[37] After Ahab's abortive attempt to buy Naboth's vineyard, Jezebel encounters a "resentful and sullen" Ahab, lying on his bed and not eating (21:4). Being "resentful and sullen" (*sar wĕzāʿēf*) seems to be a signature feature of Ahab's personality (cf. 20:43). After hearing the reason for his depression, her exclamation in 21:7, *ʾattâ ʾattâ taʿăśeh mĕlûkâ ʿal-yiśrāʾēl*, can be translated as a question, "Do you now govern Israel?" (NRSV), or as an asseverative, "Now you will exercise kingship over Israel!" Or it can be read sarcastically, "Some king

---

35. "Dragon Lady" is a stereotype of a strong, sexually seductive, duplicitous Asian woman.

36. Merecz, "Jezebel's Oath (1 Kgs 19,2)."

37. In good company with a number of scholars who see a break between vv. 16 and 17, this essay confines itself to 1 Kgs 21:1–16. (See Cronauer, *The Stories about Naboth the Jezreelite*, 116.)

of Israel you make!" (NJB). In light of the following discussion, this last rendering is to be preferred. In contrast to her sulky royal spouse, Jezebel proclaims, using the emphatic first-person pronoun, "*I* (*'ănî*) will give you the vineyard of Naboth the Jezreelite" (21:7). *She* will accomplish what her impotent husband cannot.

Taking charge, Jezebel writes letters in Ahab's name, fastening them with his seal and sending them to the elders and nobles who live with Naboth in Jezreel. She orders them to proclaim a fast, seat Naboth at the head of the assembly, have two good-for-nothings falsely accuse Naboth of cursing "God and King," and then take him out to be stoned (21:8-14). After she hears about the successful outcome of these events, Jezebel proclaims to Ahab, "Go, take possession of the vineyard of Naboth the Jezreelite, which he refused to give you for money; for Naboth is not alive but dead." Ahab then goes down and takes possession of the vineyard (21:15-16).

1 Kings 21 depicts Jezebel as the main actor of the narrative, wielding considerable authority in her position as queen. She does not hesitate to write in Ahab's name and use his seal. The elders and the nobles obey her commands without hesitation, even when they include framing an innocent person and having him put to death. Moreover, Ahab does not reprimand her for acting in his name and appropriating his royal seal, nor is there any suggestion that her exercise of power is restricted to this one instance. She is presented as an active partner in her husband's rule and a cold-blooded one at that. Nevertheless, while portraying Jezebel as a royal force to be reckoned with, the author simultaneously represents the actual king as an ineffectual leader, who could not acquire the vineyard in the first place and sulks about it like a child in his bedroom, provoking his spouse to deride his masculinity, "Some king of Israel you make!"

The ensuing depictions of Jezebel enlarge upon this portrait. According to the Deuteronomist, Jezebel "urged" her husband on to do what was evil in God's sight so that there was no other king like him in Israel (21:25). She is accused of "whoredoms and sorceries," promoting the sexual/religious apostasies of the cult of Baal and Asherah in Israel (2 Kgs 9:22). Even when confronting her imminent demise, she exhibits dramatic flair. After adorning her head and painting her eyes, she meets on her own terms Jehu, who slaughtered her family and is coming after her (9:30). If she is going to her death, she will go as a woman aware of her sexual power. She stands defiantly at the window as queen mother, as other royal women in the Bible have done (Judg 5:28; 2 Sam 6:16).

Her depiction at the window may allude to her patronage of the goddess Asherah, whose prophets she underwrites, or may even be her symbolic incarnation as the goddess, whose worship Jehu tries to eradicate through Jezebel's death.[38] She taunts Jehu with fighting words: "Is it peace, Zimri, murderer of your master?" (2 Kgs 9:31).[39] However, she dies a disgraceful death, thrown from her window by her faithless harem eunuchs. Even so, her assassinator Jehu grudgingly acknowledges that as a king's daughter, she should be buried (9:32–34). Nevertheless, fulfilling Elijah's prophecy (1 Kgs 21:23), dogs consume most of her body before it could have an honorable burial. In a wordplay on her scribally distorted name from *zebul* ("nobility") to *zebel* ("dung"), her corpse "shall be like dung (*dōmen*) on the territory of Jezreel, so that no one can say, 'This is Jezebel'" (2 Kgs 9:35–37).[40]

Much has been written about the dating and redaction of the Elijah/Elisha narratives, and the Naboth's vineyard story in particular. A number of scholars argue that the traditions about Naboth in 2 Kgs 9:25–26 are earlier than 1 Kgs 21:1–16.[41] They especially point out that in the former the crime of murder is Ahab's alone, while in the latter Jezebel is its instigator. Even the earliest tradition, the "Elijah-Naboth fragment" in 1 Kgs 21:17–19a, pins the crime only onto Ahab.[42] For these scholars, a later fifth-century author retells the older story, shifting the crime from Ahab to Jezebel, to warn those returning to Yehud of the dangers of mixed marriages with foreign women (Neh 13:23–27; Ezra 9–10).[43]

The person of Jezebel in 1 Kgs 21:1–16 thus becomes an ideological construct for dealing with a perceived fifth-century sociopolitical dilemma. She is identified with comparable foreign women in Israel's social memory (cf. Num 25:1–3; 1 Kings 11), but her portrayal has been considerably enlarged. As sexually enticing idolaters, foreign women have been disparaged because they "seduce Israel away from YHWH." Jezebel's

---

38. Ackerman, *Warrior, Dancer, Seductress, Queen*, 160–61; Everhart, "Jezebel," 689–92; McKinlay, *Reframing Her*, 88–90.

39. Zimri, who assassinated the Israelite king Elah, was only able to hold on to his kingship for seven days (1 Kgs 16:15). Jezebel is thus insinuating that Jehu's own rule will be of short duration.

40. Gray, *I & II Kings*, 551.

41. Cronauer, *The Stories about Naboth the Jezreelite*; Rofé, "The Vineyard of Naboth," 101–2; and White, "Naboth's Vineyard and Jehu's Coup," 69.

42. Cronauer, *The Stories about Naboth the Jezreelite*, 8–9, 174.

43. Cf. Yee, *Poor Banished Children of Eve*, 143–46.

Persian period representation adds ruthless, scheming, and murderous features to this stereotype, as additional reasons to avoid foreign women in Yehud. Racial and gender stereotypes of the foreign woman in the biblical text are thus not fixed static ideas that are adopted during a crisis but are concepts that undergo a continual formation and reformation as the socioeconomic, political, and cultural interests that underlie them change.

The same is also true of the characterization of Ahab, who obviously was an important powerful Israelite king, a builder of houses and cities (1 Kgs 16:32; 22:39), one who can muster a force of two thousand chariots, ten thousand foot soldiers, and an alliance of twelve kings to engage the Assyrian ruler Shalmaneser III at the battle of Qarqar (853 BCE).[44] Yet, for the Deuteronomist, he becomes the wicked king whose evil becomes the measure by which the later villainous king Manasseh will be condemned (2 Kgs 22:13). He becomes the one who, "urged on by his wife," allows her to aggressively accomplish what he himself could not do, while he snivels and pouts in his bed 'resentful and sullen'. We will also see this continual formation and reformation in racial and gender stereotypes of Asians and Asian Americans through the course of US history.

A Chinese American Perspective

Full disclosure: During my undergraduate years in the last century my nickname was "Dragon Lady" and my used Plymouth Duster was named "Dusty Dragon," because it was painted Earl Scheib green.[45] I had no idea who "Dragon Lady" was except that she was Chinese, and so was I in a very white university. Nor was I aware that Dragon Lady was a negative racist, sexist, Orientalist stereotype. In my tender earlier years, I was susceptible to any image of strong Asian women to help shape my own identity as a Chinese American female in a white dominant culture. This was certainly the case in my attraction to the Chinese woman warrior figure of Mulan.[46] The Dragon Lady appellation highlighted my "difference" from racial/ethnic Others, including whites, in my educational setting.

---

44. Grabbe, "The Kingdom of Israel from Omri to the Fall of Samaria."

45. Earl Scheib was the founder of a now defunct US automobile paint company. The green used to paint his cars was particularly bright, distinctive and hideous, marking one as working class.

46. I have written about my attraction to the Woman Warrior metaphor in Judges 4 in a number of articles (Yee, "'By the Hand of a Woman,'"; Yee, "Yin/Yang Is Not Me";

In order to understand the Dragon Lady and Fu Manchu[47] stereotypes of American Orientalism, one must recognize the construction of Asian American gender, race, and sexuality under white hegemonic masculinity. This construction was deeply rooted in the history of Chinese immigration and their experiences of racism and violence in their settlement here. From the mid-1800s onwards, Chinese arrived in the US to work in the mines and the transcontinental railroad. Most of these were male, because of xenophobic immigration restrictions in bringing wives and women from China. Anti-miscegenation laws barred Chinese men from developing heterosexual relationships with white women. US businesses wanted cheap, plentiful, and hardworking Chinese males as laborers to work in these dangerous occupations but did not want them to settle and breed. With no women around, these men formed "bachelor societies," forced to cook, clean, and launder for themselves. When jobs in mining and the railroad diminished and the competition with whites in other industries became fierce, Asian men were relegated to "women's work," taking feminized jobs as houseboys,[48] or opening restaurants and laundries.[49] "The homosocial elements of the bachelor communities and the domestic practices of men living in them had an emasculating effect on the racial discourse."[50] We will see this emasculation in the stereotypes of Asian American males.[51] The few women who were brought from China were forced into prostitution to service these bachelor societies.[52] The stigma of carnality and prostitution attached to these early women from China will eventually evolve into the sexually transgressive figure of Dragon Lady.

---

and most recently, Yee, "The Woman Warrior Revisited.").

47. Fu Manchu was a villainous fictional character in Sax Rohmer novels, which became an Asian stereotype that arose in the US during the early to middle 1900s, when US/Asian animosity was at its peak. And see further below.

48. Cf. Hop Sing on the popular US TV series *Bonanza*.

49. Hence the proverbial ethnic slur, "No tickee, no washee." See Chang, *The Chinese in America*, 48–49; Lee, *Orientals*, 97–105.

50. Chou, *Asian American Sexual Politics*, 16.

51. Chan, *Chinese American Masculinities*.

52. Chang, *The Chinese in America*, 81–92; Lee, *Orientals*, 89–91.

American Orientalism and the Cultural "Yellow Peril"

American Orientalism refocused Edward Said's *Orientalism* (1994) of the Middle East by asserting the political, social, and cultural superiority of the United States and European Americans and the inferiority of the same for Asia and Asian Americans.[53] Depending on the particular circumstances, American Orientalism constructed Asian men in contradictory and conflicting ways as "asexual, impotent, hypersexed and violent" and Asian women similarly as "obedient, servile, sexually voracious and cruel." It did not depict the lives of *real* Asian or Asian American men and women. Stereotypes of Asian men and women changed to reflect the political realities and racial and gender ideologies of the time in the US. During the late 1800s the designation "Yellow Peril" was applied to the influx of Chinese laborers that became a threat to white workers. Japan's expansion into Asia in 1910 also aroused fears of the Yellow Peril endangering the American way of life.

The Yellow Peril was epitomized in two Orientalist cultural icons of the early 1900s. The first was the beautiful but cruel Dragon Lady, embodied in the first female, Asian American film star, Anna May Wong.[54] In the role that launched her career, *Thief of Baghdad* (1924), she played a duplicitous Mongol slave girl who betrayed the princess she served by assisting an equally villainous Oriental prince, who wanted the princess's hand in marriage. Wong personified the mysterious, exotic, sexually seductive, and dangerous features of Asian and Asian American womanhood depicted in American Orientalism. She would go on to star in *Daughter of the Dragon* (1931),[55] which was based on the novel *Daughter of Fu Manchu* by Sax Rohmer, where she plays another beautiful but murderous Asian exotic, Fu Manchu's illegitimate daughter. Her role in this film was an inspiration for the "Dragon Lady" in the 1934 Chicago Tribune cartoon series *Terry and the Pirates*, the beautiful but deadly Asian ringleader of the pirates.[56]

Dr. Fu Manchu incarnated the Yellow Peril in an Oriental face and male body over a forty-year period of Sax Rohmer novels, radio shows, films, and comics that featured him. Fu Manchu wanted to bring the

---

53. Leong, *China Mystique*, 2.

54. Leong, *China Mystique*; Prasso, *The Asian Mystique*, 77–83.

55. Wikipedia, s.v. *Daughter of the Dragon*, https://en.wikipedia.org/wiki/Daughter_of_the_Dragon/.

56. Prasso, *The Asian Mystique*, 80.

world under the rule of an Oriental Empress "of incalculably ancient lineage, residing in some secret monastery in Tartary or Tibet."[57] Besides his desire to bring the world under feminine domination, the alien silken robes and long fingernails of Fu Manchu highlighted his sexual ambiguity, a blend of feminine masochism with sadistic machismo that reflected his racial and gendered background of the Chinese Orient (female) and his Western scientific education (male). The hetero/homoerotic blur of his sexuality was contrasted with the healthy, controlled masculinity of his British nemesis Nayland Smith.[58] Fu Manchu became the model for a similar villain of my youth, Ming the Merciless of the planet Mongo in the *Flash Gordon* television series, which I avidly watched. Like Fu Manchu, Ming the Merciless was a diabolical Oriental male, dead set on conquest. His archenemy was the blond all-American hero Flash Gordon.[59]

When Japan attacked China in the 1930s, the Hollywood images of the Chinese changed. Dragon Lady morphed into O-Lan of Pearl Buck's *The Good Earth*, the hard-working, long-suffering peasant, played in the film version by the white actress Luise Rainer in yellow-face (1937). Her male film counterpart, spouting fortune cookie Confucianisms, was the obsequious inscrutable detective Charlie Chan, also played by white actors in yellow-face. Contrasting the threatening Fu Manchu, here was another stereotype of Chinese American males: smart, subservient, feminine, the prototypical "model minority." Although he evidently had ten children, his virility was belied by his asexual affect.[60]

The Japanese especially became the villain after their attack on Pearl Harbor (December 7, 1941). However, with the rise of evil Communist China and the recovery of Japan after World War II, the Japanese became the "good guys." They were represented visually in films dealing with the deferential Japanese geisha girls who catered to G.I.'s stationed in Japan, such as *Teahouse of the August Moon* (1956) and *Sayonara* (1957). Dragon Lady was transformed into Lotus Blossom: docile, obedient, pampering white men and their bodily needs.[61]

Significant was the fact that the lovers of Asian women were only white men, symbolizing another feature of American Orientalism: only

57. Quoted in Lee, *Orientals*, 115.
58. Lee, *Orientals*, 116–17.
59. Ma, *The Deathly Embrace*, 3–37.
60. Chan, *Chinese American Masculinities*, 51–72.
61. Hagedorn, "Asian Women in Film"; and Tajima, "Lotus Blossoms Don't Bleed."

white men could have free sexual access to women of color. Lotus Blossom would mutate back into Dragon Lady as one of the "dirty yum-yum girls" of Hong Kong's red-light district, Suzie Wong, in the 1957 novel, *The World of Suzie Wong* (film 1960). Reflecting the entanglements of the US war in Vietnam, she would reappear again in the 1978 film, *The Deer Hunter*, but as a Vietnamese prostitute.[62] Diverse Asian ethnic groups were thus collapsed monolithically into racial and gendered stereotypes of the Asian Other, which were continuously formed and reformed to respond to, as well as reflect, different events and circumstances in US history.

Back to 1 Kings 21

Jezebel and Dragon Lady share commonalities primarily in their foreignness. They become the exotic female Other, threatening male hierarchies with their beauty, sexuality, ruthlessness, and cruelty. Ahab shares the contradictory images of Asian masculinity. The Deuteronomistic depiction of the wickedness of his rule is similar to the despotism of Fu Manchu and Ming the Merciless. However, in his Persian period incarnation he is ultimately emasculated by his wife, who carries out the task of seizing Naboth's vineyard, which he could not do himself despite his royal power. In this he is similar to the stereotypes of Asian men feminized by American Orientalism.

Conclusion

My first Asian American reading of 1 Kings 21 correlated the illegitimate seizure of Naboth's land by the crown with the "regulatory taking" of Japanese property in the US during their internment during World War II. Denying the Japanese any economic use of their property was in effect a seizure of it. Like Naboth, the Japanese were accused of treason, even though there was no substantive truth in the allegations. "Military necessity" and desire for agricultural land in both cases formed the basis for

---

62. A very helpful documentary tracing the Hollywood depictions of Asian women, correlating them to the events of US history, is Deborah Gee's *Slaying the Dragon*. For a filmic portrayal of Asian men, see Adachi, *The Slanted Screen: Asian Men in Film and Television* (2006) at FilmsOnDemand.

the unlawful seizure of land, on the one hand, and the criminal removal of people from the land, on the other.

My second reading of the passage highlighted the stereotypical depictions of Jezebel and Ahab and Asian women and men, as ideological constructs that were formed and reformed in varying ways to respond to the sociopolitical contexts to which they were applied. We saw that despite her unfavorable depiction in the Bible, Jezebel was a very imposing woman, whose power base was derived from her husband's monarchic rule and from her strong association with the foreign cult that she and her husband supported (1 Kgs 16:31–33; 18:18–19; 21:25–26). In the Persian period redaction of the story, she became the cruel mastermind behind the murder of Naboth and the confiscation of his vineyard to compensate for her husband's impotence in obtaining it. Their relationship in 1 Kgs 21:1–16 became a cautionary tale, warning the returnees from Persia against marital couplings with the "peoples of the land." Ahab who first offered Naboth a just and fair price for his vineyard became the whimpering child who did not get his own way in his postexilic incarnation. The intent here painted Ahab as one 'who sold himself to do what was evil in the sight of the Lord, urged on by his wife (1 Kgs 21:25).[63] "Resentful and sullen," he was scornfully emasculated by his formidable wife: "Some king of Israel you make!" Jezebel's expansion of the biblical stereotype of the foreign woman as a shameless, scheming, homicidal female would be a characterization that lived on in numerous literary and artistic genres and memorably embodied in the actress Bette Davis as a spoiled, conniving Southern bell in the motion picture *Jezebel* (Warner Bros. 1938).[64]

Dragon Lady has been applied to a number of very powerful Asian women who wielded power alongside their men just like Jezebel, such as Empress Tzu-hsi (Cixi), Madame Chiang Kai-shek, and Madame Nhu (Ngo Kinh Nhu).[65] Moreover, other Asian American women have recuperated and embraced the Dragon Lady appellative to communicate the politicization of their feminist power.[66] Even I took on the Dragon Lady label in my own identity formation as a Chinese American female in a dominant white society. My second reading demonstrates that

63. Cronauer, *The Stories about Naboth the Jezreelite*, 165–85.

64. Gaines, *Music in the Old Bones*; Snyder, "Jezebel and Her Interpreters"; and Beach, *The Jezebel Letters*.

65. Chang, *Empress Dowager Cixi*; Demery, *Finding the Dragon Lady*; and Leong, *China Mystique*.

66. Shah, *Dragon Ladies*.

stereotypes, both ancient and modern, are not static and monolithic, but take on substance and meaning as they are used in different historical situations and by those in diverse social locations of gender, race, class, and sexuality.

Postscript

During May–June 2015, I was fortunate to participate in the Jezreel Expedition,[67] an archaeological dig in the area whose identification with the biblical Jezreel is commonly accepted. Having never been on an archaeological dig and wanting to join one before my retirement, I chose the Jezreel Expedition for several reasons, first of all, because of the excellent reputation of its codirectors, Dr. Norma Franklin and Dr. Jennie Ebeling. I was also good friends with members of the expedition, Dr. Julye Bidmead and Dr. Deborah Appler. Finally, I wanted to experience first-hand the area to which I devoted much historical and archaeological study, not only for this article but also for one on the narratives of Elijah and Elisha.[68] I saw for myself why Jezreel was a significant piece of real estate, agriculturally and militarily. I spent many days at the spring of Jezreel ('Ein Jezreel) washing pottery, knowing that it had supplied life-giving water to the area for thousands of years. The panoramic views of the valley were astounding, underscoring the tel's strategic importance. I could well imagine the thousands of horses for Ahab's chariots and cavalry pastured in the area.[69] I could also envision Jehu driving his chariot like a madman across the valley plane from Ramoth-Gilead, to confront and eventually assassinate Joram king of Israel at the property of Naboth the Jezreelite, thus avenging Naboth's death and fulfilling Elijah's earlier prophecy (2 Kgs 9:16–26; 1 Kgs 21:17–19).

Along with Athalya Brenner-Idan and the co-directors, I visited the large ancient winery installation that was recently uncovered in 2013 by the expedition. Because of the difficulty in dating rock-cut installations, the winery may be ninth century (the era of Ahab and Jezebel) but more likely seventh century or Persian period. A modern Israeli winery tested the soil around the winery and found that it was suitable for viticulture. While they might not have been owned by the Omrides, these

67. See Jezreel Expedition; http://jezreelexpedition.com.
68. Yee, "The Elijah and Elisha Narratives."
69. Cantrell, *The Horsemen of Israel*, 53–57.

archaeological remains and soil results confirm that there were indeed vineyards in Jezreel.

In the photograph, I am sitting on the treading floor where winemakers stomped on grapes over two thousand years ago. I am holding a bottle of Jezreel wine, bottled in the local winery, carrying on the ancient tradition of the area.

Le-chayim!

Photography courtesy of the Jezreel Expedition.

Works Cited

Ackerman, Susan. *Warrior, Dancer, Seductress, Queen: Women in Judges and Biblical Israel.* Anchor Bible Reference Library. New York: Doubleday, 1998.

Adachi, Jeff, writer and director. *The Slanted Screen: Asian Men in Film and Television.* Produced by Asian American Media Mafia. DVD. San Francisco: Asian American Media Mafia Productions, 2006.

Aster, Shawn Z. "The Function of the City of Jezreel and the Symbolism of Jezreel in Hosea 1–2." *Journal of Near Eastern Studies* 71 (2012) 31–46.

Beach, Eleanor Ferris. *The Jezebel Letters: Religion and Politics in Ninth-Century Israel.* Minneapolis: Fortress, 2005.

Cantrell, Deborah. *The Horsemen of Israel: Horses and Chariotry in Monarchic Israel (Ninth–Eighth Centuries B.C.E.).* History, Archaeology, and Culture of the Levant 1. Winona Lake, IN: Eisenbrauns, 2011.

Chan, Jachinson. *Chinese American Masculinities: From Fu Manchu to Bruce Lee.* Asian Americans. New York: Routledge, 2001.

Chang, Iris. *The Chinese in America: A Narrative History.* New York: Viking, 2003.

———. *The Rape of Nanking: The Forgotten Holocaust of World War II.* New York: Basic Books, 1997.

Chang, Jung. *Empress Dowager Cixi: The Concubine Who Launched Modern China.* New York: Knopf, 2013.

Chou, Rosalind S. *Asian American Sexual Politics: The Construction of Race Gender, and Sexuality.* Lanham, MD: Rowman & Littlefield, 2012.

Cline, Eric H. *The Battles of Armageddon: Megiddo and the Jezreel Valley from the Bronze Age to the Nuclear Age.* Ann Arbor: University of Michigan Press, 2000.

Cronauer, Patrick T. *The Stories about Naboth the Jezreelite: A Source, Composition, and Redaction Investigation of 1 Kings 21 and Passages in 2 Kings 9.* LHBOTS 424. T. & T. Clark Library of Biblical Studies. London: T. & T. Clark, 2005.

Daniels, Roger, et al., eds. *Japanese Americans: From Relocation to Redress.* Rev. ed. Seattle: University of Washington Press, 1991.

Demery, Monique Brinson. *Finding the Dragon Lady: The Mystery of Vietnam's Madame Nhu.* New York: Public Affairs, 2013.

Ebeling, Jennie R., et al. "Jezreel Revealed in Laser Scans: A Preliminary Report of the 2012 Survey Season." *Near Eastern Archaeology* 75 (2012) 232–39.

Everhart, Janet S. "Jezebel: Framed by Eunuchs?" *CBQ* 72 (2010) 688–98.

Gaines, Janet Howe. *Music in the Old Bones: Jezebel through the Ages.* Carbondale: Southern Illinois University Press, 1999.

Gee, Deborah, producer and director. *Slaying the Dragon: Slicing and Dicing Representations of Asian Women in the Media.* DVD. Asian Women United of California, 1988.

Grabbe, Lester L. "The Kingdom of Israel from Omri to the Fall of Samaria: If We Only Had the Bible . . ." In *Ahab Agonistes: The Rise and Fall of the Omri Dynasty*, edited by Lester L. Grabbe, 54–99. LHBOTS 421. T. & T. Clark Library of Biblical Studies. London: T. & T. Clark, 2007.

Gray, John. *I & II Kings: A Commentary.* OTL. Philadelphia: Westminster, 1970.

Hagedorn, Jessica. "Asian Women in Film: No Joy, No Luck." In *Screaming Monkeys: Critiques of Asian American Images*, edited by M. Evelina Galang et al., 204–10. Minneapolis: Coffee House, 2003.

Jezreel Expedition. https://www.bibleodyssey.org/en/places/related-articles/jezreel-expedition.aspx/.
Kitagawa, Daisuke. *Issei and Nisei: The Internment Years.* New York: Seabury, 1967.
Lee, Robert G. *Orientals: Asian Americans in Popular Culture.* Asian American History and Culture. Philadelphia: Temple University Press, 1999.
Leong, Karen J. *China Mystique: Pearl S. Buck, Anna May Wong, Mayling Soong, and the Transformation of American Orientalism.* Berkeley: University of California Press, 2005.
Lyon, Cherstin M. "Alien Land Laws." In *Densho Encyclopedia.* http://encyclopedia.densho.org/Alien%land%laws/.
Ma, Sheng-Mei. *The Deathly Embrace: Orientalism and Asian American Identity.* Minneapolis: University of Minnesota, 2000.
McKinlay, Judith E. *Reframing Her: Biblical Women in Postcolonial Focus.* Bible in the Modern World 1. Sheffield: Sheffield Phoenix, 2004.
Merecz, Robert J. "Jezebel's Oath (1 Kgs 19,2)." *Bib* 90 (2009) 257–59.
Na'aman, Nadav. "Naboth's Vineyard and the Foundation of Jezreel." *JSOT* 33 (2009) 197–218.
Ng, Wendy. *Japanese American Internment during World War II: A History and Reference Guide.* Westport, CT: Greenwood, 2002.
Prasso, Sheridan. *The Asian Mystique: Dragon Ladies, Geisha Girls, and our Fantasies of the Exotic Orient.* New York: Public Affairs, 2005.
Robinson, Greg. *By Order of the President: FDR and the Internment of Japanese American.* Cambridge: Harvard University Press, 2001.
Rofé, Alexander. "The Vineyard of Naboth: The Origin and Message of the Story." *VT* 38 (1988) 89–104.
Shah, Sonia. *Dragon Ladies: Asian American Feminists Breath Fire.* Boston: South End, 1997.
Sison, Marites N. "Injustices toward Japanese Canadian Anglicans Acknowledged." *Episcopal News Service*, March 20, 2013. https://www.episcopalnewsservice.org/2013/03/20/injustices-toward-japanese-canadian-anglicans-acknowledged/.
Smith, Geoffrey S. "Racial Nativism and Origins of Japanese American Relocation." In *Japanese Americans: From Relocation to Redress*, edited by Roger Daniels et al., 79–87. Seattle: University of Washington Press, 1991.
Snyder, Josey B. "Jezebel and Her Interpreters." In *Women's Bible Commentary*, edited by Carol A. Newsom et al., 180–83. 3rd ed. Twentieth-anniversary ed. Louisville: Westminster John Knox, 2012.
Tajima, Renee E. "Lotus Blossoms Don't Bleed: Images of Asian Women', in *Making Waves: An Anthology of Writings by and about Asian American Women*, edited by Asian Women United of California, 308–26. Boston: Beacon, 1989.
Takaki, Ronald. *Strangers from a Different Shore: A History of Asian Americans.* Updated and rev. ed. New York: Back Bay, 1998.
US Commission on Wartime Relocation and Internment of Civilians (George Miller, chairman). *Personal Justice Denied: Report of the Commission on Wartime Relocation and Internment of Civilians; Report for the Committee on Interior and Insular Affairs.* Washington, DC: Government Printing Office, 1982. https://www.nps.gov/parkhistory/online_books/personal_justice_denied/index.htm/.
Ussishkin, David. "Samaria, Jezreel and Megiddo: Royal Centres of Omri and Ahab." In *Ahab Agonistes: The Rise and Fall of the Omri Dynasty*, edited by Lester L. Grabbe,

293–309. LHTOTS 421. T. & T. Clark Library of Biblical Studies. London: T. & T. Clark, 2007.

Weglyn, Michi N. "The Secret Munson Report." In *Asian American Studies Now: A Critical Reader*, edited by Jean Y. S. Wu and Thomas C. Chen, 193–212. New Brunswick, NJ: Rutgers University Press, 2009.

White, Marsha. "Naboth's Vineyard and Jehu's Coup: The Legitimation of a Dynastic Extermination." *VT* 44 (1994) 66–76.

Wilson, John A. "The Asiatic Campaigns of Thut-mose III." In *ANET*, 234–41.

Yamamoto, Eric K. et al. *Race, Rights, and Reparation: Law and the Japanese American Internment*. Aspen Elective Series. Gaithersburg, NY: Aspen Law & Business, 2001.

Yee, Gale A. "'By the Hand of a Woman': The Biblical Metaphor of the Woman Warrior." *Semeia* 61 (1993) 99–132.

———. "The Elijah and Elisha Narratives: An Economic Investigation." In *The Congress Volume of the 2014 International Congress of Ethnic Chinese Biblical Scholars*, edited by Gale A. Yee and John Y. H. Yieh, 21–50. Hong Kong: Chinese University of Hong Kong, 2016.

———. *Poor Banished Children of Eve: Woman as Evil in the Hebrew Bible*. Minneapolis: Fortress, 2003.

———. "The Woman Warrior Revisited: Jael, Fa Mulan, and American Orientalism." In *Joshua and Judges*, edited by Athalya Brenner and Gale A. Yee, 179–90. Texts@ Contexts. Minneapolis: Fortress, 2013.

———. "Yin/Yang Is Not Me: An Exploration into an Asian American Biblical Hermeneutics." In *Ways of Being, Ways of Reading: Asian-American Biblical Interpretation*, edited by Mary F. Foskett and Jeffrey Kah-Jin Kuan, 152–63. St. Louis: Chalice, 2006.

10

Of Foreigners and Eunuchs
An Asian American Reading of Isaiah 56:1–8[1]

As a third-generation Chinese American feminist, I have already engaged in several readings of the biblical text from this context, particularly dealing with stereotypes of Asian Americans as the "perpetual foreigner" and "model minority."[2] As will be seen in the commentary that follows, I choose to interpret Isaiah 56:1–8 from an Asian American perspective because it not only deals with foreigners, but also with eunuchs, which I interpret here as sexual minorities. By including foreigners and eunuchs, Isa 56:1–8 provides a welcome for both in the religious worship of Yehud that had formerly excluded them. Although there are exceptions,[3] Asian and Asian American churches tend to be conservative and resistant to accepting LGBTQ members. Interpreting eunuchs as sexual minorities, this chapter will argue that Isa 56:1–8 offers biblical affirmation for the acceptance of LGBTQ individuals into their religious communities.

---

1. Originally published in Yee, "Of Foreigners and Eunuchs," (2019).
2. Yee, "Inculturation and Diversity"; Yee, "Yin/Yang Is Not Me"; Yee, "'She Stood in Tears'"; Yee, "Where Are You Really From?"; Yee, "The Woman Warrior Revisited"; Yee, "Coveting the Vineyard"; Yee, "Racial Melancholia."
3. See those inclusive Asian American churches cited in Lin, "It's Lonely."

The Sociohistorical Context of Isaiah 56:1-8

Isaiah 56:1-8 opens the division of the book usually called Third Isaiah.[4] Its setting is Yehud[5] after the return of the exiles from Babylon during the early Persian period.[6] This is a time when different social groups compete to establish their own beliefs on what Israel should become after the trauma of the exile.[7] Isa 56:1-8 provides a stunning reversal for two of these groups that previously were not admitted into the worship of the temple. To the foreigners who fear that "the LORD will surely separate me from his people" (v. 3a), the prophet proclaims that God will bring them to his holy mountain and accept their offerings and sacrifices (vv. 6-7). Similarly, to the eunuch who laments that he is "just a dry tree," one who will have no offspring (v. 3b), God will give him a "monument and a name" (*yād vā-šēm*),[8] which will be "better than sons and daughters," as well as "an everlasting name that will not be cut off" (v. 5).

While it is difficult to pinpoint the *exact* historical date and sociological context of Isa 56:1-8,[9] it seems to be a time when foreigners and eunuchs were excluded from the postexilic community in Yehud. During the time of Ezra and Nehemiah, for example, some isolationist factions endorsed a policy of ethnic and religious purity that had a socioeconomic base (Neh 9:1-2; 13:1-3). This is particularly seen in the prohibition of intermarriage between the returning exiles and the women who were regarded as "foreign" (Neh 10:28-31; 13:23-30; Ezra 9-10).[10] We will see that eunuchs were disparaged as well for their otherness and strangeness. In a dramatic and radical move, the prophet appeals for their inclusion.[11] He first exhorts the community to "do the right thing," that is, implement justice and do what is right, because God's salvation and deliverance

---

4. For a review of the different methodological approaches to Isaiah 56-66, see Goldingay, *A Critical and Exegetical Commentary on Isaiah 56-66*, 1-58.

5. http://www.bibleodyssey.org/en/tools/image-gallery/b/borders-of-judah-map-2/.

6. Blenkinsopp, *Isaiah 56-66*, 43; Goldingay, *A Critical and Exegetical Commentary on Isaiah 56-66*, 7-9.

7. Hammock, "Isaiah 56:1-8"; Paul, *Isaiah 40-66*, 447-50.

8. Note that Yad Va-Shem is the Hebrew name of The World Holocaust Remembrance Center in Jerusalem (*http://www.yadvashem.org/*).

9. Goldingay, *A Critical and Exegetical Commentary on Isaiah 56-66*, 6-9, 17; Hammock, "Isaiah 56:1-8," 49.

10. Yee, "The Other Woman in Proverbs."

11. de Hoop, "The Interpretation of Isaiah 56:1-9," 690.

is near (v. 1). He then reveals the community's fundamental badge of membership, which will be the measure for the inclusion of foreigners and eunuchs, namely, the observance of the Sabbath and the avoidance of evildoing (v. 2). In chiastic fashion,[12] he launches into his discourse reversing the marginalization of foreigners and eunuchs.

Foreigners

The Hebrew Bible has three distinct terms for the foreigner. *Gēr* refers to the non-Israelite who resides in Israel and thus enjoys certain legal protection and inclusion in the religious life of the community.[13] *Zār* is the more general term for "foreigner/outsider/stranger/alien." It can refer neutrally to non-Israelites or those individuals who could be Israelite, but whose strangeness is threatening, such as the *'iššâ zārâ*, "foreign woman" (Prov 2:16–19; 5:3–6; 7:5).[14] The related third terms for foreigner are *nēkār, ben nēkār, and nokrî*, which unambiguously describe the non-Israelites who were forbidden to worship in the community (Exod 12:43; Ezek 44:9; Lev 22:25). More specifically, Deut 23:3 declares "No Ammonite or Moabite shall be admitted to the assembly of the Lord. Even to the tenth generation, none of their descendants shall be admitted to the assembly of the Lord" (Cf. Neh 13:1–3). Pertinent to our discussion of eunuchs below, Deut 23:1 will also forbid from the assembly the man "whose testicles are crushed or whose penis is cut off."

Nēkār/nokrî carry more negative connotations than *gēr* and *zār*.[15] Their "strangeness" can be dangerous, because their beliefs in gods other than YHWH may be a source of temptation for Israel (Num 25:1–3; Deut 31:13; Josh 24, 23; Judg 10:16). It is therefore significant that Isaiah 56 uses the more pejorative term, *ben nēkār*, to describe the foreigner (vv. 3, 6), the non-Israelite, who is normally excluded from the temple. In Isa 43:19, God announces to those in exile the appearance of a "new thing," wherein the eyes of the blind will be opened and prisoners will be liberated from their dungeons (42:7–9). Isaiah 61:1–2 continues this message

---

12. Foreigner/eunuch (v. 3)//eunuchs (vv. 4–5)/foreigners (vv. 6–7).

13. Begg, "Foreigner," 829; Wuench, "The Stranger in God's Land," 1142–48; Niggemann, "Matriarch of Israel or Misnomer?," 362–64.

14. Begg, "Foreigner," 829–30; Wuench, "The Stranger in God's Land." For a discussion of the *'iššâ zārâ*, see Yee, "The Other Woman in Proverbs."

15. Wuench, "The Stranger in God's Land," 1139–42; Begg, "Foreigner," 829.

of "good news to the oppressed," "liberty to the captives," and "release to prisoners" to the people of Jerusalem. This "new thing" that will soon come to pass will also include the most disparaged as members of the worshipping community.[16]

The oracle applies specifically to foreigners who are now believers in the God of Israel. These foreigners, who are "joined to YHWH" (vv. 3, 6), fear that YHWH will separate them from his people (v. 3) because of existing laws that forbid them from the cultic assembly (Exod 12:43; Ezek 44:9; Lev 22:25). However, for the foreigners (*běnē nēkār*) who minister to and serve YHWH, who love his name, who keep and not profane his Sabbath, and hold fast to his covenant, YHWH in turn will bring them to his holy mountain, the temple in Jerusalem. There he will make them joyful in his house of prayer and accept their burnt offerings and sacrifices (vv. 6-7). The three-fold repetition of keeping the Sabbath is significant. The first confers a blessing upon the members of the community who keep the Sabbath and refrains from evil doing (v. 2). The second and third are for the eunuch and foreigners who keep God's Sabbath and hold fast to God's covenant (vv. 4, 6). In contrast to circumcision as the hallmark of the covenant (Gen 17:9-14), observing the Sabbath becomes its signifier (Cf. Isa 58:13; 66:23). In turn, it becomes the chief criterion for the foreigner and the eunuch to becoming members in the worshipful gathering in the temple.[17]

Eunuchs

The Hebrew word *sārîs* refers to a castrated male.[18] Because these men usually held high positions in royal courts, the word is often (wrongly) translated as "officer" or "courtier."[19] Important for this essay, eunuchs had considerable access to power and rank in ancient Near Eastern courts primarily because of their inability to procreate. This impotence not only made them "safe" around the women of the harem, but also mitigated their threat to monarchs who wanted to centralize their rule and secure

16. Gaiser, "A New Word on Homosexuality?," 284.

17. Blenkinsopp, *Isaiah 56-66*, 135; Goldingay, *A Critical and Exegetical Commentary on Isaiah 56-66*, 77-78.

18. Tadmor, "Was the Biblical *Sārîs* a Eunuch?" Regarding castration, see Burke, "Queering Early Christian Discourse"; Taylor, *Castration*.

19. Cf. the NRSV's translations of *sārîs* in Gen 37:36; 2 Kgs 8:6; 25:19. Tadmor, "Was the Biblical *Sārîs* a Eunuch?," 318; Burke, *Queering the Ethiopian Eunuch*, 19-38.

their own dynastic houses. Because a eunuch did not establish a family line of his own, he was able to rise to top positions in the state hierarchy.[20]

According to Deut 23:1 [MT 2], "no one whose testicles are crushed or whose penis is cut off shall be admitted to the assembly of the Lord." Prohibitions in Deut 23:3 will continue with the religious exclusion of foreigners, as we saw above. Several scholars argue that Isa 56:1–8 upends this prohibition of foreigners and eunuchs in the religious gathering.[21] However, if juxtaposed with promises to the exiles in the preceding chapter, Isa 55:12–13, the eunuch's exclusion in Isa 56:3b is also literarily distinctive. According to Isa 55:13, along with the blossoming trees of cypress and myrtle, the returning exiles will burst with fertility "for a 'name/offspring' (šēm)[22] to the Lord, for an everlasting sign that shall not be cut off (lĕ' ôt 'ôlam lō' yikkārēt). In contrast, the eunuch complains that he is "just a dry tree," someone with no progeny who will carry on his name. As opposed to the sexually productive returning exiles of Isa 55:13, the eunuch will have no sons and daughters.

But as with foreigners, God responds to the eunuch's lament. Eunuchs, who observe God's Sabbath, do what pleases God, and hold fast to his covenant, will receive "a monument and a name" (yād vā-šēm) in the Jerusalem temple (vv. 4–5a). According to 2 Sam 18:18, Absalom sets up a funerary stele, which he names "Absalom's Monument" (yad), because "I have no son to keep my name alive." For the eunuchs in Isaiah 56, this monument and name will even be better than having sons and daughters (v. 5b). Amending the wording in Isa 55:13, a sly wordplay may be occurring here. Since yad can also mean "penis" (Isa 57:8, 10; Cant 5:4), the "everlasting name" (šēm 'ôlām) that "shall not be cut off" (lō' yikkārēt) might also be alluding to the eunuchs' castrated state, which will be surmounted by a monument and new name divinely bestowed in the temple.[23] These gifts are said to be better than progeny, because God's very-self guarantees the permanence of the monument and name in the temple, outliving any sons and daughters.

---

20. Wright and Chan, "King and Eunuch"; N'Shea, "Royal Eunuchs and Elite Masculinity."

21. See those cited in Wright and Chan, "King and Eunuch," 100, fn. 5.

22. Paul, *Isaiah 40–66*, 454, interprets *shem* as "offspring" in light of Isa. 66:22: 'So shall your seed and your name (šimḵem = offspring) endure.'

23. Blenkinsopp, *Isaiah 56–66*, 139.

During the Persian period, eunuchs were often negatively stereotyped.[24] Burke argues that eunuchs can be interpreted as "queering figures," because they trouble and destabilize the intersecting discourses of gender, sexuality, class, and race.[25] Certainly, eunuchs did not conform to ancient constructions of masculinity, which depended upon strict binaries between male and female, penetrator and penetrated, and free and slave.[26] Eunuchs disrupted all these categories as ambiguous bodies, who amassed much power and privilege and thus inspired fear.

Particularly with respect to Isa 56:1–8, eunuchs destabilized the binary between citizen/native and foreigner. On the one hand, eunuchs were "foreign" or "strange" because they did not conform to the hegemonic masculinity of the day. On the other hand, eunuchs of the biblical period were mainly associated with the foreign nations of Assyria, Egypt, and Persia.[27] Isaiah warns Hezekiah that some of his sons will be seized and carried away to be eunuchs in the palaces of the king of Babylon (Isa 39:7; 2 Kgs 20:18). A goodly number of royal eunuchs (*sārîsîm*) were taken away in the Babylonian exile (2 Kgs 24:12, 15). The return of these eunuchs to postexilic Yehud most likely raised concerns about their membership in the Jewish community, because of their identification with the Babylonian hierarchy and because of their sexual ambiguity. That they were both foreign and sexual minorities worked against their acceptance. However, for Isaiah 56, these eunuchs, who had once exerted foreign royal power through their sexually non-normative bodies, can now—by observing the Sabbath and the covenant—transfer their devotion and service to the empire over to YHWH (v. 4). The foreign court is replaced by the temple in Jerusalem where the eunuch now finds a monument and name.[28] What we have here may be a literary inclusio around Isaiah 40–55, in which Isa 39:5–7 prophesies that Israel will become eunuchs in exile, and Isa 56:1–8 welcomes them back into the community.[29]

Reacting to more exclusivist, ethnocentric voices during the Persian period regarding religious worship, Isa 56:1–8 argues for a radically open postexilic community in Yehud. For those who have "joined themselves

24. Thus, Wright and Chan, "King and Eunuch," 109–11, 117–19.
25. Burke, *Queering the Ethiopian Eunuch*, 95.
26. Burke, *Queering the Ethiopian Eunuch*, 113–17.
27. Wright and Chan, "King and Eunuch," 104–16; Burke, *Queering the Ethiopian Eunuch*, 102.
28. Wright and Chan, "King and Eunuch," 118–19.
29. Gaiser, "A New Word on Homosexuality?," 287.

to YHWH," who observe the Sabbath and the covenant, and do what is pleasing to the deity, God will bring them to his holy mountain, his house of prayer (v. 7). Into this inclusive assembly, the Lord will gather foreigners and eunuchs, "the outcasts of Israel," and bring them into community with "those already gathered" in the sacred assembly of the temple (v. 8).

The Asian American Foreigner and Eunuch

Particularly in our day and age, immigration policies have become more intolerant and exclusionary. Immigrants and refugees are targeted as the foreign "Other" to be subjected to discrimination, harassment, and sometimes violence. US presidential bans against refugees of certain Middle Eastern nations and the futile attempts to build walls to make our borders less porous, all exemplify and exacerbate the ethnocentric fears against those who are "not like us." This is especially the case in the history of Asian American communities.[30] Chinese immigrants to the United States suffered terribly under the 1882 Exclusion Act that not only barred new immigrants from entering, but also launched a period of terror now known as "the Driving Out," in which several Chinese communities in the western United States were subjected to a level of violence that approached genocide.[31] The United States instigated its most extreme and hateful form of racist exclusion in the internment of Japanese Americans during World War II.[32] Stereotypes regarding Asian Americans as the "perpetual foreigner" are exemplified in the irritating, micro-aggressive question often asked of them: "Where are you *really* from?," as if they were not *real* citizens of the United States.[33] In contrast, Isa 56:1–8 can provide a profoundly biblical welcome and reception for foreigners, Asian and otherwise, from religious host communities.

The acceptance of eunuchs as sexual minorities in Isaiah 56, who should be welcomed and included in the religious assembly, also presents a thoughtful reflection for the inclusion of LGBT Asian Americans in the churches. David Mura begins his essay by commenting on another racial

---

30. Zia, *Asian American Dreams*; Tan, *Introducing Asian American Theologies*, 20–35.

31. Chang, *The Chinese in America*, 132; Miller, *The Unwelcome Immigrant*.

32. Takaki, *Strangers from a Different Shore*, 357–405; Yee, "Coveting the Vineyard," 47–53.

33. Yee, "'She Stood in Tears.'"

stereotype, this one of the Asian American male. "The Japanese American actor Marc Hayashi once said to me: 'Every culture needs its eunuchs. And we're it. Asian American men are the eunuchs of America.'"[34] After seeing the portrayal of an effeminate Asian American male nerd in the movie *Fargo*, a character that he had auditioned for, Mura was grateful that he didn't get the part. He rightly observed that the depiction of Asian and Asian American men as sexless eunuchs had a long history.[35] This stereotype has its corollary in the depiction of Asian and Asian American males as sexually ambiguous and villainous Fu Manchus.[36] In their racialized[37] feminization, Asian American men are thus viewed not only as racial minorities, but also as sexual minorities, as eunuchs, in their white US context.

Because they do not conform to heteronormative sexual relations and traditional views regarding gender and sexuality, Asian American LGBTQ individuals can also fall under the category of "eunuch" as racial and sexual minorities. Asian American churches have often been resistant to accepting LGBTQ folk into their membership.[38] The reasons for this are very complex, because they go beyond theological and religious orthodoxy, involving the intersections of culture, race, gender, sexuality, class and colonialism.[39] In some Asian countries, such as China, same-sex relations were tolerated if they did not disrupt the status quo. However, with their arrival in Asia, white Christian missionaries disparaged as "inferior" the cultural and sexual expressions of intimacy which they observed among Asian populations and promulgated their own version

---

34. Mura, "*Fargo* and the Asian American Male," 295.

35. Chou, *Asian American Sexual Politics*, 103–35; Ling, "Identity Crisis and Gender Politics"; Fung, "Looking for My Penis"; Nguyen, "The Remasculinization of Chinese America"; Eng, *Racial Castration*; Chan, *Chinese American Masculinities*. For a filmic portrayal of Asian American men, see Adachi, *The Slanted Screen: Asian Men in Film and Television* at FilmsOnDemand.

36. Kim, "The Strange Love of Frank Chin"; Lee, *Orientals*, 113–17; Choi, "Asian/Asian American Interpretation," 8; Yee, "Coveting the Vineyard."

37. Racialization is a process by which unalterable and hereditary physical, mental, and moral characteristics are attributed to a group of bodies on the basis of shared factors usually related to environment and/or ancestry. See Burke, *Queering the Ethiopian Eunuch*, 116–17.

38. Maséquesmay, "How Religious Communities Can Help"; Lim, "Webs of Betrayal, Webs of Blessings."

39. I particularly want to thank Bianca Louie for sending me her 2017 master's thesis on this important topic and Dr. Russell Jeung for directing me to her. (Louie, "Queer Asian American Christians.")

of normative heterosexual relations. Under British colonialism, male homosexuality became illegal, driving gay men underground. Moreover, constructed by colonial Orientalist fantasies, Asian men became feminized and set up as human foils against white hegemonic masculinity.[40] This racialized feminization of Asian men will be carried over into the US context.[41]

When Asian immigrants settled in the United States, the evangelical churches and more fundamentalist mainstream churches[42] provided spaces for community support and social services that helped in their often-traumatic journey towards assimilation and ultimately US citizenship. Here was a place where they could speak their native languages and share the hopes and fears of people like them in this new, bewildering place. Unfortunately, these immigrants also bought into the existing homophobia that was widespread in the white evangelical church.[43] This homophobia was not new to them, since it was a carry-over from their former Asian countries under colonization. Also not new were the evangelical views regarding male superiority/female inferiority, because they cohered with the immigrants' Confucian beliefs regarding family, duty, sexuality, and honor and shame. Contributing to anti-LGBTQ biases were anxieties over Westernization and that homosexuality was a "white" phenomenon.[44]

However, there have been positive signs of change regarding discussions of sexual orientation among Asian Christian groups, not only in the US but also globally.[45] An important video produced by PANA at

---

40. Kwok, "Asian and Asian American Churches," 59; Choi, "Asian/Asian American Interpretation," 3–4, 8.

41. Chou, *Asian American Sexual Politics*, 103–17; Chan, *Chinese American Masculinities*.

42. See the studies that found that religiously observant Korean Protestant immigrants held more conservative anti-LGBTQ positions than Asian Catholics and Buddhists (Maséquesmay, "How Religious Communities Can Help"; Shrake, "Homosexuality and Korean Immigrant Protestant Churches"). Also, the section on "Views on Homosexuality and Abortion" in the 2012 Pew Forum on Asian Americans and their diversity of faiths: http://www.pewforum.org/2012/07/19/asian-americans-a-mosaic-of-faiths-social-and-political-attitudes/.

43. Louie, "Queer Asian American Christians," 52–57.

44. Lee, "Teaching Justice and Living Peace"; Shrake, "Homosexuality and Korean Immigrant Protestant Churches"; Louie, "Queer Asian American Christians," 20–21.

45. Wu, *Liberating the Church from Fear*; Kwok, "Asian and Asian American Churches," 60–61. For websites, see http://gayasianchristians.org/wp/; http://www.queerasianspirit.org/.

the Pacific School of Religion, "In God's House: Asian American Lesbian and Gay Families in the Church," deals sensitively with the generational struggles of Asian LGBTQ families and their sexual and religious beliefs.[46] An analysis of the film contextualizes the silence surrounding issues of sexuality as a cultural reaction to secure "Asian" ethnicity in white society, and also as a way to create a space to affirm the life stories and support the relationships of LGBTQ Asian Americans within their families.[47] Particularly as a result of the 2016 US presidential election, many evangelicals of color have moved beyond the white church to establish their own racial/ethnic communities, several of which are more progressive on LGBTQ issues.[48]

For anti-LGBTQ churches, biblical condemnations of homosexuality are primarily based on interpretations of three Old Testament texts (Genesis 19, Lev 18:22; 20:1) and three New Testament texts (Rom 1:26–27; 1 Cor 6:9; and 1 Tim 1:10). These fundamentalist interpretations have been challenged for their a-historical ignorance of the beliefs and practices regarding sexuality and sexual reproduction, gender, kinship, honor/shame, and so forth in ancient Israel.[49] These ancient biblical beliefs cannot be transferred *mutatis mutandis* to the present US context. Debates about how to use the Bible to address homosexuality in our own day are complicated by different understandings of same-sex relations from antiquity, homosexuality within the larger context of sexuality in the Bible, and within contemporary studies of sexuality.[50]

Because the Bible was composed over a long period by different authors, and in geographical settings, it brought together many voices regarding what it meant to be believers in the God of Israel. Sometimes these voices contradicted and clashed with each other. Others provided gentler opposition and resistance. For example, the injunctions against marriages with foreign women by Ezra and Nehemiah (Neh 10:28–31;

46. https://vimeo.com/73005802. See also the very moving video by Asian pastor Danny Cortez to his congregation when he decided to part ways with the Southern Baptist Convention's position on homosexuality after he learned that his son was gay: (https://www.thegailygrind.com/2014/06/02/baptist-pastor-chooses-gay-son-anti-gay-southern-baptist-convention/.)

47. Campos, "In God's House."

48. Lee, "Betrayed at the Polls."

49. Stewart, "Same-Sex Relations: Hebrew Bible"; Huber, "Same-Sex Relations: New Testament"; Stone, "Gender and Homosexuality in Judges 19"; Carden, "Homophobia and Rape."

50. Stone, "Homosexuality."

13:23–30; Ezra 9–10) were counter-balanced by the story of Ruth the Moabite who became the great ancestress of King David himself (Ruth 1–4). In the same way, the Bible presents an alternate voice regarding sexual minorities in Isa 56:1–8 that dialectically pushes back against the usual texts summoned to condemn them. Third Isaiah proclaimed a completely open community, extending God's universalistic vision of salvation to the "outcasts" of ancient Israel, the foreigners and the eunuchs. For Asian Americans, it is significant that God will bring these "outcasts" to his holy mountain (56:7). The Chinese term for California, the home of the first Asian immigrants to the United States, is *Gam Saan*, "Gold Mountain."[51] Coming to "Gold Mountain" embodied the hopes and dreams of many Asian immigrants fleeing poverty, war, and persecution. May this be so for LGBTQ Asian Americans who are searching for a home in an open and affirming worshipping community. Isaiah 56:1–8 can thus be a prophetic text offering biblical support for them to be welcomed in Asian American churches.[52]

Conclusion

The postexilic period in Persian Yehud was a conflicted time. The Israelites had just returned to their homeland from their exile in Babylon and were determined not to let it happen again. Exile was their punishment for transgressing God's covenant. In the cacophony of voices proclaiming the "right" way now to follow and serve God, Third Isaiah utters a new message. Against the narrow nationalism and ethnocentrism that was becoming prevalent, Third Isaiah preached a radically new universalism that seemingly overturned some old laws and traditions. While Exod 12:43, Ezek 44:9, Lev 22:25, and Deut 23:3 barred any foreigners from worship in the assembly, Isa 56:6–7 promised that any faithful foreigner who observed the Sabbath and adhered to God's covenant will be joyfully brought to Jerusalem. There in his holy house of prayer, the temple itself, God will accept their burnt offerings and sacrifices at the altar. It will be a house of prayer for *all* peoples.

Third Isaiah then focuses on a particularly marginal section of that people, the eunuchs. Although wielding much power, their castration left them incapable of passing on any of that power to their descendants. In

---

51. Takaki, *Strangers from a Different Shore*, 31–42.
52. Gaiser, "A New Word on Homosexuality?"; Gaiser, "Open-Door Policy."

his own and the eyes of his countrymen, a eunuch was "just a dry tree." Moreover, like foreigners, he too was banished from God's temple, according to Deut 23:1. However, God promised the eunuch that if he kept the Sabbath, did what was pleasing to God, and adhered to the covenant, God would give him a "monument and a name" that would be a greater gift than children. This monument would be enduring, his everlasting name "never cut off." Transcending the purity laws and proscriptions endorsed at the time by postexilic traditionalists, the markers for religious membership for both the foreigner and the eunuch in Third Isaiah were primarily their observance of the Sabbath and obedience to the covenant. As outcasts of Israel, God will gather them to join with those already assembled to become a new worshipping community in the Lord.

This essay also made parallels between ancient foreigners and eunuchs with modern day ones: Asian and Asian American immigrants and sexual minorities. As violence and political unrest in South Asia and the Middle East continue to soar, large numbers of Asian immigrants from countries or regions in conflict have entered the United States as refugees and as asylum seekers. As a result, a significant share of new legal permanent residents from Bhutan (100 percent), Burma (88 percent), Iraq (71 percent), Nepal (47 percent), and Thailand (41 percent) attained permanent residency by adjusting from refugee or asylee status. Although most arrive through legal channels, Asian immigrants represent a significant and growing portion of the illegal population. In the 2009–2013 period, approximately 1.5 million unauthorized immigrants from Asia resided in the United States, according to Migration Policy Institute (MPI) estimates, representing 14 percent of the total 11 million unauthorized population. China is the fifth-largest origin country of unauthorized immigrants.[53] Although many of these immigrants may not be Christian, Isa 56:1–8 urges churches to provide a safe hospitable space for them as they deal with the trauma of their various passages.

Isa 56:1–8 can also be used to advocate for an open and warm acceptance for LGBTQ folks as eunuchs. Asian LGBTQ persons operate under a double oppression as both racial and sexual minorities in the United States. They have been targeted by racist bullies and gay bashers because they threaten white heteronormativity. Moreover, they have been particularly unwelcomed in Asian and Asian American churches. These churches need to hear the alternate voice of Third Isaiah who proclaims a

---

53. Taken from http://www.migrationpolicy.org/article/asian-immigrants-united-states/.

newness in God's work of salvation, which will be "good news to the oppressed," "liberty to the captives," binding "up the brokenhearted" (61:1). These include the Asian American sexual minorities in our midst. One prays that the Spirit opens our ears to hear what she is saying to these churches, to bring these outcasts to "Gold Mountain:" God's holy mountain in our Asian American churches.

Works Cited

Begg, Christopher T. "Foreigner." In *ABD* 2 (1992) 829–30.
Blenkinsopp, Joseph. *Isaiah 56–66: A New Translation with Introduction and Commentary*. AB 19B. New York: Doubleday, 2003.
Burke, Sean D. *Queering the Ethiopian Eunuch: Strategies of Ambiguity in Acts*. Emerging Scholars. Minneapolis: Fortress, 2013.
Campos, Michael Sepidoza. "In God's House: Of Silences and Belonging." *Theology & Sexuality* 17 (2011) 265–77.
Carden, Michael. "Homophobia and Rape in Sodom and Gibeah: A Response to Ken Stone." *JSOT* 82 (1999) 83–96.
Chan, Jachinson. *Chinese American Masculinities: From Fu Manchu to Bruce Lee*. New York: Routledge, 2001.
Chang, Iris. *The Chinese in America: A Narrative History*. New York: Viking, 2003.
Choi, Jin Young. "Asian/Asian American Interpretation." In *Oxford Encyclopedia of the Bible and Gender Studies*, edited by Julia M. O'Brien, 1:1–15. 2 vols. Oxford: Oxford University Press, 2014.
Chou, Rosalind S. *Asian American Sexual Politics: The Construction of Race, Gender, and Sexuality*. Lanham, MD: Rowman & Littlefield, 2012.
Eng, David L. *Racial Castration: Managing Masculinity in Asian America*. Durham: Duke University Press, 2001.
Fung, Richard. "Looking for My Penis: The Eroticized Asian in Gay Video Porn." In *Queer in Asian America*, edited by David L. Eng and Alice Y. Hom, 115–34. Asian American History and Culture. Philadelphia: Temple University Press, 1998.
Gaiser, Frederick J. "A New Word on Homosexuality? Isaiah 56:1–8 as Case Study." *Word & World* 14 (1994) 280–93.
———. "Open-Door Policy: Homosexuality and the Message of Isaiah." *Christian Century* 123/9 (May 2, 2006) 26–27.
Goldingay, John. *A Critical and Exegetical Commentary on Isaiah 56–66*. International Critical Commentary. London: Bloomsbury, 2014.
Hammock, Clinton E. "Isaiah 56:1–8 and the Redefining of the Restoration Judean Community." *BTB* 30 (2000) 46–57.
Hoop, Raymond de. "The Interpretation of Isaiah 56:1–9: Comfort or Criticism?" *JBL* 127 (2008) 671–95. https://doi.org/10.2307/25610149.
Huber, Lynn R. "Same-Sex Relations: New Testament." In *The Oxford Encyclopedia of the Bible and Gender Studies*, edited by Julia M. O'Brien, 2:274–80. 2 vols. Oxford: Oxford University Press, 2014.
Kim, Daniel. "The Strange Love of Frank Chin." In *Q & A: Queer in Asian America*, edited by David L. Eng and Alice Y. Hom, 270–303. Asian American History and Culture. Philadelphia: Temple University Press, 1998.

Kwok, Pui Lan. "Asian and Asian American Churches." In *Homosexuality and Religion: An Encyclopedia*, edited by Jeffrey S. Siker, 59–62. Westport, CT: Greenwood, 2007.

Lee, Boyung. "Teaching Justice and Living Peace: Body, Sexuality, and Religious Education in Asian-American Communities." *Religious Education* 101 (2006) 402–19.

Lee, Deborah Jian. "Betrayed at the Polls: Evangelicals of Color at a Crossroads." *Religion Dispatches*, April 27, 2017. http://religiondispatches.org/betrayed-at-the-polls-evangelicals-of-color-at-a-crossroads/.

Lee, Robert G. *Orientals: Asian Americans in Popular Culture*. Asian American History and Culture. Philadelphia: Temple University Press, 1999.

Lim, You-Leng Leroy. "Webs of Betrayal, Webs of Blessings." In *Queer in Asian America*, edited by David L. Eng and Alice Y. Hom, 323–34. Asian American History and Culture. Philadelphia: Temple University Press, 1998.

Lin, Liz. "It's Lonely Being a Liberal Asian-American Christian." *HuffPost*, January 9, 2017. Updated January 10, 2017. http://www.huffingtonpost.com/entry/the-loneliness-of-the-progressive-asian-american-christian_us_587025a5e4b0a5e600a78ad5

Ling, Jinqui. "Identity Crisis and Gender Politics: Reappropriating Asian American Masculinity." In *An Interethnic Companion to Asian American Literature*, edited by King-Kok Cheung, 311–37. Cambridge: Cambridge University Press, 1997.

Louie, Bianca Heather. "Queer Asian American Christians: Redemptive Reclamation and Subversive Imagination." MA thesis, San Francisco State University, 2017.

Maséquesmay, Gina. "How Religious Communities Can Help LGBTIQQ Asian Americans to Come Home." *Theology & Sexuality* 17 (2011) 319–35.

Miller, Stuart Creighton. *The Unwelcome Immigrant: The American Image of the Chinese, 1785–1882*. Berkeley: University of California Press, 1974.

Mura, David. "*Fargo* and the Asian American Male." In *Screaming Monkeys: Critiques of Asian American Images*, edited by M. Evelina Galang et al., 295–97. Minneapolis: Coffee House Press, 2003.

Nguyen, Viet Thanh. "The Remasculinization of Chinese America: Race, Violence, and the Novel." *American Literary History* 12 (2000) 130–57.

Niggemann, Andrew J. "Matriarch of Israel or Misnomer? Israelite Self-Identification in Ancient Israelite Law Code and the Implications for Ruth." *JSOT* 41 (2017) 355–77.

N'Shea, Omar. "Royal Eunuchs and Elite Masculinity in the Neo-Assyrian Empire." *Near Eastern Archaeology* 79 (2016) 214–21.

Paul, Shalom M. *Isaiah 40–66: Translation and Commentary*. Eerdmans Critical Commentary. Grand Rapids: Eerdmans, 2012.

Shrake, Eunai. "Homosexuality and Korean Immigrant Protestant Churches." In *Embodying Asian/American Sexualities*, edited by Gina Maséquesmay and Sean Metzger, 145–56. Lanham, MD: Lexington, 2009.

Stewart, David Tabb. "Same-Sex Relations: Hebrew Bible." In *The Oxford Encyclopedia of the Bible and Gender Studies*, edited by Julia M. O'Brien, 2:257–63. 2 vols. Oxford: Oxford University Press, 2014.

Stone, Ken. "Gender and Homosexuality in Judges 19: Subject-Honor, Object-Shame?" *JSOT* 67 (1995) 87–107.

———. "Homosexuality." In *The New Interpreter's Dictionary of the Bible* 2 (2007) 882–83.

Tadmor, Hayim. "Was the Biblical *Sārîs* a Eunuch?" In *Solving Riddles and Untying Knots: Biblical, Epigraphic, and Semitic Studies in Honor of Jonas C. Greenfield*, edited by Ziony Zevit et al, 317–25. Winona Lake, IN: Eisenbrauns, 1995.

Takaki, Ronald. *Strangers from a Different Shore: A History of Asian Americans*. Updated and rev. ed. New York: Back Bay, 1998.

Tan, Jonathan Y. *Introducing Asian American Theologies*. Maryknoll, NY: Orbis, 2008.

Taylor, Gary. *Castration: An Abbreviated History of Western Manhood*. Routledge, 2000.

Wright, Jacob L., and Michael J. Chan. "King and Eunuch: Isaiah 56:1–8 in Light of Honorific Royal Burial Practices." *JBL* 131 (2012) 99–119.

Wu, Rose. *Liberating the Church from Fear: The Story of Hong Kong's Sexual Minorities*. Kowloon, Hong Kong: Hong Kong Women Christian Council, 2000.

Wuench, Hans-Georg. "The Stranger in God's Land: Foreigner, Stranger, Guest: What Can We Learn from Israel's Attitude towards Strangers." *Old Testament Essays* 27 (2014) 1129–54.

Yee, Gale A. "Coveting the Vineyard: An Asian American Reading of 1 Kings 21." In *Samuel, Kings, and Chronicles, I*, edited by Athalya Brenner-Idan and Archie C. C. Lee, 46–64. Texts@Contexts. London: Bloomsbury T. & T. Clark, 2016.

———. "Inculturation and Diversity in the Politics of National Identity." *JAAAT*.

———. "Of Foreigners and Eunuchs: An Asian American Reading of Isa. 56.1–8." In *The T & T Clark Handbook to Asian American Biblical Hermeneutics*, edited by by Uriah Y. Kim and Seung Ai Yang, 261–72. London: Bloomsbury T. & T. Clark, 2019.

———. "Racial Melancholia in the Book of Ruth." In *The Five Scrolls*, edited by Athalya Brenner-Idan et al., 61–70. Texts@Contexts. London: Bloomsbury T. & T. Clark, 2018.

———. "'She Stood in Tears amid the Alien Corn': Ruth, the Perpetual Foreigner and Model Minority." In *They Were All Together in One Place? Toward Minority Biblical Criticism*, edited by Randall C. Bailey et al., 119–40. Semeia Studies 57. Atlanta: Society of Biblical Literature, 2009.

———. "The Other Woman in Proverbs: 'My Man's Not Home . . . He Took His Money Bag with Him.'" In *Marxist Feminist Criticism of the Bible*, edited by Roland Boer and Jorunn Okland, 98–133. Sheffield: Sheffield Phoenix, 2008.

———. "The Woman Warrior Revisited: Jael, Fa Mulan, and American Orientalism." In *Joshua and Judges*, edited by Athalya Brenner and Gale A. Yee, 175–90. Texts@Contexts. Minneapolis: Fortress, 2013.

———. "Where Are You Really From? An Asian American Feminist Biblical Scholar Reflects on Her Guild." In *New Feminist Christianity: Many Voices, Many Views*, edited by Mary E. Hunt and Diann L. Neu, 79–85. Woodstock, VT: Skylight Paths, 2010.

———. "Yin/Yang Is not Me: An Exploration into an Asian American Biblical Hermeneutics." In *Ways of Being, Ways of Reading: Asian-American Biblical Interpretation*, edited by Mary F. Foskett and Jeffrey K. Kuan, 152–63. St. Louis: Chalice, 2006.

Zia, Helen. *Asian American Dreams: The Emergence of an American People*. New York: Farrar, Straus & Giroux, 2000.

11

Jerusalem, Samaria, and Sodom
A Sisterly Urban Triad in Ezekiel 16:44–63[1]

THIS FINAL ARTICLE IS dedicated to my dear colleague and friend Dr. Kwok Pui Lan. For years Pui Lan encouraged me to gather my essays in an anthology for Asian American biblical interpretation. She had even written a sample proposal and table of contents to compel me to start working on such a volume. So, it is with joy and gratitude for her encouragement and support in the formation of this volume that I write this essay. In a dim sum restaurant after a PANAAWTM[2] meeting in Toronto back in 1998, Pui Lan passed around a xeroxed sheet to us faculty advisors, advertising a two-year interim position in studies in feminist liberation theologies at Episcopal Divinity School (EDS). Even though I was already a tenured full professor at my former institution, I eagerly applied and was hired for it. When the two years ended, I jubilantly became a tenured full professor at EDS. For eighteen years, Pui Lan and I lived through the joys and sorrows of being colleagues at one of the most progressive, antiracist, anti-oppression institutions in the US. At EDS we became presidents of the major guilds of our fields, she for the American Academy of Religion, and I for the Society of Biblical Literature. She introduced me to postcolonial theory, which deeply influenced my work on Ezekiel 23 regarding the two sisters, Oholah (Samaria) and Oholibah (Jerusalem).[3] This es-

---

1 I would like to thank Corrine L. Carvalho for her insightful feedback on this paper. Any mistakes are completely my own.

2. Pacific Asian North American Asian Women in Theology and Ministry.

3. Yee, "The Two Sisters in Ezekiel."

say will examine Ezek 16:44–63, which adds another sister, Sodom, to make a sororal trinity in Israel's sordid covenantal history with YHWH. It will argue that 16:44–63 reflects a post–582 BCE social landscape of Jews beyond the usual binary of Babylonia/Yehud (returning exiles and peoples of the land), which is the book's perspective, to include ethnically and religiously mixed communities in Egypt (Sodom) and Samaria. In 16:44–63, other voices emerge that present alternate understandings of Jewishness during the exilic period.

Like Ezekiel 23, Ezekiel 16 relates the history of YHWH's covenantal relationship with his people through a violent sexualized and racialized metaphor of a marriage gone wrong. YHWH becomes the cuckolded and shamed husband of Jerusalem, his fornicating wife. Although many feminists have analyzed and critiqued this chapter, they have primarily focused their attention on Ezek 16:1–43.[4] I too have been guilty of this in my previous work on Ezekiel 16.[5] Ezek 16:1–43 centers on the story of Jerusalem's birth and abandonment as a newborn by her foreign parents (vv. 1–7), on her covenantal marriage to YHWH (vv. 8–14), on her idolatry and promiscuity with sexy foreign lovers (vv. 15–34), and on her merciless punishment for betraying her marital vows (vv. 35–43).[6] A rhetorical tripling device[7] unites 16:1–43 in the threefold references to the days of the woman's birth and youth (vv. 4, 22, 43) and to her stark nakedness (vv. 7, 22, 39). The third reference to Jerusalem's "days of your youth" in v. 43 seems to conclude the unit. YHWH declares that Jerusalem is punished, "because you have not remembered the days of your youth but have enraged me with all these things; therefore, I have returned your deeds upon your heads, says the LORD GOD."[8]

---

4. Galambush, *Jerusalem in the Book of Ezekiel*; Shields, "Multiple Exposures"; Day, "Rhetoric and Domestic Violence"; Day, "The Bitch Had It Coming"; Day, "Adulterous Jerusalem's"; Day, "A Prostitute Unlike Women"; Day, "Yahweh's Broken Marriages"; Kamionkowski, "Gender Reversal"; Runions, "Violence and the Economy"; Moughtin-Mumby, *Sexual and Marital Metaphors*, 170.

5. Yee, "'Your Mother Was a Hittite'"; Yee, "'Spreading Your Legs to Anyone Who Passed.'"

6. According to Brad Kelle ("Wartime Rhetoric," 98–101), the prophetic imagery of physical and sexual violence *only* appears in the context of the destruction of a *city* that is personified as a woman.

7. Cf. Boadt's suggestion ("Rhetorical Strategies," 188) that a rhetorical device of tripling connects Ezek 4–7.

8. All translations from the NRSV unless otherwise noted.

Context

The introduction of Jerusalem's sisters, Samaria and Sodom, in 16:44–63 seems to signal a new unit and a new theme.[9] For this reason, many feminists did not include these verses in their analyses, preferring to focus on the sexual violence in vv. 1–43. The question is whether vv. 44–63 are from the same author as vv. 1–43. I follow a number of scholars who see a threefold division in the chapter: A (vv. 1–43); B (vv 44–58); and C (vv. 59–63), although they differ in dealing with editorial provenance and dating of the sections.[10] Ezekiel is customarily referred to as the prophet of the Babylonian exile. However, one must remember that there were several forced migrations from Jerusalem and Judah to Babylonia, and the book of Ezekiel reflects this in its editorial history. According to 2 Kgs 24:10–17, King Jehoiachin, the queen mother, and his officers, palace officials, and the elite of the land were taken in captivity from Jerusalem to Babylon. It is this forced migration that can properly be called an "exile."[11] Ezekiel the prophet-priest was most likely a part of this first-generation exile in 597 BCE, ending up as a corvée laborer on the irrigation canals of Babylon with other displaced elites.[12] Because Judah was already a subjugated entity of the Babylonian empire, the forced migration that occurred when Nebuchadnezzar attacked Jerusalem a second time in 587 BCE (2 Kgs 25:1–21) should more correctly be termed "an internal displacement of peoples" from the periphery (Judah) to the center (Babylonia).[13] This migration witnessed the destruction of the Jerusalem temple. A third internal displacement to Babylonia occurred in 582 BCE, perhaps in retaliation for the assassination of Gedaliah, whom Nebuchadnezzar had installed as governor of those who remained in Judah (2 Kgs 25:22–26; Jer 52:30).[14] At the same time, another group in Judah, fearing Babylonian retribution, fled to Egypt, taking the prophet Jeremiah with them (Jer 43:4–7). Because this group voluntarily crossed international borders,

---

9. Joyce, *Ezekiel*, 133.

10. Eichrodt, *Ezekiel*, 216–17; Allen, *Ezekiel 1–19*, 233; Zimmerli, *Ezekiel*, 1:333–35, 348–53; Greenberg, *Ezekiel 1–20*, 292; Greenberg, "Ezekiel 16," 143–45; Darr, "The Book of Ezekiel," 1220–21; and Block, *Book of Ezekiel*, 464, recognize the three-part divisions but see more consistency in authorship.

11. Ahn, "Forced Migrations," 182.

12. Ahn, "Ezekiel 15: A *Māšāl*," 103; Wilson, "Forced Migration," 103.

13. Ahn, "Forced Migrations," 182.

14. Betlyon, "Neo-Babylonian Military Operations," 266–67; Klein, "Exile," 368.

they should be described as "refugees," rather than exiles or internally displaced persons.[15]

It is within this more nuanced understanding of "the exile" that we should situate Ezek 16:44-63. While A (Ezek 16:1-43) was probably composed before the destruction of Jerusalem and second deportation in 587 BCE,[16] I will argue below that B (vv. 44-58) and C (vv. 59-63) were added to this core sometime after the third forced and voluntary migrations from Jerusalem in 582 BCE.[17]

We must also reckon with several social groups who had their own needs and concerns during this period of forced and voluntary migration.[18] The *first* were those elites transported to Babylonia in the first exile in 597. This group was divided between those whom Jeremiah encouraged to "seek the welfare of the city" and come to terms with the major urban and multicultural area of Babylon itself (Jer 29:5-7), and those like Ezekiel, who were sent to dig in the remote, isolated, mono-ethnic setting of Babylonia's irrigation ditches.[19] It was this latter faction that developed a separatist ideology of "extreme exclusivity" over and against the *second* group, namely, those who remained in the land (2 Kgs 25:22; Jer 40:7-12).[20]

This second group continued to live south or north of Jerusalem, many as rural farmers, paying taxes in wine, oil, and other farm products, as they had done before Jerusalem's destruction.[21] Specifically included in this group were the elites who were still functioning in Jerusalem (2 Kgs 25:1-21). These elites were excoriated by Ezekiel (see Ezek 33:23-29), who depicted them metaphorically as YHWH's unfaithful wife of foreign origin who is doomed to destruction in Ezek 16:1-43 (A).[22] They be-

15. Ahn, "Forced Migrations," 183; Cf. Kessler, *Social History*, 126-27, who refers to this event as the Egyptian exile, although he does acknowledge that it as voluntary.

16. Zimmerli, *Ezekiel*, 1:348-50; Allen, *Ezekiel 1-19*, 233.

17. Cf. those who simply say that these verses are post-587: Allen, *Ezekiel 1-19*, 243; Zimmerli, *Ezekiel*, 1:348-50.

18. Middlemas, *The Templeless Age*, Location 85-100.; Rom-Shiloni, "Forced/Involuntary Migration," 384-89.

19. Distinguishing here between the city of Babylon and the country it is set in, viz. Babylonia. Strine, "Is 'Exile' Enough?," 291; Pearce, "Continuity and Normality," 180; Rom-Shiloni ("Forced/Involuntary Migration," 397) contends that there were no internal differences or conflicts between these two communities in exile.

20. Rom-Shiloni, "Ezekiel as the Voice."

21. Lipschits, "Shedding New Light," 73-85.

22. Rom-Shiloni, "Ezekiel as the Voice," 20-34.

came a segment of the forced migration in 587 BCE. Those who were not deported in either 587 or 582 BCE, the so-called "poorest of the land" (2 Kgs 24:14; 25:12; Jer 39:10; 40:7; 52:16), took over the lands and vineyards of the elites and, urged on by Gedaliah at Mizpah, produced a plentiful economic harvest of summer fruits and oil (Jer 40:9–10). Undoubtedly, a good portion of this harvest was destined as taxes for their Babylonian overlords.[23] Joining these farmers were many Judeans who had fled to Moab, Ammon, and Edom because of the conflicts (Jer 40:11–12). These ex-patriots returned to Judah when they heard that the Babylonians left a remnant in Judah, appointing Gedaliah as governor. It is not inconceivable that in joining the remnant in working the land, they brought with them Moabite, Ammonite, and Edomite spouses and children, creating more ethnically mixed communities in Judah after 582 BCE.[24]

The third population were those Judeans who had settled, evidently for some time before the exile, "in the land of Egypt, at Migdol, at Tahpanhes, at Memphis, and in the land of Pathros" (Jer 44:1).[25] By the late sixth century, a Jewish military colony was in place at the island of Elephantine in Upper Egypt. More about this colony and its origins will be discussed below. Besides these settlements in Egypt, we must also include the communities of those Judean men and women who fled to Egypt after Gedaliah's assassination (Jer 43:4–7).[26] Each of these social groupings will figure in some way in Ezekiel's prophecy.

Analysis

In Ezek 16:44, the literary character known as Ezekiel[27] continues his diatribe against the capital city, Jerusalem, and her elites by lobbing a proverb[28] against her foreign parentage: "Like mother, like daughter." We are

---

23. Graham, "Vinedressers and Plowmen."
24. Ahn, "Ezekiel 15: A *Māšāl*," 115–16; Kessler, *Social History*, 122–23.
25. Holladay, "Judeans (and Phoenicians)," 423–29.
26. Kessler, *Social History*, 126–27; Becking, "A Fragmented History," 156–57.
27. "The reader of the final form of the text should also recognize that the author and Ezekiel are not identical: Ezekiel is a character within the prophetic narrative, through whom the reader experiences the exile." Thus, Patton, "Priest, Prophet, and Exile," 73.
28. In Hebrew, *māšāl*. According to Polk ("Paradigms, Parables," 575), the *māšāl* is not a neutral saying, but one that should issue in a judgment: "The *māšāl* forces upon Jerusalem a self-evaluation, one with an obvious enough conclusion, which, were it

reminded of her loathsome pedigree in v. 45, "your mother was a Hittite, your father an Amorite," inverting the previous accusation that begins his oracle in v. 3, in order to focus on Jerusalem's mother. By betraying her husband YHWH (vv. 15–34), Jerusalem is like her Hittite mother, who also loathed her husband. Historically, Jerusalem was actually a Jebusite city before it was conquered by David (2 Sam 5:6–10//1 Chr 11:4–9), but by highlighting her Hittite and Amorite ancestry, Ezekiel binds Jerusalem with the seven peoples of Canaan, whom God commanded Israel to drive out (Josh 3:10, 24:11; Deut 7:1). Hittite women are particularly censured as marital partners for Israelite men, because of their foreignness. For example, Rebekah relates her fears to Isaac that Jacob will marry a Hittite woman just like his brother Esau (Gen 27:34, 46). Or, the downfall of King Solomon will be his foreign wives, which included Hittite women (1 Kgs 11:1).[29]

Complicating the dysfunctional family history is the fact that Jerusalem's Hittite mother not only loathes her Amorite husband but also her children. These include not only Jerusalem herself, but also her sisters, Samaria and Sodom. And like Jerusalem, these sisters are guilty of despising their own husbands and children (vv. 45–46). This antipathy toward one's spouses and children has been described as a "hereditary defect of character" that runs in the family because of the sisters' foreign progenitors.[30]

The NRSV translates the description of Samaria as the "elder" sister (*haggĕdôlâ*) and of Sodom as the "younger" one (*haqqĕṭānâ*). However, both Jerusalem and Sodom are actually older than Samaria. Jerusalem existed before Samaria was established by King Omri (1 Kgs 16:23–24), and Sodom was a city-state during the so-called Patriarchal period (Gen 13:12–13). The comparison among the three cities is only effective if their descriptions refer to geographic size.[31] Therefore, Jerusalem's bigger sister is Samaria, the former capital of the Kingdom of Israel to her north, the traditional home of the ten tribes. To her south is her smaller sister, the city of Sodom, whose actual location is debated. Although Sodom

---

taken to heart, should issue in shame and disgrace (v. 52); and, on from that, in aid to the poor and needy (v. 49), renewed covenant and a true knowledge of God (vv. 60–63)."

29. For more on the Hittites, see McMahon, "The History of the Hittites."
30. Pope, "Mixed Marriage Metaphor," 394–95.
31. See Block, *Book of Ezekiel*, 507, n. 256; Also, Allen, *Ezekiel 1-19*, 244.

is claimed to be north of the Dead Sea,[32] the more persuasive evidence points to a location southeast of the Dead Sea.[33] In our text, Jerusalem is geographically positioned between these northern and southern cities.

Both Samaria and Sodom are said to have daughters (*běnôtēhâ*, v. 46). Given the geographic thrust of the passage, these daughters are the dependent towns of these cities.[34] These daughters also manifest the foreignness of their mothers. Along with these "nieces," Jerusalem too has her own satellite towns or "daughters" (v. 48). The focus on these cities with their dependencies will be important for the interpretation of this passage, as we will see. Ezekiel accuses Jerusalem of following in the ways of Sodom and Samaria according to their abominations (*tô' ēvôt*) and becoming even more corrupt than they (v. 47).[35] Traditionally, Sodom is the archetypically wicked and sinful city,[36] which God destroys because of its iniquity.[37] A smattering of biblical verses,[38] such as Gen 19:1–28 about the attempted male-male rape of Lot's two guests at Sodom, have become proof texts against homosexual desire and relationships for some evangelical Christians.[39] However, studies that contextualize same-sex relations within the ancient Mediterranean sexual milieu provide a more balanced interpretation of the biblical text.[40] Inhospitality to the male guest is Sodom's most likely transgression in Gen 19.[41] From a literary

---

32. Collins, "Where Is Sodom?"

33. Rast, "Bab Edh-Dhra," 196–97; Howard, "Sodom and Gomorrah," 399–400; Shanks, "Have Sodom and Gomorrah"; Westermann, *Genesis 1–11*, 300; Arnold, *Genesis*, 184.

34. According to Josh 15:45, Ekron has its "daughters" (*běnôtēhâ*) or satellite dependencies. See also Josh 17:11; Num 21:25; Jer 49:2. Allen, *Ezekiel 1–19*, 244; Zimmerli, *Ezekiel*, 1:350; Sweeney, *Reading Ezekiel*, 87.

35. According to Goldstein, sexuality was never a core issues for *tô' ēvôt*, "abominations." The core concern of *tô' ēvôt* was idolatry and foreign cultic practices, and it became sexualized in the marriage metaphor of Ezekiel: "*Toevah* is what is unacceptable to the community—i.e., what is inherently dangerous to one's identity as an Israelite." Goldstein, "Reading Toevah," 53–57; For another take, see Stone, "Hermeneutics of Abomination."

36. Gen 13:12; 18:20; Deut 32:32; Isa 3.9; Jer 23:14.

37. Deut 29:23; Isa 13:19; Jer 49:18; 50:40; Lam 4:6; Amos 4:11; 2 Esdr 2:8; Matt 10:15.

38. Besides Gen 19:1–28, see Lev 18:22; 20:13; Rom 1:26–28; 1 Cor 6:9; 1 Tim 1:10.

39. Cf. Peterson, "The Sin of Sodom Revisited"; Gagnon, *The Bible and Homosexual Practice*; Gagnon, "The Old Testament and Homosexuality."

40. Nissinen, *Homoeroticism*; Stewart, "Same-Sex Relations."

41. Matthews, "Hospitality and Hostility"; Morschauser, "'Hospitality.'" On the

perspective, this inhospitality toward the stranger contrasts with both Abraham's and Lot's hospitality toward God's messengers (Gen 18:1–8 and Gen 19:1–3, respectively).[42] In commissioning his followers, Jesus warns that it will be more tolerable for Sodom than for any town that does not welcome them hospitably (Luke 10:10–12). It was only in later Jewish and Christian traditions that Sodom became a signifier of sexual sins in their interpretations of Gen 19:1–28.[43]

Ezekiel is very precise about Sodom's guilt or iniquity (ʿăwôn): She and her "daughters" had pride, excess of food, and prosperous ease, but did not aid the poor and needy (Ezek 16:49). There is no mention here of the male-male gang rape of Gen 19.[44] Rather, Sodom is guilty of arrogance, gluttony, materialistic comfort, and neglect of the impoverished and destitute. In Sodom, we encounter an economically stratified urban center whose wealth and greed has made its people proud and indifferent to the marginal populations within it. Israelite and Jewish traditions support Ezekiel's particular denunciation of Sodom's social injustices recounted here. The prophet Isaiah scathingly addresses the leaders and people of Jerusalem as "you rulers of Sodom, you people of Gomorrah" (Isa 1:10). After spurning their sacrifices and feasts, God commands them to "cease to do evil, learn to do good; seek justice, rescue the oppressed, defend the orphan, plead for the widow" (Isa 1:16–17). Isaiah accuses Jerusalem of being a prostitute (zônâ), connecting this to her lack of justice and righteousness and to the oppression and thievery of her leaders, who do not defend the orphan or the widow's cause (Isa 1:21–23). Sir 16:7–8 and 3 Macc 2:4–5 condemn both the giants of Gen 6 and the inhabitants of Sodom for their arrogance and trust in their strength. Both were destroyed because they committed injustices (3 Mac 2:4).[45]

According to Carden, references to Sodom and Gomorrah are pervasive in rabbinic literature, highlighting their oppression, injustice, and hostility towards strangers. In particular, the hospitality of Abraham and Lot is contrasted with the inhospitality of Sodom in Gen 19.[46] Relevant

---

importance of hospitality in the social world in which ancient Israel is embedded, see, Herzfeld, "As in Your Own House."

42. Alter, "Sodom as Nexus," 150–51; Nissinen, *Homoeroticism*, 47–48.

43. See the conclusions of Carden's extensive study: Carden, *Sodomy*, 76–77.

44. Thus, Block, *Book of Ezekiel*, 509; Woudstra, "Everlasting Covenant," 36; Pace, Peterson, "Identifying the Sin of Sodom."

45. Carden, *Sodomy*, 47–48.

46. Carden, *Sodomy*, 86, 113, and the rest of Chapter 4.

for Ezek 16:48–50 is *Pirķê de Rabbi Eliezer* 25.[47] According to Rabbi Ze'era, the men of Sodom were wealthy and prosperous because of the fertility of their land and their mother lodes of gold and precious stones. In their arrogance, they trusted not their Creator, but their immense wealth. Their lack of hospitality is exhibited in the wall they built around their fruit trees so that the traveler and the stranger could not partake from them.[48] According to Rabbi Jehudah, a proclamation was made in Sodom that whoever gave bread to the poor and needy shall be burnt by fire. One of these "offenders" was Lot's own daughter Peleṭith, who was married to one of Sodom's peers. Feeding a poor man on the street from her household provisions, she is condemned to die by fire. She prays to God, "Maintain my right and my cause at the hands of the men of Sodom," and God hears her cry.[49] These various traditions cumulatively attest to Ezekiel's depiction of Sodom's manifold offenses.

Turning to the bigger sister, Ezekiel only accuses Samaria of not committing half the sins of Jerusalem (v. 51a). Unlike Sodom's, these sins are not specified. Verse 47 declares that Jerusalem not only followed in the ways of the two cities but became more corrupt than them. Therefore, the catalogue of Sodom's offenses rhetorically presumes that Jerusalem was even more abominable than her sister in her own pride, excess of food, prosperous ease, and neglect of the poor and needy.[50] Ezekiel contains a number of oracles condemning Jerusalem's own social injustices. Ezekiel 18:7–8 extols the righteous man—who does not oppress anyone, but restores to the debtor his pledge, commits no robbery, gives his bread to the hungry and covers the naked with a garment, does not take advance or accrued interest, withholds his hand from iniquity, executes true

---

47. Eighth–ninth cent. CE. I am relying here on the page numbers of the Friedlander translation, *Pirķê de Rabbi Eliezer*.

48. *Pirķê de Rabbi Eliezer*, 181–82. See also *Tosefta Soṭah* 3:2, accessed in Sefaria, 6/25/20 1:34 PM. In his condemnation of Sodom, Rabbi Joshua, son of Korchah, cites Ezek 16:49: "Behold, this was the iniquity of thy sister Sodom: pride, fullness of bread, and prosperous ease was in her and her daughters, but she did not strengthen the poor and needy."

49. *Pirķê de Rabbi Eliezer*, 182–83. Peleṭith is nameless in *Sanhedrin* 109b:9, where her punishment for feeding the poor is more gruesomely described. She is covered with honey and put on the city wall to be attacked by hornets. Her act of kindness and her horrific execution that followed sealed the fate of Sodom's destruction. Accessed in Sefaria, William Davidson edition, 6/25/20 12:57 PM. See also the rendition in Ginzberg et al., *Legends of the Jews*, 1:209.

50. Eichrodt, *Ezekiel*, 215.

justice between contending parties—and reviles the man who does not (18:12–13). Ezekiel 22:6–7 denounce the "princes of Israel" in Jerusalem, who extort the alien living within her and oppress the orphan and widow. Ezekiel continues in 22:12 to condemn those who take bribes for murder, overcharge interest on loans, and profit from extortion. In 34:1–6, he lambasts the "shepherds of Israel" for their gluttony and materialism, and for not feeding their people or strengthening the weak, healing the sick, or binding up the injured in their charge.[51] The abominations of Jerusalem in these social injustices make both these errant sisters of hers appear righteous in their stead (16:51b). The favorable judgment for her sisters, in spite of their own corruption, is intended to make Jerusalem feel a profound shame for her own deeds.[52]

> Bear your disgrace, you also, for you have brought about for your sisters a more favorable judgment; because of your sins in which you acted more abominably than they, they are more in the right than you. So be ashamed, you also, and bear your disgrace, for you have made your sisters appear righteous. (v. 52)

Who Are Samaria and Sodom?

Before we proceed, let us ask why the feminized Samaria and Sodom become signifiers to highlight Jerusalem's own crimes. The most obvious reason is that they are both cities that enflamed God's wrath so much by their sinfulness that God destroyed them.[53] By comparing Jerusalem to these destroyed cities, Ezekiel assumes Jerusalem's apparent fate as well. Ezekiel also highlights the foreign ethnic parentage that they share with Jerusalem. The geographical locations of Sodom south of Jerusalem may refer to those mixed ethnic farming communities in Judah after 582 BCE, that formed when Judeans who had fled to Moab, Edom, and Ammon returned with their spouses and children (see above). Clues for the text's interpretation also lie in the mention of the "daughters" or dependent towns/villages of these cities. Astonishingly, God will restore "the fortunes

---

51. On social justice in Ezekiel, see Mein, *Ezekiel and the Ethics of Exile*, 94–100.

52. Regarding shame as self-awareness, see Lapsley, "Shame and Self-Knowledge," 163–68.

53. Thus, Eichrodt, *Ezekiel*, 214–15; and Woudstra, "Everlasting Covenant," 35. Eichrodt thinks that Samaria and Sodom were "capriciously chosen" as Jerusalem's sisters. I will argue differently.

of Sodom and her daughters and Samaria and her daughters" and restore Jerusalem and her daughters along with theirs, so that Jerusalem will become more disgraced and ashamed (vv. 53–54). God will restore Sodom, Samaria, and their towns to their former state, and Jerusalem and her towns along with them (v. 55). At the beginning of this passage, Ezekiel accuses Jerusalem, Sodom, and Samaria of being offspring of foreign ethnicities (vv. 44–45). In contrast to the ideology of the "empty land," that the land was supposedly empty because the true "people of Israel" were in the Babylonian diaspora,[54] mixed ethnic communities ("daughters") already inhabit the land and will, according to Ezek 16:55, be restored to their former state.

Along with those who already live in the land, we must also remember that two competing centers exist in the Judean diaspora, particularly after the forced and voluntary migrations in 582 BCE. These centers are Babylon and Egypt, although the one that becomes normative biblically will be the former.[55] Egypt has been allied with Judah several times during the course of its history, and its attraction to Judeans lies not only in its military support but also in its agrarian economic power.[56] I mentioned previously the flight of elite Judean refugees in 582 BCE after the assassination of the Babylonian-appointed governor, Gedaliah, and their settling in the already established Israelite communities in Egypt (Jer 44:1). Jeremiah warns the refugees in Egypt that war and famine will overwhelm them, because of their worship of other deities (Jer 44:1–14). They, in turn, rebuke him, saying that they and their ancestors have always prospered while they offered libations to the queen of heaven, but now suffer war and famine when they ceased presenting them (Jer 44:15–19). In short, the exilic population in Egypt, just like their preexilic ancestors in Judah, is a mixed lot.[57]

Augmenting this exilic diversity in Egypt, the community of Elephantine has its own complex diasporic history. According to van der Toorn, the ancestors of the Elephantine Jews were from Jerusalem's northern sister Samaria rather than from Judah.[58] Based on his analysis of Pa-

---

54. Barstad, *Myth of the Empty Land*; Barstad, "After the 'Myth of the Empty Land.'"

55. With grateful thanks to John Ahn for pointing me in this direction and directing me to the work of Gary Knoppers and Karel van der Toorn.

56. Carvalho, "A Serpent in the Nile," 205.

57. Knoppers, "Exile, Return and Diaspora," 41.

58. Van der Toorn, *Becoming Diaspora Jews*, 3.

pyrus Amherst 63, van der Toorn argues that a group of Samarians[59] fled to Judah at the time of its fall in 721 BCE, becoming mercenaries under Judean command. When the Assyrians under Sennacherib attacked Judah, they fled again, this time north to Palmyra in Aram (Syria).[60] In Palmyra, they encountered and intermingled with ethnically and religiously pluralistic populations of Syrians and Babylonians, relinquishing their Hebrew language in favor of Aramean. Sometime toward the end of the seventh century BCE, a significant population from Syria and Palestine journey to Egypt, drawn by the promise of houses, land, and perhaps salary in exchange for military service at Elephantine. They continue to worship their warrior god Yaho as they did in Samaria and Palmyra, equating him with the storm god Bethel, as well as adopting several Aramean deities associated with Bethel.[61] Because of a completely different diasporic history than those of the Babylonian diaspora, the Elephantine Jews had a mixed ethnic and religious ancestry:

> At Elephantine, it was possible to be a Jew and a polytheist. It was possible to be a Jew and have your own temple far away from Jerusalem. It was possible to be a Jew, marry an Egyptian wife, and still have Jewish children. It was possible to be a Jew and never read the Torah because there was, as yet, no Torah. To anyone who hears it, the story of the Elephantine community is a reminder of the fact that the story of the Jews has many chapters. To believe that every chapter tells the same story in a slightly different way would be a big mistake.[62]

A connection between Egypt and Sodom appears in Wis 19:13–17. Sodom "had refused to receive strangers when they came to them," but Egypt is far worse in making "slaves of guests who were their benefactors" (Wis 19:14). An even stronger analogy between Egypt and Sodom is found in a celebratory poem in the later Samaritan text *Memar Marqah*,

---

59. Both van der Toorn and Knoppers refer to the residents of Yehud and Samaria (Assyria province of Samerina) as Judeans and Samarians to distinguish them from the later Jews and Samaritans of the later Roman period. Knoppers, *Jews and Samaritans*, 14–15.

60. Van der Toorn, *Becoming Diaspora Jews*, 87–88; For an abbreviated version of van der Toorn's thesis, see van der Toorn, "Egyptian Papyrus."

61. Van der Toorn, *Becoming Diaspora Jews*, 87–88, 102–3.

62. Van der Toorn, *Becoming Diaspora Jews*, 147; Both Knoppers ("Exile, Return and Diaspora," 46) and Granerod (*Dimensions of Yahwism*, 2–3) concur that in the Neo-Babylonian and Persian periods there were multiple and multi-dimensional Yahwisms.

comparing Moses and Aaron who enter Egypt with the two angels who enter Sodom:

> How excellent to see them [Moses and Aaron] enter Egypt like the two angels who entered Sodom! // The two angels entered Sodom at eventide, sent to open the storehouse of wrath upon all the inhabitants therein. // Moses and Aaron entered Egypt at eventide, sent to open the storehouse of judgement therein. // The angels were sent to destroy Sodom. Moses and Aaron were sent to destroy Egypt. // The angels ate unleavened bread in Sodom. Moses and Aaron celebrated the feast of unleavened bread in Egypt. // The angels burnt the young in the deep. Moses and Aaron smote Pishon, tributary of Eden. // The angels drove Lot out in the morning. // Moses and Aaron led the Israelites out before morning. (MM I§3)[63]

The link between Egypt and Sodom is a tradition that is carried over in the triangulation of Sodom, Egypt, and Jerusalem in Rev 11:8. The implication to be drawn in Ezek 16:46 is that Jerusalem's southern sister Sodom and her "daughters" become signifiers for the diverse Judean communities in Egypt in this passage. Although the move is speculative, the prophet appropriates a very sinful city south of Jerusalem, already entrenched in the tradition as one destroyed by God, as his avatar for these Judean settlements in Egypt. While the author of Ezek 16:1–43 reflects the "extreme exclusivity" of Babylonian exiles and the book itself, Ezek 16:44–58, written after the forced and voluntary migrations in 582 BCE, suggests a perspective cognizant of Judean communities in Egypt that have different experiences of diaspora. Assuming van der Toorn is correct about the origin of the Elephantine Jews, this perspective will also include communities of Jerusalem's sister Samaria. These communities are more ethnically, religiously, and culturally diverse than the Judean elites in Babylonia. Ezekiel accuses them of being like Sodom: sinful because of their pride, excess of food, prosperous ease, and neglect of the poor and needy (16:49). Nevertheless, while Sodom and Samaria are still abominable in their sinful ways, these sisters will be judged more favorably and appear more righteous when compared to Jerusalem's own transgressions and shame (v. 52).

The prophet continues by declaring that YHWH will restore the fortunes of Sodom, Samaria, and their daughters (v. 53a). Jerusalem's fortunes will also be restored along with those of her sisters and nieces, but

---

63. Cited in Carden, *Sodomy*, 48–49, n. 3.

only to compel her to bear her disgrace and be ashamed (v. 53b–54). The promised restoration of Samaria and her daughters/towns by YHWH will actually come to pass in the future (vv. 55). In contrast to Judah, the region of Samaria seemed to have escaped large-scale destruction by the Babylonians.[64] While some of its population eventually landed in Elephantine, the population in Samaria itself was an ethnic mix of mostly former Israelites and foreign populations transplanted earlier by the Assyrians and absorbed into the local population (see 2 Kgs 17:24–41).[65] After 582 BCE, Samaria and her dependent towns were developing into the larger and more prosperous entity that will confront the Babylonian elites in Yehud when they return: "During the Achaemenid era, members of the Judean elite were not dealing with a depopulated outback to the north. Quite the contrary, they were dealing with a province that was larger, better-established, wealthier, and considerably more populous than Yehud."[66]

The restoration of the fortunes and former state of Sodom and her daughters (vv. 53–55) is problematic if, as argued, it represents the communities in Egypt. Perhaps what is also alluded to here is the revitalization of Sodom's southern location around the Dead Sea and its environs in Judah (Ezek 47:3–12; cf. Zech 14:8).[67] Or more likely, it may refer to God's restoration of those scattered in Egypt, who will return to the land under the united kingdom of Israel and Judah:

---

64. Zertal, "Province of Samaria," 405–6; Knoppers, "Revisiting the Samarian Question," 272.

65. Knoppers disagrees with both the maximalist position (that maintains a great devastation of Samaria by the Assyrians and massive bidirectional populations exchange between Samaria and Assyria) and the minimalist position (that the conquests of Samaria were mainly localized at major urban centers). Rather the picture is mixed. There was not wholesale replacement of one population with another, but rather a diminution of the local population. The number of foreign transplants was not high, and these seemed to have been gradually absorbed into the local population. The religious divergence of Samaria from the normative Yahwism in the Deuteronomistic History is due to the resurgence during the exilic/postexilic periods of the "old time religion" of YHWH practiced in the former Northern Kingdom. The springboard of Knoppers's thesis here is 2 Kgs 17:25–28, which describes the Assyrian king repatriating an exiled Samarian priest to teach the foreign settlers of the God of the land, taking up residence at one of the former major Israelite sanctuaries, Bethel (Knoppers, *Jews and Samaritans*, 21–44, 48–57).

66. Knoppers, "Revisiting the Samarian Question," 272–73.

67. Block, *Book of Ezekiel*, 513; Zimmerli, *Ezekiel*, 1:352.

> I will take the people of Israel from the nations among which they have gone, and will gather them from every quarter, and bring them to their own land. I will make them one nation in the land, on the mountains of Israel; and one king shall be king over them all. Never again shall they be two nations, and never again shall they be divided into two kingdoms. (Ezek 37:21–23)[68]

In any case, the restorations of Samaria, Sodom, and their daughters serve not to return them to their former wickedness, but to compel Jerusalem to suffer her own disgrace and shame (vv. 53–54). Contrasting Jerusalem with Sodom, the prophet declares, "Was not your sister Sodom a byword in your mouth in the day of your pride, before your wickedness was uncovered? Now you are a mockery to the daughters of Aram and all her neighbors, and to the daughters of the Philistines, those all around who despise you. *You*[69] must bear the penalty of your lewdness and abominations, says the Lord" (vv. 56–58, italics in the text).

We now arrive at the concluding verses: Ezek 16:59–63 (C). Most likely written by the author of vv. 44–58 (B), they recapitulate themes found in both vv. 1–43 (A) and (B).[70] Although Jerusalem flagrantly broke the covenant (v. 59) that she entered with YHWH (v. 8), YHWH will establish an "everlasting covenant" with her (*bĕrît ʿôlām*, v. 60).[71] In contrast to Jerusalem, who did not remember (*zkr*) the days of her youth (vv. 4, 22, 43), YHWH[72] will remember (*zkr*) the covenant he made with her in the days of her youth (v. 60). Jerusalem will in turn remember *zkr*) her sinful ways and be ashamed when God takes her bigger and smaller sisters, Samaria and Sodom, and gives them to her as daughters (v. 61), perhaps alluding to the eventual reunification of Israel and Judah. As Jerusalem's daughters, Samaria and Sodom will be included in the same *bĕrît ʿôlām*.

If Sodom and her daughters stand for Egypt, and Samaria and her daughters represent the former Northern Kingdom, whom does Jerusalem personify? There are two possibilities: the ethnically mixed groups living in Yehud or the Babylonian exiles. The more radical interpretation,

---

68. Such a promise of restored unification was also uttered by preexilic prophets: Amos (Amos 9:11–12), Hosea (Hos 3:5), and Micah (Mic 5:2–5), and the exilic prophet Jeremiah (Jer 30:1–17).

69. With the emphatic feminine form, "You" (*ʾat*).

70. Zimmerli, *Ezekiel*, 1:352.

71. Cf. also Ezek 37:26.

72. With the emphatic "I" (*ʾănî*).

and the one suggested, would be Jerusalem symbolizing the exiles in Babylonia. When the Judean elites return from Babylonia in the late sixth and early fifth centuries BCE, they encounter an ethnically and religiously pluralistic Yehud, Samaria, and Egypt (cf. Ezra 4:1–23; Neh 4:1–23). According to Knoppers,

> In dealing with the political, social and cultic evidence from the Diaspora and the homeland in the 6th and 5th centuries BCE, one is confronted with a plurality of Judean communities within the larger context of the Neo-Babylonian and Achaemenid empires. Multiple Yahwisms, rather than a single Yahwism, characterised the social and religious landscape.[73]

The pluralism of "the peoples of the land(s)" and their real or imagined ethnic and religious foreignness (Ezra 10:2, 11; Neh 10:28–31) will clash with the returnees' ideologies of "extreme exclusivity," embodied and critiqued in the person of Jerusalem in our passage. The "peoples of the land" are identified with those seven peoples whom God commanded the Israelites to drive out (Ezra 9:1–2), of which two were the Hittite and Amorite parents of Jerusalem herself (Ezek 16:3, 45). The ideologies of "extreme exclusivity" will define "true Israel" as those belonging to the children of the *golah*, the returning exiles from Babylonia (Ezra 6.19–21; 8:35; 10.7, 16). These ideologies will be manifested in narrow injunctions against mixed marriages (Ezra 9; Neh 13:23–27). Non-*golah* Jewish women will be lumped with ethnically foreign women as objectionable women for *golah* men to marry, because they contaminate the "holy seed" that will be sown into the "new" land (Ezra 9:2, 11–15).[74]

Ezek 16:44–63 presents an alternative outlook. By asserting the foreign origins of Samaria and Egypt/Sodom, by making them more righteous and favored than Jerusalem, who also shares their foreignness, the text has those who will regard themselves as the "true Israel" becoming the chastened Other. By recognizing and accepting the ethnic and religious plurality of other diasporic Judeans, the text forces Jerusalem (the *golah*) to acknowledge and accept her own guilt and sinfulness and to be purified by God's very self. It accomplishes this through the shared

---

73. Knoppers, "Exile, Return and Diaspora," 46.

74. For a discussion of the politics and economics of *golah* endogamy, see Yee, *Poor Banished Children of Eve*, 143–46.

foreign parentage of all these characters and their future inclusion in the same "everlasting covenant."[75]

When YHWH establishes this covenant, "you (Jerusalem) will know that I am YHWH" (*wĕyādaʿ at kî-ʾ ănî yhwh*, v. 62). The marriage metaphor of Ezek 16:8 might be recurring here in the renewal of God's covenant. The climax of God's covenantal rebetrothal of the wife/Israel in Hos 2:16–20 (MT 2:18–22) declares, "I will take you for my wife in faithfulness; and you shall know YHWH" (*wĕyādaʿ at ʾet-yhwh*). However, the covenant God establishes with Jerusalem in Ezek 16:62–63 does not end on a happy note, like Hosea's. The knowledge of God that results from YHWH's covenant with Jerusalem intends that she remember (*zkr*) and be ashamed, never opening her mouth again because of her disgrace, "when I have purified her of all that she has done" (v. 63).[76]

Conclusion

Ezekiel 16:44–63 marks the conclusion of a chapter filled with sexual violence against the personified city of Jerusalem (16:1–43). It veers from this theme by providing a reflection on the ethnically foreign parentage of Jerusalem as a product of a Hittite mother and Amorite father—a parentage that was asserted in 16:3. The family metaphor is extended to provide Jerusalem with sisters and nieces: Sodom and Samaria and their "daughters," two vanquished cities with their dependent towns. Jerusalem is accused of following in their sinful ways, becoming even more corrupt than they. Only Sodom's sin is specified: her arrogance, gluttony, materialistic comfort and her disregard of the poor and needy in her midst. On the basis of other texts that associate Sodom with Egypt, I argued that Sodom becomes Ezekiel's avatar for the Judean communities settled in Egypt. These include not only those already established at Migdol, Tahpanhes, Memphis, and in the land of Pathros, but also the military community of Elephantine. Along with the exilic populations in Samaria and Judah, these ethnically and religiously mixed communities exhibit a different diasporic history than those deported in the three Babylonian exiles. Ezekiel 16:44–63 reveals that the post–582 BCE social landscape extends beyond the usual binary of Babylonian exiles and peoples of the

---

75. Thank you, Corrine L. Carvalho!

76. While the NRSV refers to God "forgiving" Jerusalem, I follow Galambush, Block, and Odell in translating *kippēr* as "purify" or "cleanse."

land (*golah/'am hā-' āreṣ*). There are actually four groups: the *golah*, or Babylonian exiles represented by Jerusalem; the internally mixed non-*golah* groups in Yehud; the internally remixed groups in Samaria; and the various diasporic Jews in Egypt. In Ezek 16:44–63, other voices emerge that present alternate understandings of Jewishness during the exilic period, all of them included in the "everlasting covenant."

Postscript

Although this essay concludes a volume on Asian American biblical interpretation, you will notice that the term "Asian American" does not appear anywhere in it. This is deliberate. In my essay "Coveting the Vineyard" (Chapter 9), I initially struggled in trying to read 1 Kgs 21 through an Asian American lens. I could not separate into silos the various parts of my identity as a female, Asian American trained in diverse methods of biblical interpretation, etc. etc., to distill a distinctively Asian American reading. When one idea sparked in my brain, I dismissed as too historical-critical or literary-critical or sociological or comparative, because I could not figure out how to relate it to Asian American issues. It did not seem to "look like" an Asian American reading. Well, this concluding chapter is what an Asian American reading "looks like." It is a product of a hybrid self, where all aspects of my identity inform my interpretation of the biblical text. Whatever analysis I conduct will be an Asian American, feminist, intersectional, middle-class, historical- and/or literary-critical, multi-cultural, and multi-methodological investigation.

My feminist self was attracted to a prophetic text involving mothers, daughters, sisters, and nieces in a chapter filled with sexual violence. My class-based self was curious about the depiction of Sodom as a proud, wealthy glutton who slighted the poor and needy, in contrast to its depiction by fundamentalist evangelicals as a city of murderous perverts. My Asian American self exists in a society that conceives of race in a white/black binary, making those of Asian descent to feel "betwixt and between" and "neither here nor there" here in the US. And yet, this very phenomenon of my daily experience directly influences my ability to detect a similar binary (Yehud/people of the land) in the typical studies of the book of Ezekiel in general and Ezekiel 16, in particular. In turn, my ethnic Asian American self disrupts this binary as it detects the submerged voices of mixed-ethnic communities within and around Yehud, farther beyond in Egypt, and those still in Babylon. All of these communities attempt to come to grips with and assert their multifaceted identities as Jews and Yahwists. Finally, my biblically trained self is able to assess the complex historical events and sociological challenges of the Babylonian "exile" and critically assess the scope and diversity of scholarly investigations of it. It is the intersection of all these aspects of who I am that come together as an Asian American interpreter of the biblical text.

Works Cited

Ahn, John. "Ezekiel 15: A *Mšl*." In *The Prophets Speak on Forced Migration*, edited by Mark J. Boda, Frank Ritchel Ames, John Ahn, and Mark Leuchter, 101–19. Ancient Israel and Its Literature 21. Atlanta: SBL Press, 2015.

———. "Forced Migrations Guiding the Exile: Demarcating 597, 587, and 582 B.C.E." In *By the Irrigation Canals of Babylon: Approaches to the Study of the Exile*, edited by John J. Ahn and Jill Middlemas, 173–89. LHBOTS 525. New York: Continuum, 2012.

Allen, Leslie C. *Ezekiel 1–19*. Word Biblical Commentary 28. Dallas: Word, 1994.

Alter, Robert. "Sodom as Nexus: The Web of Design in Biblical Narrative." In *The Book and the Text: The Bible and Literary Theory*, edited by Regina M. Schwartz. Cambridge, MA: Blackwell, 1990.

Arnold, Bill T. *Genesis*. New Cambridge Bible Commentary. Cambridge: Cambridge University Press, 2009.

Barstad, Hans M. "After the 'Myth of the Empty Land': Major Challenges in the Study of Neo-Babylonian Judah." In *Judah and the Judeans in the Neo-Babylonian Period*, edited by Oded Lipschits and Joseph Blenkinsopp, 3–20. Winona Lake, IN: Eisenbrauns, 2003.

———. *The Myth of the Empty Land: A Study in the History and Archaeology of Judah during the 'Exilic' Period*. Symbolae Osloenses. Oslo: Scandinavian University Press, 1996.

Becking, Bob. "A Fragmented History of the Exile." In *Interpreting Exile: Displacement and Deportation in Biblical and Modern Contexts*, edited by Brad E. Kelle et al., 151–69. Ancient Israel and Its Literature 10. Atlanta: Society of Biblical Literature, 2011.

Betlyon, John W. "Neo-Babylonian Military Operations Other Than War in Judah and Jerusalem." In *Judah and the Judeans in the Neo-Babylonian Period*, edited by Oded Lipschits and Joseph Blenkinsopp, 263–83. Winona Lake, IN: Eisenbrauns, 2003.

Block, Daniel I. *The Book of Ezekiel*. Vol. 1, *Chapters 1–24*. 2 vols. Grand Rapids: Eerdmans, 1997.

Boadt, Lawrence. "Rhetorical Strategies in Ezekiel's Oracles of Judgment." In *Ezekiel and His Book: Textual and Literary Criticism and Their Interrelation*, edited by Johan Lust, 182–200. Bibliotheca Ephemeridum theologicarum Lovaniensium 74. Leuven: Leuven University Press, 1986.

Carden, Michael. *Sodomy: A History of a Christian Biblical Myth*. Bible World. London: Equinox, 2004.

Carvalho, Corrine L. "A Serpent in the Nile: Egypt in the Book of Ezekiel." In *Concerning the Nations: Essays on the Oracles against the Nations in Isaiah, Jeremiah and Ezekiel*, edited by Else K. Holt et al., 195–220. LHBOTS 612. London: Bloomsbury T. & T. Clark, 2014.

Collins, Steven. "Where Is Sodom? The Case for Tall el-Hammam." *BAR* 39/2 (2013) 32.

Darr, Katheryn Pfisterer. "The Book of Ezekiel: Introduction, Commentary, and Reflections." In *The New Interpreter's Bible*, edited by Leander E. Keck 6:1073–607. 13 vols. Nashville: Abingdon, 2001.

Day, Linda M. "Rhetoric and Domestic Violence in Ezekiel 16." *BibInt* 8 (2000) 205–30.

Day, Peggy L. "Adulterous Jerusalem's Imagined Demise: Death of a Metaphor in Ezekiel XVI." *VT* 50 (2000) 285–309.

———. "The Bitch Had It Coming to Her: Rhetoric and Interpretation in Ezekiel 16." *BibInt* 8 (2000) 231–54.

———. "A Prostitute Unlike Women: Whoring as Metaphoric Vehicle for Foreign Alliances." In *Israel's Prophets and Israel's Past: Essays on the Relationship of Prophetic Texts and Israelite History in Honor of John H. Hayes*, edited by Brad E. Kelle and Megan Bishop Moore, 167–73. LHBOTS 446. New York: T. & T. Clark, 2006.

———. "Yahweh's Broken Marriages as Metaphoric Vehicle in the Hebrew Bible Prophets." In *Sacred Marriages: The Divine–Human Sexual Metaphor from Sumer to Early Christianity*, edited by Martti Nissinen and Risto Uro, 219–41. Winona Lake, IN: Eisenbrauns, 2008.

Eichrodt, Walther. *Ezekiel: A Commentary*. Translated by Cosslett Quin. OTL. Philadelphia: Westminster, 1970.

Gagnon, Robert A. J. *The Bible and Homosexual Practice*. Nashville: Abingdon, 2001.

———. "The Old Testament and Homosexuality: A Critical Review of the Case Made by Phyllis Bird." *ZAW* 117 (2005) 367–94.

Galambush, Julie. *Jerusalem in the Book of Ezekiel: The City as Yahweh's Wife*. SBLDS 130. Atlanta: Scholars, 1992.

Ginzberg, Louis, et al. *Legends of the Jews*. Vol. 1. 2nd ed. JPS Classic Reissues. Philadelphia: Jewish Publication Society, 2003.

Goldstein, Seth. "Reading Toevah: Biblical Scholarship and Difficult Texts." *Reconstructionist* 67/2 (2003) 48–60.

Graham, J. N. "Vinedressers and Plowmen: 2 Kings 25:12 and Jeremiah 52:16." *Biblical Archaeologist* 47 (1984) 55–58.

Granerød, Gard. *Dimensions of Yahwism in the Persian Period: Studies in the Religion and Society of the Judaean Community at Elephantine*. Beihefte zur Zeitschrift für die alttestamentliche Wissenschaft 488. Berlin: de Gruyter, 2016.

Greenberg, Moshe. *Ezekiel 1–20: A New Translation with Introduction and Commentary*. AB 22. Garden City, NY: Doubleday, 1983.

———. "Ezekiel 16: A Panorama of Passions." In *Love & Death in the Ancient Near East*, edited by John H. Marks and Robert M. Good, 143–50. Guilford, CT: Four Quarters, 1987.

Herzfeld, Michael. "'As in Your Own House': Hospitality, Ethnography, and the Stereotype of Mediterranean Society." In *Honor and Shame and the Unity of the Mediterranean*, edited by David D. Gilmore, 75–89. A Special Publication of the American Anthropological Association 22. Washington, DC: American Anthropological Association, 1987.

Holladay, John S. "Judeans (and Phoenicians) in Egypt in the Late Seventh to Sixth Centuries B.C." In *Egypt, Israel, and the Ancient Mediterranean World: Studies in Honor of Donald B. Redford*, edited by Gary N. Knoppers and Antoine Hirsch, 405–37. Probleme der Ägyptologie 20. Leiden: Brill, 2004.

Howard, David M., Jr. "Sodom and Gomorrah Revisited." *Journal of the Evangelical Theological Society* 27 (1984) 385–400.

Joyce, Paul M. *Ezekiel: A Commentary*. LHBOTS 482. London: T. & T. Clark, 2007.

Kamionkowski, S. Tamar. "Gender Reversal in Ezekiel 16." In *The Prophets and Daniel: A Feminist Companion to the Bible*, edited by Athalya Brenner, 170–85. FCB, 2nd ser., 8. London: Sheffield Academic, 2001.

Kelle, Brad E. "Wartime Rhetoric: Prophetic Metaphorization of Cities as Female." In *Writing and Reading War: Rhetoric, Gender, and Ethics in Biblical and Modern Contexts*, edited by Brad E. Kelle and Frank Ritchel Ames, 95–111. SymS 42. Atlanta: Society of Biblical Literature, 2008.

Kessler, Rainer. *The Social History of Ancient Israel: An Introduction*. Translated by Linda M. Maloney. Minneapolis: Fortress, 2006.

Klein, Ralph W. "Exile." In *The New Interpreter's Dictionary of the Bible* 2 (2007) 367–70.

Knoppers, Gary N. "Exile, Return and Diaspora: Expatriates and Repatriates in Late Biblical Literature." In *Texts, Contexts and Readings in Postexilic Literature: Explorations into Historiography and Identity Negotiation in Hebrew Bible and Related Texts*, edited by Louis C. Jonker, 29–61. Forschungen zum Alten Testament 2/53. Tübingen: Mohr/Siebeck, 2011.

Knoppers, Gary N. *Jews and Samaritans: The Origins and History of Their Early Relations*. New York: Oxford University Press, 2013.

———. "Revisiting the Samarian Question in the Persian Period." In *Judah and the Judeans in the Persian Period*, edited by Oded Lipschitz and Manfred Oeming, 265–86. Winona Lake, IN: Eisenbrauns, 2006.

Lapsley, Jacqueline E. "Shame and Self-Knowledge: The Positive Role of Shame in Ezekiel's View of the Moral Self." In *The Book of Ezekiel: Theological and Anthropological Perspectives*, edited by Margaret S. Odell and John T. Strong, 143–73. SymS 9. Atlanta: Society of Biblical Literature, 2000.

Lipschits, Oded. "Shedding New Light on the Dark Years of the 'Exilic Period': New Studies, Further Elucidation, and Some Questions Regarding the Archaeology of Judah as an 'Empty Land.'" In *Interpreting Exile: Displacement and Deportation in Biblical and Modern Contexts*, edited by Brad E. Kelle et al., 57–90. Ancient Israel and Its Literature 10. Atlanta: Society of Biblical Literature, 2011.

Matthews, Victor H. "Hospitality and Hostility in Genesis 19 and Judges 19." *BTB* 22 (1992) 3–11.

McMahon, Gregory. "The History of the Hittites." *Biblical Archaeologist* 52 (1989) 62–77.

Mein, Andrew. *Ezekiel and the Ethics of Exile*. Oxford Theological Monographs. Oxford: Oxford University Press, 2006.

Middlemas, Jill. *The Templeless Age: An Introduction to the History, Literature, and Theology of the "Exile."* Kindle ed. Louisville: Westminster John Knox, 2007.

Morschauser, Scott. "'Hospitality', Hostiles and Hostages: On the Legal Background to Genesis 19.1–9." *JSOT* 27 (2003) 461–85.

Moughtin-Mumby, Sharon. *Sexual and Marital Metaphors in Hosea, Jeremiah, Isaiah, and Ezekiel*. Oxford Theological Monographs. Oxford: Oxford University Press, 2008.

Nissinen, Martti. *Homoeroticism in the Biblical World: A Historical Perspective*. Translated by Kirsi Stjerna. Minneapolis: Fortress, 1998.

Patton, Corrine L. "Priest, Prophet, and Exile: Ezekiel as a Literary Construct." In *Ezekiel's Hierarchical World: Wrestling with a Tiered Reality*, edited by Stephen L. Cook, 73–89. SymS 31. Atlanta: Society of Biblical Literature, 2004.

Pearce, Laurie E. "Continuity and Normality in Sources Relating to the Judean Exile." *Hebrew Bible and Ancient Israel* 3 (2014) 163–84.

Peterson, Brian Neil. "Identifying the Sin of Sodom in Ezekiel 16:49–50." *Journal of the Evangelical Theological Society* 61 (2018) 307–20.

———. "The Sin of Sodom Revisited: Reading Genesis 19 in Light of Torah." *Journal of the Evangelical Theological Society* 59 (2016) 17–31.

Pirķê de Rabbi Eliezer = *(The Chapters of Rabbi Eliezer, the Great): According to the Text of the Manuscript Belonging to Abraham Epstein of Vienna)*. Translated by Gerald Friedlander. London: Kegan Paul, 1916.

Polk, Timothy. "Paradigms, Parables, and *Mešālîm*: On Reading the *Māšal* in Scripture." *CBQ* 45 (1983) 564–83.

Pope, Marvin H. "Mixed Marriage Metaphor in Ezekiel 16." In *Fortunate the Eyes That See: Essays in Honor of David Noel Freedman in Celebration of His Seventieth Birthday*, edited by Astrid B. Beck, 384–99. Grand Rapids: Eerdmans, 1995.

Rast, Walter W. "Bab Edh-Dhra and the Origin of the Sodom Saga." In *Archaeology and Biblical Interpretation: Essays in Memory of D. Glenn Rose*, edited by Leo G. Perdue et al., 185–201. Atlanta: John Knox, 1987.

Rom-Shiloni, Dalit. "Ezekiel as the Voice of the Exiles and Constructor of Exilic Ideology." *Hebrew Union College Annual* 76 (2005) 1–45.

———. "Forced/Involuntary Migration, Diaspora Studies, and More: Notes on Methodologies." *Hebrew Bible and Ancient Israel* 7 (2018) 376–98.

Runions, Erin. "Violence and the Economy of Desire in Ezekiel 16:1–45." In *The Prophets and Daniel: A Feminist Companion to the Bible*, edited by Athalya Brenner, 156–69. FCB, 2nd ser., 8. London: Sheffield Academic, 2001.

Shanks, Herschel. "Have Sodom and Gomorrah Been Found?" *BAR* 6/5 (1980) 26–36.

Shields, Mary E. "Multiple Exposures: Body Rhetoric and Gender Characterization in Ezekiel 16." *JFSR* 14 (1998) 5–18.

Stewart, David Tabb. "Same-Sex Relations: Hebrew Bible." In *The Oxford Encyclopedia of the Bible and Gender Studies*, edited by Julia M. O'Brien, 2:257–63. 2 vols. Oxford: Oxford University Press, 2014.

Stone, Ken. "The Hermeneutics of Abomination: On Gay Men, Canaanites, and Biblical Interpretation." *BTB* 27 (1997) 36–41.

Strine, C.A. "Is 'Exile' Enough? Jeremiah, Ezekiel, and the Need for a Taxonomy of Involuntary Migration." *Hebrew Bible and Ancient Israel* 7 (2018) 289–315.

Sweeney, Marvin A. *Reading Ezekiel: A Literary and Theological Commentary*. Reading the Old Testament Series. Macon, GA: Smyth & Helwys, 2013.

Toorn, Karel van der. *Becoming Diaspora Jews: Behind the Story of Elephantine*. 1 online resource vol. Anchor Yale Bible Reference Library. New Haven: Yale University Press, 2019.

———. "Egyptian Papyrus Sheds New Light on Jewish History." *BAR* 44/4 (2018) 33–39, 66–68.

Westermann, Claus. *Genesis 1–11: A Commentary*. Translated by John J. Scullion. Continental Commentary. Minneapolis: Augsburg, 1984.

Wilson, Robert R. "Forced Migration and the Formation of Prophetic Literature." In *By the Irrigation Canals of Babylon: Approaches to the Study of the Exile*, edited by John J. Ahn and Jill Middlemas, 125–39. LHBOTS 525. New York: Continuum, 2012.

Woudstra, Marten H. "The Everlasting Covenant in Ezek 16:59–63." *Calvin Theological Journal* 6 (1971) 22–48.

Yee, Gale A. *Poor Banished Children of Eve: Woman as Evil in the Hebrew Bible*. Minneapolis: Fortress, 2003.

———. "The Two Sisters in Ezekiel: They Played the Whore in Egypt." In *Poor Banished Children of Eve: Woman as Evil in the Hebrew Bible*, 111–34. Minneapolis: Fortress, 2003.

———. "'Spreading Your Legs to Anyone Who Passed': The Pornography of Ezekiel 16 and 23." Paper read at the 1990 Annual Meeting of the Society of Biblical Literature, New Orleans, Louisiana.

———. "'Your Mother Was a Hittite': The Image of the Harlot in Ezekiel 16." Paper read at the 1988 Annual Meeting of the Catholic Biblical Association, Santa Clara, California.

Zertal, Adam. "The Province of Samaria (Assyrian Samerina) in the Late Iron Age (Iron Age III)." In *Judah and the Judeans in the Neo-Babylonian Period*, edited by Oded Lipschits and Joseph Blenkinsopp, 377–412. Winona Lake, IN: Eisenbrauns, 2003.

Zimmerli, Walther. *Ezekiel: A Commentary on the Book of the Prophet Ezekiel*. Vol. 1. Translated by Ronald E. Clements. 2 vols. Hermeneia. Philadelphia: Fortress, 1979.

Subject Index

African American women, 15,
    20–22, 28, 40, 42, 78
Ahab, 9, 147–48, 151–52, 160
    feminization of, 151–52, 154,
    158–59
American Academy of Religion, 5,
    65, 180
American Orientalism (*see*
    Orientalism)
Anna May Wong, 156
Asian American, 69–71, 111
    advocacy stance, 3, 70–71,
    73–74
    anti-immigrant laws, 145, 155
    identity, 3, 54–59, 69, 72–73
    immigrants, 10, 54–55, 94, 112–
    13, 120, 173, 175–76
    many ethnicities of, 57–58, 63,
    73, 128–29, 144
    churches, 10, 165, 171, 173–74,
    176–77
    theologians, 61–64
Asian American Biblical
    Hermeneutics/
    Interpretation, 1, 2, 4–6,
    9–10, 43, 59, 65–75, 78–81,
    142–43, 165–79, 197–98
Asian American stereotypes
    Dragon Lady, 9, 102, 151,
    154–60
    Charlie Chan, 157
    Fu Manchu, 9, 154, 156–57, 172
    Yellow Peril, 77, 156
    sexually insatiable Asian
    women, 102–3, 155–56, 158

meek and submissive Asian
    women, 157
feminization of Asian men/
    emasculation, 155–56, 158,
    172–73
Asian American Studies, 7, 68
Asian religions, 61–63, 66
    Asian Christianity, 63
Assimilation, 2, 105, 113, 116–17,
    120

Babylonia, Babylon, 166, 182–84,
    190–92, 195, 198
Bathsheba, 37
Berit 'olam, 194, 196–97
Biblical methods/criticisms, 5 14–53
    Cultural Criticism, 15, 34
    Deconstructive Criticism, 34
    Gender Criticism, 36–37
    Historical Criticism, 3, 34, 143,
    197
    Ideological Criticism, 14
    Interdisciplinary, 34–38
    Literary Criticism, 3, 34, 143,
    197
    Marxist/materialist Criticism,
    15, 101–2, 147
    Minoritized criticism (Racial/
    ethnic), 9, 71–72, 85–87,
    142–43, 197–98
    Postcolonial criticism, 15, 41,
    143
    Psychoanalytic Criticism, 8,
    111–22
    Queer Theory, 41, 170
    Social History, 143, 197

SUBJECT INDEX

Binaries, 10
　white/black, 19, 88, 95, 116, 197
　male/female, 19, 36–37, 130–31, 170
　heterosexual/homosexual, 19–20
　citizen/native, 170
　golah/people(s) of the land, 10, 181, 196–97
　normative/non-normative, 20
Boaz, 101–5, 115

Castration, 168–69
Chinese Americans, 54–55, 89–90, 144, 171
　American-born vs. immigrant, 90–94
　Chinese Exclusion Act, 89, 171
　economic exploitation, 55, 89, 95, 100, 105, 112–13
Christine de Pizan, 27
Citizenship, 88, 95
Class, 20, 101–2
　class exploitation, 21, 101, 105, 112, 117
Coercive mimeticism (*see* mimeticism)
Colonialism, colonization, 24–25, 41, 103, 116, 173
　colonialist move, 25–26
Combahee River Collective, 20–22
Confucius, Confucianism, 125, 173
Critical White Studies, 79

Deborah, 8, 34, 124
Deconstructive Criticism (*see* Biblical methods/criticisms)
Diaspora, 190–91, 195
Discourse, 19, 116
Diversity, 54
Dragon Lady (*see* Asian American stereotypes)
Dworkin, Andrea, 16–17, 22

Egypt, 10, 190 (*see also* Elephantine)
　Jews in, 184, 190, 192–93, 195, 198
Elephantine, 190–93, 196

Episcopal Divinity School, ix, 1, 6, 91, 138, 180
Ethnic Chinese Biblical Colloquium, ix, 4
Eunuch, 9, 165–72, 175–76
Exile (*see* Migration)
Extreme exclusivity. 183, 192, 195
Eve, 27–29, 31
Everlasting Covenant (*berit 'olam*), 194. 196–97
Ezekiel, 10, 46, 180–202
Ezra, 42, 97, 99, 116, 174, 195

Fa Mulan, 9, 80, 123, 154
　as warrior, 124–26, 138
　ethnicity of, 127–28, 138
　(trans)gendering of, 129–30, 136, 138
　reception history of, 129–30, 133–34
　Disney *Mulan*, 9, 135–38
Femininity, femaleness, 19, 26, 130, 170
　white hegemonic, 77
Feminism, 14, (*see also* Stereotypes of Third World Women)
　White feminism, 21–22, 24–26, 104
　Liberal Feminism, 16, 19, 25, 34
　Radical Feminism, 16–19, 25
　Marxist Feminism, 15, 22, 26, 102, 114–16
　Postcolonial Feminism, 15, 24–25
　Postmodern Feminism, 15, 26
　Queer theory, 19, 26
　African American, 20–23, 26, 38–39
　Latina American, 23–24, 26
　Asian American, 23–24, 26
Feminist biblical scholarship, 15, 18–19, 29–47
　African American/Womanist/black, 15, 23, 38–39, 41
　Asian American, 43–44
　Cultural criticism, 37–38, 47
　Deconstructive criticism, 35, 47

SUBJECT INDEX   205

Gender and Queer approaches, 36–37, 47
Historical criticism, 29–32, 34, 47
Literary criticism, 29–32, 34, 47
Marxist/Materialist readings, 35–36, 46–47
Postcolonial readings, 44–47
Feminist Companion to the Bible Series, 33
Foreigner, 9, 41, 70, 96–97, 165–68, 175–76, 189
  foreign women, 154, 166, 174–75, 185
Fu Manchu (see Asian American Stereotypes)

Gedaliah, 182, 184, 190
Gender (see also masculinity, femininity), 15, 19, 25, 125
  as performance, 19, 26, 137
  reversal, 124–25, 130
  gender blur (sexual ambiguity), 131–32, 170
  (trans)gendering, 129–32
Gender criticism (see Biblical methods/criticisms)
Gender/race/class, etc. (see Intersectionality)
Golah (returning exiles), 115–16, 119–20, 169, 190, 192, 194–97

Heteronormativity (see also Sexism), 20, 27, 132
Heterosexism (see also Sexism), 42, 74, 173
Hildegard of Bingen, 27
Historical Criticism (see Biblical methods/criticisms)
Hittite women, 185, 196
Homophobia, 3, 42
Homosexuality (see also LGBTQ), 20, 93, 174, 186, 197
Hospitality, inhospitality, 186–88
Hybridity, 23, 73, 143, 197

Ideological Criticism (see Biblical methods/criticisms)
Ideology, 15, 34, 97, 119–20, 195
Immigration, Immigrants, 99, 171, 173
  Asian (see Asian Americans)
Inculturation, 54–59
Indigenous American women (see Racial/ethnic women)
Interdisciplinary Criticism (see Biblical methods/criticisms)
Intermarriages, 42, 93, 99, 166, 174–75, 195
  anti-miscegenation laws, 155
Intersectionality (gender/race/class, etc.), 5, 15, 21–23, 26, 41, 47, 54, 56, 86–87, 170, 197
Isaiah, 10, 165–79, 187

Jael, 34, 79–80, 123–41
  as warrior, 8–9, 124–26, 138
  ethnicity of, 126–27, 138
  (trans)gendering of, 129–32, 137
  reception history of, 132–33
Japanese internment, 88, 144–50, 158, 171
  Pearl Harbor, 146, 157
  Executive Order 9066, 146
  Personal Justice Denied, 146
  regulatory taking, 150, 158
Jeremiah, 180, 190
Jerusalem, 10, 183–85, 189, 195–97
  as wife, 181, 183, 196
  as sister of Samaria and Sodom, 180, 182, 186, 189, 192, 196
  daughters of, 190, 194, 196
  social injustices of, 188–89
Jezebel, 9, 151–53, 158–59
  as an ideological construct, 153–54
Jezreel, 147–48, 160–61
Judges 4–5, 79–80, 123–41

LGBTQ, 10, 41–42, 131–32, 165, 171, 173–77
Liberal Feminism (see Feminism)
Literary Criticism (see Biblical methods/criticisms)

SUBJECT INDEX

Lot's daughters, 45, 98, 103, 116, 188

Marx, Karl, 17
Marxist/materialist Criticism (*see* Biblical methods/criticisms)
Marxist Feminism (*see* Feminism)
Masculinity, maleness, 19, 26, 41, 130, 158, 170
   white hegemonic, 77
Matrix of domination, 22, 42
Melancholia (*See* Racial Melancholia)
Memar Marqah, 191–92
Migration, 196, 198
   exile, 166, 175, 182–83
   forced migration, 182–83, 192
   voluntary migration, refugees, 171, 176, 182–83, 192
Mimeticism, 67
   coercive mimeticism, 67–68
Minoritized criticism (*see* Biblical methods/criticisms)
Missionaries, Missionary position, 6, 60–64, 172–73
Mixed marriage (*see* Intermarriage)
Model minority (*see also* Asian American Stereotypes), 7, 77, 85, 87, 92–96, 111, 157, 165
Mulan (*see* Fa Mulan)
Multiculturalism, 90

Naboth's vineyard, 9, 142, 145, 147–53, 158, 160
Naomi, 100–101, 105, 114–15
   as melancholic subject, 113, 118–19
Native American women (*see* Racial/ethnic women)
Nehemiah, 97, 99, 116, 174, 195

Oppressions, 22, 26, 41
   internalized oppression, 77–78
Orientalism (*see also* Asian American stereotypes), 68–69, 154, 173
   American Orientalism, 9, 75–77, 134–35, 138, 155–56, 158

Orientals, 72, 76
Orpah, 46, 99, 114
Other, Othering, 78, 119
   Asian other, 158
   racial other, 78, 89, 99, 112, 154
   foreign other, 89, 116, 171
   familiar/familial other, 116–20
   female other, 117–18, 120, 158

PANAAWTM, ix, 4, 6, 180
Patriarchy, 20–21, 132
   definition of, 17n9
   in the Hebrew Bible, 30, 34–35
   Asian, 61, 77, 124–25
People(s) of the land, 184, 195
Perpetual foreigner (*see also* Asian American stereotypes), 7, 10, 72, 85, 87–92, 100–105, 111, 165, 171
Persian Period, Achaemenid period, 9, 97, 115, 119, 158, 160, 170, 175, 193
Pocahontas Perplex, 46
Postcolonial Feminism (*see* Feminism)
Postmodern Feminism (*see* Feminism)
Prostitutes (*see also* Sex Workers), 155, 158, 187
Psychoanalytic Criticism (*see* Biblical methods/criticisms)

Queer Theory (*see* Biblical methods/criticisms)

Rabbinic literature, 188
Racial melancholia, 8, 111–20
   Melancholic Object, 112–13, 119
   Melancholic Subject, 112–13
   Misremembering, 113, 115, 117, 119
Racial/Ethnic women (women of color), 22, 26, 39, 58
   African American, 22, 26
   Asian American, 23–24, 26
   Latina American, 23–24, 26

Native/Indigenous American, 45–46
Third World, 24–25, 27, 104
Racialization
    Asian American, 87–88
    African American, 87–88
Racism, 3, 7, 24, 42, 56, 74, 77–78, 89, 95, 112, 119
Radical Feminism (*see* Feminism)
Rape, 40
    male-male rape, 10, 186–87
Refugees (*see also* voluntary migration)
Returnees from Babylon (*see golah*)
Ruth the Moabite, 8, 46, 85–105, 175
    as a model minority, 96–100
    as a perpetual foreigner, 96, 100–105
    as a melancholic object, 113–18
    Multicultural perspectives on, 85–87
    Homoerotic perspectives on, 86n3

Samaria, 10, 180–81, 185–86, 188–97
    daughters of, 186, 190, 192–94
Same-sex relations (*see* Homosexuality)
Sex/gender system, 17
Sex workers, 35–36
Sexism, 3, 15, 74
Sexuality, 20, 45, 171–74
    non-normative, 20n21, 103, 117, 172–73
    sexual minority(ies) (*see also* eunuch), 10, 165, 171–72, 175–77
Sexual ambiguity (*see* gender blur)
Sexual exploitation, 102–3
Sexual violence, 40, 103, 182, 196

Society of Biblical Literature (SBL), ix, 1, 4, 6, 180
Sodom, 181, 185–98
    daughters of, 186–87, 189–90, 192–94
    its neglect of the poor and needy, 187–88, 192, 196–97
    as signifier of Egypt, 191–92, 194–96
Sojourner Truth, 28–29
Standpoint Theory, 18, 26
Stereotypes
    racial/ethnic, 102, 154
    sexual, 102–3
    of Asian American (*see* Asian American stereotypes)
    of Third World women, 24–27

The Woman's Bible, 28, 31
The Women's Bible Commentary, 33
(Trans)gendering (*see* Gender)

White feminism (*see* Feminism)
Whiteness, 7, 56, 76–79, 94–95, 99–100, 112–13, 173
    white male/men, 62–63, 65–66, 89, 102, 157–58
    white privilege, 8
    white supremacy, 42
    (*See also* Critical White Studies)
Widows, 96–97, 102, 105, 187, 189
Woman Warrior (*See also* Fa Mulan), 8, 37, 58, 79, 123
Women of Color (*See* Racial/ethnic women)

Yad Va-Shem, 166, 169, 176
Yehud, 9–10, 166, 170–71, 175, 193
    Mixed ethnic groups, 181, 184, 189–90, 192, 194, 197
Yellow Peril (*See* Asian American stereotypes)

Author Index

Ackerman, Susan, 101n79, 105, 126n16, 127n17, 139, 153n38, 162
Adaci, Jeff, 158n62, 162, 172n35
Ahn, John, 182n11-13, 183n15, 184n24, 190n55, 198
Allen, Leslie, 182n10, 183n16-17, 185n31, 186n34, 198
Alpert, Rebecca, 83n3, 105
Alter, Robert, 187n42, 198
Ancheta, Angelo N., 87n30, 88n32, n34, 105
Anderson, Cheryl B., 41-42, 47-48
Ang, Ien, 87n31, 106
Anzaldúa, Gloria, 24, 48
Arnold, Bill T., 186n33, 198
Aster, Shawn Z., 148n22, 162
Ayers, Brenda, 136n57, 139

Bach, Alice, 38n89-90, 48
Back, Les, 79n45, 83
Bailey, Randall E., 4, 7n17-18, 11
Baker-Fletcher, Karen, 29n51, 48
Bal, Mieke, 35, 48
Barrett, Michèle, 18n14, 48, 102n83, 106
Barstad, Hans M., 190n54, 198
Beach, Eleanor Ferris, 159n64, 162
Beal, Timothy, 96n60, 108, 117n35, 121
Becking, Bob, 184n26, 198
Begg, Christopher T., 96n61, 97n62, 106, 167n13-15, 177
Bell, Elizabeth, 136n57, 139
Bennett, Harold V., 96n61, 106

Berger, Maurice, 79n45, 81
Bethel, Lorraine, 21, 48
Betlyon, John W., 182n14, 198
Bhabha, Homi K., 112n8, 120
Bird, Phyllis A., 31-32, 48
Blenkinsopp, Joseph, 166n6, 168n17, 169n23, 177
Block, Daniel, 182n10, 185n31, 187n44, 193n67, 196n76, 198
Boadt, Lawrence, 187n7, 198
Boer, Roland, 36n80, 48, 86n5, 101-2, 106, 117n34, 120
Bohn, Babette, 133n43, 139
Boling, Robert, 127n18, 139
Bottigheimer, Ruth B., 133n47, 139
Bow, Leslie, 23n35, 48, 87n30, 106
Brenner, Athalya, 32-33, 48, 86n2-3, 87n28, 100, 106, 116n36, 117n34, 118n37, 120
Brenner-Idan, Athalya, ix, 33n64, 49, 142n1
Brock, Rita Nakashima, 103n85, 106
Brode, Douglas, 136n57, 139
Brodkin, Karen, 79n45, 81
Bruner, Edward M., 88n35, 106
Burke, Sean D., 168n18-19, 170, 177
Bush, Frederic, 97n65, 101n81, 106
Butler, Judith, 8, 11, 19-20, 49, 125n12, 139
Byron, Gay L., 39n96, 49

Campos, Michael Sepidoza, 174n47, 177

AUTHOR INDEX

Cantrell, Deborah, 148n24, 160n69, 162
Carasik, Michael, 103n86, 106, 117n35, 120
Carden, Michael, 174n49, 177, 187n43, n45-46, 192n63, 198
Carter, Warren, 44n116, 52
Carvalho, Corrine L., 30n53, 49, 180n1, 190n59, 196n75, 199
Caspi, Mishael Maswari, 98n68, 106
Cavalcanti, Tereza, 86n15, 106
Chan, Jachinson, 155n51, 157n60, 162, 172n35, 173n41, 177
Chan, Joseph M., 135n54, 139
Chan, Michael J., 169n20-21, 170n27-28, 179
Chan, Sucheng, 77n38, 81
Chang, Iris, 89n37, 90n39, 106, 113n14, 120, 144n4-5, 155n49, n52, 162, 171n31, 177
Chang, Juliana, 112n6, 120
Chang, Jung, 159n65, 162
Cheng, Anne Anlin, 8, 11-13, 118n39-40, 120
Cheng, Lucie, 93n49, 106
Chin, Frank, 76n36, 81, 135n53, 139
Cho, Sumi, 15n5, 49
Cho, Sumi K., 92n47, 106
Choi, Jin Young, 172n36, 173n40, 177
Chou, Rosalind S., 155n50, 162, 172n35, 173n41, 177
Chow, Rey, 67-68, 70n13, 72, 81
Christiansen, Keith, 133n43, 139
Christianson, Eric S., 133n46, 140
Chu Julie Li-Chuan, 86n20, 106
Chuh, Kandice, 70n70, 72n22, 81
Clavell, James, 76, 81
Cline, Eric H., 148n21, 162
Collins, Adela Yarbro, 33, 49
Collins, Patricia Hill, 22-23, 49
Collins, Steven, 186n32, 199
Combahee River Collective, 15n4, 20-21, 22, 49
Crenshaw, Kimberlé Williams, 15, 22, 49

Cronauer, Patrick T., 147n19, 151n37, 153n41-42, 159n63, 162
Crowell, Bradley, 44n116, 49

Daly, Mary, 17-18
Daniels, Roger, 77n38, 80n49, 81, 146n16, 162
Darr, Katheryn Pfisterer, 98n68, 106, 182n10, 199
Davis, Angela Y., 15n4, 49
Dawson, Jenny, 87n23, 106
Day, Linda M., 181n4, 199
Day, Peggy L., 181n4, 199
De La Torre, Miguel A., 86n13, 107
Delgado, Richard, 79n45, 82
Demery, Monique Brinson, 159n65, 162
Dill, Bonnie Thornton, 15n5, 49
Donaldson, Laura E., 45-46, 49, 87n24, 96n60, 107
Dong, Lan, 124n6, n8, 124n9, 125n9, n11, 128n22-23, 130n29, n31, 133n48, 135n54, 140
Du Bois, W. E. B., 71, 74, 81-82
Dube, Musa, 45, 49, 86n9, 96n58, 101n79, 107
Duncan, Celena M., 86n3, 107
Dweeb, 137n58, 140
Dworkin, Andrea, 16-17, 22
Dyk, Alta C. and Peet J. van, 87n29, 96n59, 107

Ebeling, Jennie R., 148n21, 160, 162
Ebron, Paulla, 88n35, 107
Edwards, Katie B., 38n91, 49
Eichrodt, Walther, 182n10, 188n50, 189n53, 199
Eng, David L., 75n28, 78n41, n44, 82, 111-13, 120, 172n35, 177
Eoyang, Thomas, 143n3
Erbele-Küster, D. Dorothea, 87n26, 107
Eskenazi, Tamara Cohn, 116n27, 117n32, 120
Espiritu, Yen Le, 75n29, 82

Everhart, Janet S., 153n38, 162
Exum, J. Cheryl, 37–38, 49, 86n3, 107

Feng, Peter X., 76n36, 82
Fenton, Steve, 74n27, 82
Ferber, Abby L., 79n45, 82
Fewell, Danna Nolan, 35, 49, 96n60, 107, 117n35, 120, 125n13, 140
Fisch, Harold, 103n87, 107
Flax, Jane, 113n11, 120
Fleming, Robyn C., 131–32, 140
Foskett, Mary F., 1, 6, 50, 65
Foulkes, Irene, 86n12, 107
Frankenberg, Ruth, 79n45, 82
Franklin, Norma, 160
Freud, Sigmund, 111, 121
Frymer-Kensky, Tikva, 114–16, 117n32, 120–21
Fuchs, Esther, 34–35, 50, 103n87, 107
Fung, Richard, 172n35, 177
Furth, Charlotte, 76n32, 82

Gafney, Wilda C., 39, 50
Gagnon, Robert A. J., 186n38, 199
Gaines, Janet Howe, 159n64, 162
Gaiser, Frederick J., 168n16, 170n29, 175n52, 177
Galambush, Julie, 181n4, 196n76, 199
Gallares, Judette A., 87n22, 107
García-Treto, Francisco, 96n60, 107
Gee, Deborah, 77n37, 82, 158n62, 162
Gillingham, Susan, 116n25, 121
Ginzberg, Louis, 188n49, 199
Goldingay, John, 166n4, n6, n9, 168n17, 177
Goldstein, Seth, 186n35, 199
Gossai, Hemchand, 86n14, 107
Gottheimer, Josh, 29n51, 50
Gottwald, Norman K., 1–2, 11
Gow, Murray D., 97n66, 107
Grabbe, Lester L., 148n21, 154n44, 162
Graham, J. N., 184n23, 199

Granerød, Gard, 191n62, 199
Gray, John, 153n40, 162
Greenberg, Moshe, 182n10, 199
Guest, Deryn, 36–37, 50, 130–32, 137, 140
Guglielmo, Jennifer, 79n45, 82
Gulik, Robert Hans van, 76, 82
Gunn, David M., 37n86, 50, 96n60, 107, 117n35, 120, 125n13, 133, 140

Haas, Lynda, 136n57, 139
Haber, Beth K., 133n43, 140
Hagedorn, Jessica, 157n61, 162
Hall, Stuart, 73n26, 82
Halpern, Baruch, 80n48, 82, 126n16, 127n19, 140
Hamamoto, Darrell Y., 76n36, 82
Hammock, Clinton E., 166n7, 177
Han, Shinhee, 111–12, 120
Hanson, K. C., ix
Harrington, D. J., 132n40, 140
Harte, F. Bret, 72n20, 82
Hartmann, Heidi, 18, 50, 102n83, 107
Hartsock, Nancy S. M., 18, 50
Havrelock, Rachel, 98n68, 106
Hawkins, Peter S., 114n17, 121
Heneghan, Bridget T., 79n45, 82
Herzfeld, Michael, 187n41, 199
Hill, Mike, 79n45, 82
Hobgood, Mary E., 79n45, 82
Holladay, John S., 184n25, 200
Honig, Bonnie, 86n4, 99, 100n76, 108, 114n16, 121
hooks, bell, 15, 38, 50
Hoop, Raymond de, 166n11, 177
Houten, Christiana van, 96n61, 108
Howard, David M., Jr., 186n33, 200
Huber, Lynn R., 174n49, 177
Hübinette, Tobias, 112n7, 121

Ipsen, Avaren E., 36, 50

Jackson, Beverley, 130n28, 140
Jacobson, Matthew Frye, 79n45, 82
Jen, Gish, 70, 82
Johnson, Denise L., 77, 83

AUTHOR INDEX

Jordan, June, 23, 50, 83n86, 108
Joyce, Paul M., 182n9, 200
Junior, Nyasha, 30n54, 38–39, 50

Kamionkowski, S. Tamar, 132, 140, 181n4, 200
Kang, Laura Hyun Yi, 72n22, 75n28, 82
Kanyoro, Musimi R. A., 86n9, 104n90, 108
Kates, Judith A., 86n2, 108
Kay, Toy, 5, 11
Kelle, Brad E., 181n6, 199
Kessler, Rainer, 183n15, 184n24, n26, 199
Killebrew, Ann E., 129n26, 140
Kim, Chan-Hie, 72n19, 82
Kim, Daniel, 172n36, 177
Kim, Seung-Kyung, 14n2, 19n17, 51
Kim, Uriah Y., 1n1, 9, 11
Kincheloe, Joe L., 79n45, 82
King, Deborah, 22n28, 50
Kingston, Maxine Hong, 66, 76–77, 79, 83, 123, 133, 140
Kirk-Duggan, Cheryl A., 87n25, 108
Kitagawa, Daisuke, 145n8, 163
Klein, Ralph W., 182n14, 200
Knoppers, Gary N., 190n55, n58, 191n62, 193n64–66, 195n73, 200
Koosed, Jennifer L., 114–15, 116n30, 121
Koyama, Kosuke, 92n45, 108
Kuan, Jeffrey Kah-jin, 1n1, 6n12, 11, 43n111, 50, 65, 72n19, 83
Kuo, Sui May, 87n21, 108
Kuruvilla, Carol, 7n15, 11
Kwok Pui Lan, 4, 6, 86n19, 96n60, 108, 173n40, n45, 178, 180

LaCocque, André C., 97n65, 98–99, 108, 118, 121
Lan, Feng, 128n22, 140
Lanyer, Amelia, 27–28, 51
Lapsley, Jacqueline E., 189n52, 200
Larkin, Katrina J., 97n65, 108
Lee, Archie C. C., 142n1
Lee, Boyung, 173n44, 178

Lee, Deborah Jian, 174n48, 178
Lee, Peter K. H., 86n19, 108
Lee, Robert G., 75n29, 83, 92n47–48, 94n51, 108, 134n52, 140, 144n6, 155n49, 157n57–58, 163, 171n36, 178
LeMon, Joel M., 30n53, 51
Leneman, Helen, 133n44, 140
Leong, Karen J., 156n53–54, 159n65, 163
Lerner, Gerda, 27n46, 47, 51
Levine-Rasky, Cynthia, 79n45, 83, 100n74
Levine, Amy-Jill, 86n2, 96n60, 100n74, 108, 118n37, 121
Li, Siu Leung, 125n11, 130n30 n32, 141
Liew, Tat-siong Benny, 3, 7n17–18, 43n111–12, 51, 71–72, 83
Lim, You-Leng Leroy, 172n38, 178
Lin, Liz, 165, 178
Linafelt, Tod, 96n60, 108, 117n35, 121
Ling, Amy, 71n16, 83
Ling, Jinqui, 172n35, 178
Lipschits, Oded, 183n21, 200
Lipsitz, George, 79n45, 83
Lorde, Audre, 21–22, 26, 51
Louie, Andrea, 90n40, 91n42, 92n46, 108
Louie, Bianca Heather, 172n39, 173n43–44, 178
Lovelace, Vanessa, 39n96, 49
Lowe, Lisa, 23–24, 51, 70n14, 72n22, 73, 83
Lugones, Maria, 24n39, 51
Lundström, Catrin, 112n7, 121
Lustbader, Eric Van, 76n34, 83
Lyon, Cherstin M., 145n7, 163

Ma, Sheng-Mei, 75n29, 76n31, 83, 134n52, 135n54, 141, 157n59, 163
Maldonado, Robert D., 86n11, 96n60, 108, 117n32, 121
Mann, Judith, 133n43, 140
Mann, Susan, 124n6, 125n10, 140

Mann, Susan Archer, 20n20, 24n40, 51
Marchetti, Gina, 76n36, 83
Marcus, Jane, 79n45, 83
Masenya, Madipoane, 86n7, 96n59, 108
Maséquesmay, Gina, 172n38, 173n42, 178
Matthews, Victor, 96n65, 108, 186n41, 200
Mayfield, Tyler D., 123n4, 141
McCann, Carol R., 14n2, 19n17, 51
McKinlay, Judith E., 87n23, 108, 153n38, 163
McMahon, Gregory, 185n29, 200
Mein, Andrew, 189n51, 200
Merecz, Robert, 151n36, 163
Mesters, Carlos, 86n16, 109
Meyers, Carol, 32, 51
Middlemas, Jill, 183n18, 200
Miller, Max, 98n67, 109
Miller, Stuart Creighton, 88n34, 109, 171n31, 178
Milne, Pamela, 34, 51
Mohanty, Chandra Talpade, 24–25, 26–27, 51
Moraga, Cherrie, 24, 51
Morschauser, Scott, 186n41, 200
Moughtin-Mumby, Sharon, 181n4, 201
Mura, David, 171–72, 178

N'Shea, Omar, 169n20, 178
Na'aman, Nadav, 147n19, 163
Nadar, Sarojini, 86n8, 109
Nayap-Pot, Dalila, 86n12, 109
Newman, Louise Michele, 79n45, 83
Newsom, Carol A., 33n69, 51
Ng, Wendy, 146n16, 149n26, 150n32, 163
Ngan, Lai Ling Elizabeth, 44, 52
Nguyen, Mimi, 137–38, 141
Nguyen, Viet Than, 172n35, 178
Nicholson, Linda, 16n6, 52
Niggemann, Andrew J., 167n13, 178
Nissinen, Martti, 186n40, 187n42, 201

Okihiro, Gary Y., 77n38, 83, 134n52, 141
Økland, Jorunn, 36n80, 48
Omi, Michael, 88n33, 94n53, 109
Oppenheim, Jamie, 7n14, 11
Osajima, Keith Hiroshi, 92n47, 109

Parikh, Crystal, 112n6, 121
Patton, Corrine, 184n27, 201
Paul, Shalom, 166n7, 169n22, 178
Pearce, Laurie E., 183n19, 201
Perdue, Leo G., 44n116, 52
Peterson, Brian Neil, 186n39, 187n44, 201
Pirkê de Rabbi Eliezer, 188, 201
Polk, Timothy, 184n28, 201
Pope, Marvin, 185n30, 201
Prasso, Sheridan, 156n56, 163
Pyke, Karen D., 77, 83

Raheb, Viola, 86n17, 109
Rast, Walter W., 186n33, 201
Räterlink, Lennart E. H., 112n7, 121
Reimer, Gail Twersky, 86n2, 108
Rendtorff, Rolf, 96n61, 97n62, 109
Richards, Kent H., 30n53, 51
Ringe, Sharon H., 33n69, 51
Robinson, Greg, 146n12, 149n28, 163
Robnolt, I'Laine, 133n45, 141
Rofé, Alexander, 153n41, 163
Rom-Shiloni, Dalit, 183n18–20, n22, 201
Routledge, Bruce, 116n29–30, 121
Ruane, Nicole, 32n82, 52
Rubin, Gayle, 17, 20
Runions, Erin, 181n4, 201
Russell, Letty M., 33, 52

Sakenfeld, Katharine Doob, 87n22, 97n65, 104, 109
Salerno, Salvatore, 79n45, 82
Sasson, Jack M., 100, 109
Schearing, Linda S., 38n88, 52
Schipper, Jeremy, 115, 117, 121
Scholz, Susanne, 30n55, 52
Segovia, Fernando F., 4, 7n17–18
Sells, Laura, 136n57, 139

Shah, Sonia, 76n31, 83, 159n66, 163
Shanks, Herschel, 186n33, 201
Shepherd, David, 103n86, 109, 117n35, 121
Sherwood, Yvonne, 35, 52
Shields, Mary E., 181n4, 201
Shiu, Anthony Sze-Fai, 112n6, 121
Shrake, Eunai, 173n42–43, 178
Silber, Ursul, 87n27, 109
Sison, Marites N., 163
Smith, Geoffrey S., 146n13, 163
Snijders, L. A., 96n61, 109
Snyder, Josey B., 159n64, 163
Sojourner Truth, 28–29
Soggin, J. Alberto, 127n19, 141
Spelman, Elizabeth V., 21–22, 52
Spencer, John R., 96n61, 109
Stanton, Elizabeth Cady, 16, 28, 31, 33, 52, 86n2, 109
Stefancic, Jean, 79n45, 82
Stewart, David Tabb, 174n49, 178, 186n40, 201
Stokes, Mason, 79n45, 83
Stone, Ken, 36n82, 52, 174n49–50, 178, 186n35, 201
Strine, C. A., 183n19, 201
Sun, Chloe, 1n1, 11
Sweeney, Marvin A., 186n34, 201

Tadmor, Hayim, 168n18–19, 179
Tajima, Renee E., 157n61, 163
Takaki, Ronald, 55n2, 59, 77n38, 83, 89n37, 110, 113n9, 121, 144n6, 146n12, 147n18, 163, 171n32, 175n51, 179
Tan, Jonathan Y., 171n30, 179
Tang, Jun, 135n54, 141
Taylor, Gary, 168n18, 179
Taylor, Marion Ann, 4n4, 11, 29n52, 52
Thistlethwaite, Susan Brooks, 103n85, 106
Thompson, Becky, 23n36, 26n44, 52
Thompson, J. A., 101n79, 110
Tolbert, Mary Ann, 33, 53
Tong, Rosemarie, 15n3, 16n7, 18n11, 19n17, 24n40, 52
Toorn, Karel van der, 190–91, 201

Travis, Irene S., 87n25, 110
Trevanian, 76, 83
Trible, Phyllis, 28, 30–31, 33n65, 35, 53
Tsing, Anna Lowenhaupt, 88n35, 107
Tuan, Mia, 70n15, 78n43, 83, 87n30, 88n34, 94n55, 110

Uchida, Aki, 76n33, 83, 102n84, 110
US Commission on Wartime Relocation and Internment of Civilians, 146n17, 163
Ussishkin, David, 148n23, 163

Van Wolde, Ellen, 103n87, 110

Walker, Alice, 38, 53
Wang, Georgette, 135n54, 141
Waren, Vron, 79n45, 84
Weems, Renita J., 39–41, 53, 87n25, 110
Weglyn, Michi N., 145n9, 164
Weir, Heather E., 29n52, 52
West, Traci C., 38n94, 53
Westermann, Claus, 186n33, 201
White, Marsha, 153n41, 164
Wiegman, Robyn, 79n45, 84
Williams, Dolores S., 87n25, 110
Wilson, John A., 147n20, 163, 201
Wilson, Karina, 137n58, 141
Wimbush, Vincent L., 71, 84
Winant, Howard, 88n33, 94n53, 109
Wong, Angela Wai Ching, 86n19, 96n60, 110
Woudstra, Marten, 187n44, 189n53, 201
Wright, Jacob L., 169n20–21, 170n27–28, 179
Wu, Frank H., 70n15, 80n49, 84, 87n30, 88n32, 92n47, 93n50, 94n52, 95n56, 110
Wu, Rose, 173n45, 179
Wuench, Hans-Georg, 167n13–15, 179

Xing, Jun, 72n23, n25, 74n27, 76n36, 84

Yamamoto, Eric K., 149n29, 164
Yamamoto, Margie, 143n3, 146n14
Yamashita, Karen Tei, 128, 141
Yang, Philip Q., 93n49, 106
Yang, Seung Ai, 1n1, 9, 11
Yeh, Emilie Yueh-yu, 135n54, 141
Yellow Bridge, 127n7, 141
Yieh, John Y. H., 4n5 13
Yoshihara, Mari, 75n29–30, 84
Yoshikawa, Mako, 76n33, 83, 102n84, 110

Yu, Henry, 68–69, 75n29, 78n42–43, 84

Zambrana, Ruth Enid, 15n5, 49
Zertal, Adam, 193n64, 201
Zia, Helen, 75n29, 77n38, 84, 90n38, 95n57, 110, 171n30 179
Ziegler, Valarie H., 38n88, 52
Zimmerli, Walther, 182n10, 183n16–17, 186n34, 193n67, 194n70, 201

www.ingramcontent.com/pod-product-compliance
Lightning Source LLC
Chambersburg PA
CBHW031357230426
43670CB00006B/567